ALEXANDER FU SHENG
Biography of the Chinatown Kid

Terrence J. Brady

Copyright © 2018 Terrence J. Brady
All rights reserved.
ISBN: 1717363679
ISBN-13: 978-1717363671

DEDICATION

To my wife, my daughters,
and our beloved dog Maggie (rip)

CONTENTS

	Acknowledgments	vii
	Introduction	1
Chapter 1	Origins	7
Chapter 2	The Cheungs	11
Chapter 3	The Shaw Brothers	22
Chapter 4	Chang Cheh	29
Chapter 5	Ti Lung and Chiang Da-Wei	38
Chapter 6	Alex the Actor	45
Chapter 7	Chang's Film Company	57
Chapter 8	The Shaolin Monastery	70
Chapter 9	Along Comes Jenny	76
Chapter 10	The Boxer Rebellion	86
Chapter 11	Lau Kar-Leung	93
Chapter 12	Changgong Goes to War	103
Chapter 13	Back to Movietown	117
Chapter 14	Wedding Bells	123
Chapter 15	The Brave Archer	132
Chapter 16	Sun Chung	143
Chapter 17	Black September 1978	149
Chapter 18	Chor Yuen	157
Chapter 19	Black September: The Sequel	174
Chapter 20	The Return of Alex	181
Chapter 21	Trouble in Paradise	190
Chapter 22	Fatal Crash	197
Chapter 23	The Funeral of Fu Sheng	205
Chapter 24	Jenny After Alex	214
Chapter 25	Fu Sheng's Legacy	218
	Film Summaries	221
	Bibliography	309
	Index	319

Terrence J. Brady

ACKNOWLEDGMENTS

Six years in the making and this endeavor would not have come to fruition without the considerable assistance of a large group of people. Several translators were utilized for this project but I wish to openly praise Winnie Seko and Carrie Cheung. Translating text from a source language into a target language is more than just reiteration. To be an exceptional translator, one must have a superior grasp of the subtleties or nuances of a dialect, its culture, and the context in order to successfully convey the same message into another language. Both Winnie and Carrie were first-rate linguists who went above and beyond the call of duty and I cannot thank them enough.

To my editor, John McConnell, who provided a splendid set of fresh eyes and delivered superb feedback. I recommend him without reservation. To my illustrator, Kung Fu Bob O'Brien. A gifted artist whose passion for the genre is exemplified in his art. Check out his webpage for more info. Another round of praise goes to Monica Brady for her tolerance over the last six years and assistance in chiseling away my choppy composition to allow the prose to progress.

I also wish to acknowledge a forum I've been a member of since 2002. The Kung Fu Fandom membership has provided years of entertaining and enlightening dialogue on this genre of film. I have learned so much from so many, that it would be impossible to name them all. Nevertheless, I tip my hat to my KFF brothers and sisters.

Finally, I want to express my appreciation to the following individuals who helped in a variety of ways. Big or small, they all played a role: Alex Tan, Alexander Fu Sheng: Biography of the Chinatown Kid (Facebook group), Bey Logan, Brian Dyer, Chen Kuan Tai, Chi Fai Man, Chu Ko, Conrad Niem, Craig Reid, Daniel O'Leary, Diane Wardle, Frank Bolte, Gary Bettinson, Gerard Muttrie, Guiqin Zhang, Gus Lam, Hsiao Ho, Hui Ying-hung, Ian Polson, Isabel Li, James Valentino Santi, Jana Stanley, Jean-Paul Delisle, Jeanne Lau, Jeffrey Bona, Jenny Lie, Jesse Easley, Joe

Keit, Josephine Ng, Kakalina Cheung, Lo Mang, Man Hon Lam, Man Kit Cheung, Marion Mixdorff, Michael Ng, Mike Horner, Mike Leeder, Patty Keung, Paul Bramhall, Paul Kilianski, Richard Harrison, Russell Boos, Sandra Tsukiyama, Scott Blasingame, Stanley Hui, Stephan Zahner, The Cheung Family, Tai Chi-Hsien, Tim Kwan, Toby Russell, Todd Ashbaugh, Tommy Wan, Vaughan Savidge, Vincent Ng, Wang Lung-wei, Wong Ka Hee, and Yukio Someno.

Alexander Fu Sheng: Biography of the Chinatown Kid

Terrence J. Brady

Introduction

Beijing: Summer of 1900

A noon haze blanketed the city's one million inhabitants. The sun, merciless in an empty sky, bombarded blistering heat upon the layers of choking smog that hung over Beijing this mid-August day. Once thriving marketplaces were vacant, and the bustling avenues deserted. Heat, smoke, and death were their only occupants. Unburied corpses now littered the forsaken streets and Christian churches burned unchecked. Whole neighborhoods were eerily silent and Empress Dowager Cixi's massive Forbidden City abandoned. A manufactured day of judgement was upon the land and its people.

Not even seven days before, an 18,000 strong Eight-Nation Alliance pushed into the Chinese capital to liberate their countrymen held hostage by a peasant crusade known as the Yìhéquán Movement or Boxer Uprising. While this Alliance gave the impression that it was a savior of the embattled city, it proved to be just the contrary. The foreign forces chopped up Beijing into districts and commenced a systematic operation of plundering not seen since the Mongols of yore. The liberators were ravenous, ruthless, and highly motivated to execute atrocities to further their own means. Most of the Boxers were now on the run as the Alliance pressed inward to the heart of the city.

One Boxer remained behind. He was barely a man, twenty-years-young, but the past few years of sweeping social and institutional changes forced him to grow up fast. The loyal pugilist witnessed his country become divided after the failed Hundred Days' Reform and the wave of growing hostilities caused by the Boxer movement. He was now a wanted man and needed to escape the city's walls before the Alliance soldiers found him. Before the walls became his tomb.

The Boxer's teen sweetheart accompanied him as they searched the twisting labyrinth of alleyways and courtyard homes hoping to find a way out. Despite all, it was only a matter of time before they happened upon a marauding band of Imperial Japanese Army troops hell-bent on recreation. When the barbarian officer spotted the native girl, he sneered and summoned his men to separate his war trophy from her unarmed chaperone. Unabashed, the Boxer stood his ground and hurled his slender frame at them. Feet and fists were his weapons of choice and the man-child warrior brushed off the soldiers as if they were of no consequence. The Japanese Commander finally became roused and joined the fray but the Boxer taunted his new attacker and derided the officer's inferior martial arts skills.

The Chinese patriot's attitude of the skirmish was child's play until the troops once again attempted to seize his companion. The Boxer disarmed one of them and sliced through the man's snowy-white uniform with his bayonet. Panicked, the other soldiers regrouped as one fired off a round, yet the pugilist seemed unfazed and continued to hurl himself against his aggressors. Reinforcements then arrived. A volley of explosive rounds pelted the defying warrior. Riddled with bullet holes and soaked in blood, the Chinese fighter turned to the new aggressors and unleashed his fury. Amid the madness, he heard a frail cry for help. The Boxer turned his attention to his companion who had been critically wounded and hastened to her side.

Time froze for a fleeting moment. Heartbeats grew louder and slower. The young man knelt and cradled the girl's head. His love gasped her last breaths, short and labored, until her spirit drifted off. Her body went limp as he slowly lowered her head to the ground. The pugilist was in disbelief; however, there was no time to mourn for the incensed Japanese officer stood over the couple with his unsheathed Kyū guntō. He raised his sword for a fatal strike but the Boxer spun and stood, rifle in hand, and fired multiple shots until the commander's body gave out and crumpled over into the dirt.

More alliance troops arrived; Americans, Germans, Russians. They looked over the carnage of Japanese soldiers and then to their vanquisher. The Boxer, now lifeless as well, stood erect over his fallen love. The rifle he used was jammed into the ground, keeping him propped upright, as his dead eyes were wide open and staring beyond them.

One American soldier removed his cavalry hat and held it over his heart. The others followed suit in showing respect for this great warrior. Their moment of silence was then interrupted. An older Chinese gentleman, dressed from a different era, ambled into the foreground. He didn't seem concerned by the troops or the corpses lying about. The man gazed around for a moment, taking in the ambiance like an artist critiquing a canvas. He pulled a well-loved corona from his mouth and a plume of smoke filled the air. In his other hand, the man held a megaphone, which he put to his lips.

"Cut..!" he barked.

The fallen soldiers rose from the dead like Lazarus of Bethany. They brushed themselves off and were surrounded by members of the Changgong Film Company. The crew rearranged butterfly frames, fans, and camera dollies with assembly line precision. The young Boxer and his fallen love were immediately lost in the sea of workers.

The cigar chomping director peered about and was promptly besieged by a legion of assistants. He grunted at them in Putonghua as they exchanged papers and pointed off to the distance, giving them their marching orders for the next shot. Not finding his lead actor and actress, he returned to his director's chair that read "Chang Cheh" in modest Chinese characters. The director reached over for his cup of tea but it was empty. He scowled — who dare drink his beverage?

Chang spied the young Boxer standing nearby with remnants of tea leaves on his chin and made a beeline to him. Nonchalant, the actor pretended not to notice and hastily rubbed the evidence from his face. The director stopped and eyeballed him but the performer said nothing, looking up and around to profess his innocence. Father Chang smiled for the first time and patted him on the shoulder. Chang's laughter was echoed by his cinema son, Alexander Fu Sheng.

Hong Kong film fans will surely recognize this battle scene from Chang Cheh's larger-than-life production, *Boxer Rebellion*, released by Shaw Brothers Studio of Hong Kong in January 1976. Director Chang is considered by his supporters as the "Godfather of Hong Kong Cinema," a flag-bearer of the martial arts motion picture who helped reinstate the dominance of the masculine movie star during the 1960s & '70s. Chang

Cheh advocated films that were visceral, raw, and reveled in exploring the settling of scores with stoic heroes that often met with tragic consequences. His tales were driven by genuine interpretations of the martial arts entwined with elaborate choreography delivered by authentic practitioners.

Shaw Screen deemed Chang an *"innovator"* and his visual signatures provided him with a *"refreshingly bold image befitting the new school label."*[1] American film theorist David Bordwell wrote that the filmmaker nurtured a *"Theatre du Grand Guignol approach to swordplay"* and provided the genre a technical sophistication.[2] Hong Kong movie critic Sek Kei stated that Chinese cinema experienced a surge of the "aesthetics of violence" and while international stars such as Bruce Lee, Jackie Chan, and Jet Li didn't belong to the Chang Clan, *"they all had to thank Chang for paving their success."*[3]

Chang Cheh was also acknowledged for nurturing protégés including Wu Ma, John Woo, and Lau Kar-Leung and adept at discovering and grooming new talent for his employer, Shaw Brothers Studio. Superstars Jimmy Wang Yu, Lo Lieh, Ti Lung, and Chiang Da-Wei were just a few who cut their teeth under Chang's direction. Another of his most successful prodigies was a 17-year-old native from the New Territories.

Zhang Fu Sheng (Mandarin) or Cheung Fu Sing (Cantonese) was the ninth child of eleven.[4] Later to be more commonly known as Alexander Fu Sheng, he was born into an affluent family in 1954 whose patriarch was an influential leader in the local government. Alex chose not to coast through life living off his family's wealth but took on the perilous path of cinematic uncertainty. He entered a career pursuit that was untested and used his charisma and genius to set himself apart from thousands of others. Signing his initial contract with Shaw Brothers Studio in 1972, he embarked on an impressive eleven-year career in which he appeared in 43 completed films (28 directed by his cinema dad). Alex initially honed his skills as a background actor and made his official debut in *Police Force (1973)*. The following year, he was bestowed with an award for the Most Talented Newcomer in the production *Friends (1974)*.

Alex became a staple in Chang's group, appearing opposite leading men Ti Lung, Chiang Da-Wei, and Chen Kuan-tai. His ingenuous ways and playful flairs were in stark contrast to Shaw Brothers Studio's matinee idols. At a time when newcomers were trying to emulate the recently deceased Bruce Lee, Alex was a trendsetter, and his persona would eventually be imitated.

The young star followed Chang to Taiwan in 1974 and acted in a series of Shaolin Temple themed productions when the director set up a base of operations on the island nation. Chang's films featured accurate presentations of traditional Chinese martial arts choreographed by Lau Kar-Leung. Sifu Lau later defined the look and tone of the genre, combining intense choreography with showmanship and comedy. A lifelong practitioner of the Hung Gar Kuen discipline, he's a fourth-generation direct disciple of martial arts legend Wong Fei-Hung. Lau took Fu Sheng on as his student which galvanized Alex's own athletic adeptness in becoming a full-fledged action hero.

Fu Sheng's 1976 marriage to songstress Jenny Tseng solidified his status as a power player in the Hong Kong entertainment industry. The duo became the darlings of the local press and likened to the Orient's version of Sony and Cher. Jenny appeared in several films with Alex and they performed in a variety of TV shows. The couple started multiple businesses together, including the music label JenFu Records. Regrettably, their celebrity status also brought the prying eyes of the public and tabloid speculation haunted them for most of their life together.

Despite a pair of serious work-related accidents in 1978/79, Alex showed his amazing resilience to bounce back and work on multiple film projects. The star appeared in all four productions of Chang's *Brave Archer* series; however, it was the contemporary kung fu drama, *Chinatown Kid (1977),* that allowed his name to go global. He expanded his resume by joining up with Sun Chung for the highly acclaimed, *The Avenging Eagle,* and *The Deadly Breaking Sword,* both starring opposite mega-star Ti Lung, and *My Rebellious Son* with Ku Feng. Alex also served under the direction of Chor Yuen (*The Proud Twins, Return of the Sentimental Swordsman,* and *Heroes Shed No Tears*), Lau Kar-Leung (*Legendary Weapons of China, The 8 Diagram Pole Fighter,* and *Cat vs Rat*), Lau Kar-wing (*Treasure Hunters* and *Fake Ghost Catchers*), and Wong Jing (*Hong Kong Playboys* and *Wits of the Brats*).

Fu Sheng was the complete package. His carefree façade, playful grin, and animated eyes balanced with physical agility, an arsenal of martial skills, and charismatic performances that placed him among Asia's most beloved movie personalities. Though he didn't fit the role of the conventional leading man, his knack to execute comic relief with slapstick kung fu antics endeared him to a worldwide audience; years before Jackie Chan's rise and the late '70s kung fu comedy craze.

"Crowned by a mop of black hair, his visage bore the graphic features of a comic-strip figure: thick, agile brows; eyes shifting from doe-eyed naivety to a shrewd or steely squint; lips apt to swell into a sulky pout. His fighting style combined mercurial speed with supple poise."[5]

In the early '80s, Fu Sheng was preparing to take his career to a higher tier by directing motion pictures for the company he exclusively worked for despite receiving multiple offers elsewhere. His accomplishments in the martial arts genre served as a testament that he was destined for greater things. Regrettably, his chance to solidify his position amongst Hong Kong's greatest talents was left unfulfilled. At the pinnacle of his career, only 28 years of age, fate reared its unpredictable head. Alex's life prematurely ended in a horrific car wreck one evening on a haphazard road in Clear Water Bay. His departure left a devastating void in the industry and an even more substantial hole in the hearts of his fans, his family, and his beloved.

---

[1] See Books, The Shaw Screen, page 146.
[2] See Books, Planet Hong Kong, page 248.
[3] See Books, Chang Cheh: A Memoir, page 15.
[4] Those older than Alex also called him "Sing Jai" meaning little Sing or simply Ah Sing (Cantonese) or Ah Sheng (Mandarin).
[5] See Books, Directory of World Cinema: China 2, page 47.

1

Origins

Alexander Fu Sheng was born in the original Kowloon Hospital, on Argyle Street, during the Chinese Zodiac Year of the Horse on October 20, 1954. People born under the sign of the Horse are extremely animated and energetic. They are masters of repartee, possess a deft sense of humor, and relish in taking center stage and delighting audiences everywhere. Horses are healthy, possess a positive attitude towards life, and are warm-hearted and generous. Conversely, heavy responsibility or pressure from their job can also weaken them.

Alex's parents hailed from the backwater village of Sheung Shui in the New Territories. It's a stone's throw from the Sham Chun River which serves as a natural border between Hong Kong and mainland China. For more than six centuries, the New Territories have been home for numerous migrants from the southern Guangdong Province. The earliest settlers were called Punti (local people) and established themselves on the fertile plains in the northwest. Later, immigrants came down from points farther north and took residence on the hilly part in the northeast or rented the less fruitful parcels from the Punti. They became to be known as Hakka (guest people). No matter the period, many of these inhabitants claim lineage from what is known as the Five Great Clans of Hong Kong.

Alex's mother, Angela Fung Wo Liu, is from the Liu (Liao) family, which is one of the Five Great Clans. She was one of 11 children and raised in Sheng Shui where her father, Liu Siu Yin, was an affluent figure in the Liu lineage. He worked for the Royal Hong Kong Police and possessed a large amount of land besieged by two catastrophic fires that ravaged the village around the time of Alex's birth. One of Angela's brothers, Liu Hing-chai, developed a fascination with astronomy at an early age and became well-known in the region as a pioneer amateur astronomer.[1] In the 1930s, the evening skies in the village were so dark and clear, the stars littered the heavens and one could witness the Milky Way stretching from horizon to horizon.

For Liu Siu Yin, like many before him, the importance of lineage for the clan members came only after family. An individual's personal safety, property rights, and so forth relied on their membership in a specific lineage faction. The origin of the Liu Clan was in Henan, a province in Central China's Yellow River Valley, which is widely accepted as the place where Chinese civilization originated. Angela Liu's ancestors migrated south towards the end of the Yuan Dynasty (A.D. 1271-1368). They first came to Tuen Mun, then to Futian (Shenzhen), and finally settled in the Sheung Yue River area. Some generations later, the Liu drew up plans for the walled village of Wai Loi Tsuen.

The region's original settlement completed construction near the end of the 16th century and the population grew to 500 in less than 100 years. As the clan continued to grow, other settlements were added during the 17th century: Chung Sum Tsuen, Po Sheung Tsuen, and Mun Hau Tsuen. Over time, the four villages have come to be communally known as Sheung Shui Heung. This walled village is only a handful of rural settlements that have retained its original moat dating back to 1646. In the 18th century, the power of the Liu Clan was at a crowning point when they erected their central ancestral hall named Liu Man Shek Tong.

The three-hall, two-courtyard building is richly adorned with plaster moldings, wood carvings, and paintings of lucky themes and imageries. The halls are lined with name tablets that pay tribute to the Liu ancestors that include Sheung Shui's founding father, Liu Chung-kit. The structure was restored in 1983 with funding provided by the clan, and again in 1994, with funds from the local government. Today, Liu Man Shek Tong is considered protected property by the government and classified as a "Declared Monument of Hong Kong."

It was in Sheng Shui, during the 1930s, that Angela Liu became acquainted with a young man named Benton Cheung Yan-lung and in due course would raise a family together. He was not part of the Liu Clan, but despite being an outsider, rivaled and eventually became more powerful than many of its membership. His father, Cheung Chi-hang, was a doctor of traditional Chinese medicine. Chi-hang was a principal member of another influential single-patrilineage village in Bao'an, Shenzhen that was located a few miles inside Chinese territory.

Cheung Chi-hang received shelter by the Liu in Sheung Shui during the 1920s when Kuomintang forces were resolved on assassinating him for alleged pro-communist activities. He opened a modest grocery business and later established "Chi Sheung Hong," a wholesale company in staple goods which flourished and brought wealth to the family. His wife, Siu Tai Choi, bore him three sons and four daughters. Their eldest son was born in 1922 and named Cheung Yan-lung.

Cheung Chi-hang's arrival at Sheng Shui was fortuitous as the old adjoining market town, Shek Wu Hui, was about to enter a new era of prosperity. This spot was originally known as Stone Lake Market as there's a river inside the town, and at the bottom of a nearby slope, a lake formed by quarry stones. During its earliest days, there was only one street called Ja Po Alley that was dotted with small shops. Competition from the market town of Shenzhen caused Shek Wu Hui to fall into neglect in the late 19th century but the town underwent a revival in 1925 when the Luen Hing Wet Market was set up. Business people from neighboring villages poured into the area and soon the population surged.

"Markets were an important part of our lives. They were great social gatherings and were very colorful and noisy occasions in comparison with the more regulated markets of today," explained Cheung Yan-lung looking back at the market's humble beginnings.[2]

Beyond the standard foodstuffs for sale, the markets featured vendors of Chinese cures and remedies, letter-writers, and even acrobats who provided entertainment for the shoppers. The markets at Shek Wu Hui, Tai Po, and Yuen Long were scheduled on fixed days of the Lunar month so they wouldn't overlap with the main market in Shenzhen. Despite living amid paddy fields in a primarily agricultural area, the youngster Cheung didn't feel as if he was cut off from the rest of the world.

The Cheung family had access to the Kowloon-Canton Railway and Cheung Yan-lung spent a good bit of his childhood traveling to the government primary school in Tai Po. He later commuted to Kowloon while attending La Salle College which was a highly selective secondary school for boys. When Cheung first traveled to Kowloon at the age of eleven, he commented that it was like *"visiting another world."*[3]

Luckily for Cheung Yan-lung, he escaped from the British colony shortly before the Japanese occupation in 1941 and went to live on the mainland. He majored in Economics at Sun Yat-sen University aka Zhongshan University in Guangzhou and carried out translation work for the Kuomintang, ironically the very outfit that chased his father from the mainland. Cheung befriended several affiliates of their membership during the war years, including Heung Chin. Heung served as a military officer in the Kuomintang but is better known as the founder of the Sun Yee On Commercial and Industrial Guild. Years after the war, many Kuomintang members fled to Sheung Shui, and as late as the 1970s, "Blue Sky with a White Sun" flags were found hanging everywhere in Shek Wu Hui on Double Ten Day.[4]

---

[1] Alex's uncle, Joseph Liu Hing-chai, became the eminent pioneer of astronomical popularization in Hong Kong. In 1972, he built HK's first private observatory in the backyard of his ancestral home in Sheung Shui. He played a leading role in establishing the Hong Kong Space Museum (1980) and was its first director. In 1994, a minor planet was named in his honor.
[2] See Books, Hong Kong Remembers, page 36.
[3] Ibid, 35.
[4] Known as the National Day of the Republic of China.

2

The Cheungs

Life for many, including Angela Liu and Benton Cheung Yan-lung, was extremely difficult during the dark days of the Japanese occupation. They married in 1942 and started a family the following year but the war was taking its toll. The Japanese soldiers confiscated most of the food stocks and many villagers were forced to survive on tree bark. Those who were landowners were slightly better off as they still grew some basics, such as yams and rice, but canned meats, diary, and sugar were all luxuries. Hong Kong locals loathed the arrogant and brutal invaders and did their best to avoid them. They did nevertheless assist in the war effort by helping civilians and British soldiers escape to safety through the New Territories and on into the Chinese mainland.

After the war ended, Cheung Yan-lung assisted his father with the grocery business. Shek Wu Hui saw a surge of refugees with the end of the Japanese occupation and the establishment of the People's Republic on the mainland. The population swelled to 5000 by 1955, which now surpassed the Liu lineage village of Sheung Shui. Many pint-sized industrial enterprises took off in Shek Wu Hui and an agricultural revolution swept across the region. Liu lineage members now allowed immigrants to rent land from them and grow produce for the urban market. With such rapid transformations occurring in the region, the colonial system of administration was becoming more complex. This opened a new avenue of prospects for Cheung.

"In response to both local changes and the more general democratization of the empire, a system of political representation was introduced throughout the New Territories. Under this new structure, Stone Lake was not only to become the seat of the local rural committee but in addition was accorded its own village representative."[1]

In 1947, Cheung Yan-lung was nominated as the Chairman of the

Shek Wu Hui Chamber of Commerce, a position he held for sixteen consecutive terms, as well as, joined the Heung Yee Kuk membership. The Kuk, as they're locally known, are a council of rural leaders who initiated a forum for the New Territories leaders to discuss their grievances and opinions. Created in the 1920s, the Kuk had limited official powers but they commanded the support of the New Territories indigenous population. Over the decades, the Kuk became a powerful and wealthy alliance and its members reaped financial benefits from their allegiance.

The refugee incursion into the region, primarily after the communist takeover of the mainland, caused many small-scale cottage industries to spring up which led to an economic boom in the New Territories. There was a rapid expansion of numerous villages and wooden factories were hastily erected. Unfortunately, these poorly built structures posed a deadly fire hazard as there were few or no housing codes at the time. In 1955, and again in the ensuing year, Shek Wu Hui paid the ultimate price.

Alex was only a few months old, in late February 1955, when the first disaster struck. The blaze started around 4:00am. Fanned by strong winds, the fire swept south engulfing multiple businesses and homes. The densely-populated market included rice merchants, fireworks dealers, groceries, goldsmiths, photographic shops, tea houses, and numerous squatter huts.

Within a few hours, the market was a smoldering ruin. Four thousand people were left homeless and over 270 shops and huts were destroyed. Before major restorations began, another fire struck the area just two days before Christmas 1956. Cheung Yan-lung set up a relief task force and funded the rescue efforts by distributing rice and foodstuffs to the victims. He later assisted in the market town's reconstruction which laid the foundation for his ultimate rise in becoming the head of Shek Wu Hui. Alex recalled his early days and how they were once destitute like many of the others.

"...when the village was in disaster and many were starving and homeless, my father took out all of his hard-earned savings to help them. This is something remarkable. He helped them then and later they helped him in return and he became rich again. It was probably because of this that he got the support of the villagers and became a village gentry."[2]

Cheung's command of the English language was an important asset during negotiations between local landowners and the colonial government throughout Shek Wu Hui's reconstruction. He was adept at comprehending the problems of the modern world and willing to embrace Western values. The colonial administration gave Cheung face by listening to his sentiments on local interests and made him their key adviser on these matters.

As a result, the shrewd entrepreneur formed the United Association of Small Property Holders in Shek Wu Hui. Through this organization, Cheung demonstrated that he possessed the support of nearly 75 percent of all small landowners affected by the fires and those involved in the reconstruction of the town. He not only secured a sizable loan from the government to assist these small property-owners with the rebuilding but also received special concessions over the financial terms in future land development projects. His undertakings proved quite successful as, several years later in 1964, he chaired the committee in charge of the major celebrations for the rebuilding of Shek Wu Hui.

Cheung used his strategic position to keep the Sheung Shui LIC from an active role in the market town's repairs by convincing the colonial administration that the SSL was likely to undermine the interests of the peasant landowners.[3] Additionally, he hashed out a system of redistributing post-fire land amongst pre-fire property owners in which the SSL ultimately had a constricted role.

While this was a strong political move on his part, Cheung's amalgamation of small business owners pitted him against certain members of the Liu lineage. The clan contended the administration should have never granted Cheung a position in the rural committee system of local government. They argued that his position as Shek Wu Hui's village representative was inappropriate as he wasn't a member of the area's long-established settlements but an outsider who simply rose to power. Moreover, they held that Shek Wu Hui wasn't even a traditional village but merely a marketplace. Periodic markets occupied a lowly station in Cantonese notions of human settlement, and only those traditional communities were supposed to function as constituents for this new system of local government.

Despite these protests, Cheung Yan-lung was further celebrated by the region's colonial rulers who awarded him the esteemed Member of the Order of the British Empire which is a much sought-after status in the colony. The honor is primarily bestowed upon prestigious, but not necessarily politically powerful, individuals. Attaining this position provided him even broader commercial and political networks within the colony. Cheung's political success in the rebuilding of Shek Wu Hui, as well as other acts equally obstructive to the Liu, caused him to now be considered by some within the lineage as a man who "*turned upside down the bowl from which he has eaten rice.*"[4]

Alex was only nine-years-old when Shek Wu Hui held its grand re-opening on March 15, 1964. An ambitious celebration organized by the Committee of All Circles of the Sheung Shui District marked the completion of the redeveloped market town. Attractions comprised a large procession of floats including a one-hundred-foot long, silver dragon. The festival drew upwards of two thousand visitors and was attended by the Governor and the Colonial Secretary. Deemed as a proud moment for the villagers of Shek Wu Hui, the ceremony became a defining achievement in Cheung Yan-lung's career. The businessman and politician continued to reward the community by instituting new schools and clan associations and became the chairman of Shek Wu Hui Merchants Association for nineteen years. Kei-kong Wong, fellow committee member and Atom Studio director, was the appointed photographer for Cheung and recalled those initial years.

"*In the past, there was not even a mourning hall to keep ancestral tablets. It was him [Cheung Yan-lung] who first built Xiao Si Tang so people could burn joss papers and keep the ancestral tablets. Also, there were many refugees at that time who had only Renminbi. He was willing to exchange Renminbi for Hong Kong currency and help others.*"[5]

Of course, by allocating so much time to his career and the reconstruction, there was a heavy price to pay. Cheung's limited amount of time for the family grew even more hampered. Alex reflected on those days and commented,

"*I rarely saw my father when I was small. He was always out and coming home after midnight. When he got home, we were all sleeping.*"[6]

Cheung admitted in an interview that he did not discipline his children much and rarely interfered with their interests. Alex remarked,

"Occasionally when he was around, he'd lecture us. Tell us to line up and call us over one by one and reprimand us for our wrongdoings. Although I didn't get along with him as a child, I know he's a kind man."[7]

Family was still a treasured part of Cheung's life despite not being able to spend as much time with his children as he would have enjoyed. A testament to his firm belief in family was his financing of the Hang Lok Theatre with the profits he gained from his real estate investments. Opening its door in October 1957, the theater was the first entertainment venue in the northern part of the New Territories and allowed free admission for children to encourage family unity. A hawker who sold food outside of Hang Lok recanted the vibrant streets around the theatre full of vendors and filmgoers before and after a show. The food seller pointed out that the theatre helped to foster local community bonding and commented,

"We got to know the regulars because they came really often. Teenagers spent the whole night around the theatre. Some factory workers who lived locally also came together to enjoy leisure time after work."[8]

During the 1967 Leftist riots, Cheung Yan-lung expressed support for the government and was decried as one of the four running dogs, so the colonial administration permitted him to carry a sidearm. After the riots, officials arranged his visit to the United Kingdom in which he briefed the conditions of his hometown to prevent the Communist infiltration into London's Chinatown. In later years, Cheung was awarded The Order of St. John and sat on various boards that included the Hong Kong Jockey Club, The Hong Kong Housing Authority, the Kowloon-Canton Railway Corp, and the highly lucrative Simsen International Corp. in which two of his children would later become involved.

The right time and the right place. The story of Cheung Yan-lung's success was the portrayal of ruling the New Territories during the unsettled years after the war. He managed to get close to the colonial government at an opportune time in exchange for advantage and resolved the administration problems in the New Territories. Though Cheung was not an indigenous inhabitant of Sheung Shui, he transcended the village culture typically ruled by ancestral relationships and came to be even more respected than the locals.

Lineage was only second to family, as mentioned previously, and between 1943 and 1957, Angela Liu and Benton Cheung Yan-lung had eight sons and three daughters. While Cheung Yan-lung was bestowed with a long list of accomplishments in politics, his first born mirrored his accomplishments in the field of medicine.

Herman Shing-Chung came to the U.S. in 1964 and received his undergrad in Biological Sciences at Loyola Marymount in Los Angeles. In 1974, he obtained a Ph.D. in Cellular Molecular Biology from USC and spent the next 40 years building a prestigious career. Currently, he is a leading expert in biomedical engineering, renowned in his research in stem cells and regenerative medicine. Dr. Cheung serves on the editorial boards for several journals, consultant to biotech companies, and recipient of numerous national and international awards.

The Cheung's second child, the first of three daughters, named Amy Heung-Ping arrived New Year's Day 1946. Horatio Chun-Sing was born two years later and received his formal education at the University of Leeds in the U.K. He later returned home and became director of a non-profit advisory service for would-be immigrants. The Hong Kong Freedom of Movement and Rights of Abode Ltd. addressed citizen concerns on how they might emigrate from the colony before the 1997 handover. Mass migrations occurred in the 1990s with the looming handover on the horizon and the Tiananmen Square protests. Approximately 1% of the population departed from the colony each year, up to the handover, as would assets worth billions.

The 1940s concluded with the birth of the Cheung's second daughter, May Mei-Ping. The following year, another son was born. His name was Edmund Leung-Sing who lived a luxurious and playful life in his early years. Edmund studied in Canada during the seventies where he met his future wife. Her name was Anita Heung and she was the eldest daughter of Heung Wah-yim who was the first-born son of Heung Chin; Cheung Yan-lung's Kuomintang associate. In 1953, Heung Chin was deported to Taiwan for illicit activities and eldest son, Wah-yim, inherited the Dragon Head title for the infamous Sun Yee On Triad organization.

In 1987, Edmund was detained after a police raid at Lica Property

Mgmt., a business owned by Cheung Yan-lung, netted a large list of Sun Yee On members. Billed as the biggest organized-crime trial in Hong Kong's history, Edmund, Wah-yim, and others were indicted and sentenced for underworld related offenses.[9] A few years after, the decision was reversed and the charges dropped. Edmund soon distanced himself from his father-in-law and became a shareholder of a Macau gaming club in the New Century Hotel. His love of bookmaking proved to be ill-fated as he imprudently gambled while managing the casino. Sadly, with mounting debts and declining quality of life, Edmund passed in July 2013.

The Cheung's would have a pair of sons, children #6 and #7, born in 1951 and 1952 respectively. Danny Shue-Shing emigrated to Canada where he raised a family and worked as a chef. Norman Lok-Ching headed slightly south arriving in the U.S. where he followed in his eldest siblings' footsteps. He attended both Loyola Marymount and USC before his residency and fellowship at the Medical College of Wisconsin. Norman has been an Orthopedic Surgeon for over two decades, specializing in orthoscopic procedures, knee and hip replacements, and spinal surgeries.

The Cheung's 8th child was their third and final daughter, Eva Yuen-Wah. Eva was the closest in age to Alex, being his senior by a year and three weeks. She was also educated in the U.S. and followed in Fu Sheng's footsteps in 1980 by becoming a student of Lau Kar-Leung. Alex was the Cheung's next child, and soon after, Angela gave birth to her final two children; David in '56 and Simon in '57.

David Chin-Pang was born between the time of the two great Shek Wu Hui fires. He later relocated to Canada and attained his degree in psychology from the University of Calgary. David returned to Hong Kong, not to pursue a career in his field, but to join his brother in the film industry. He worked on seven films for Shaw Brothers Studio before abruptly retiring. David briefly joined a Chinese heavy metal band called The Crystal Zone who released their debut album in 1989. David is an avid snooker player and even played professionally in the U.K.

Simon Leung-Kwan was number eleven and the third son to pursue a career in medicine. He trained in medical microbiology and virology and received his Master of Science in Radiotherapy & Cancer research in 1981. He continued his instruction in the People's Republic of China at the Traditional Medical School in Nanjing before returning to the U.K. to set up his practice.

While Alex and most of his siblings were born in Kowloon, the family still had close ties to the village. Alex and his brothers spent many weekends visiting their grandfather and great grandmother in Sheung Shui. They would ride their bicycles near the communist border and stare over the fortified zone as the red star capped guards patrolled the area. Alex loved all his brothers and sisters, but when questioned about his large family, said he felt apathy for his mother's plight and joked,

"Mum has been giving birth all her life. She has given birth way too many times, almost like laying eggs in the end. You know, I have a brother who was born on the way to the hospital in the car?"[10]

As a youngster, Fu Sheng admitted he exhibited a poor disposition while attending school. Some sources state he was introduced to the martial arts by Wah-yim's younger brother, Charles Heung, and was a quick study.[11] Whenever someone upset him, Alex fought them no matter who it was: classmate, teacher, or even the headmaster. The principal though never wanted to suspend Alex as he excelled in sports (track and field, tennis, basketball) and medaled in whatever event he entered. Despite his short fuse, Alex knew right from wrong and injuring someone was not the answer.

"I once participated in a hurdle race when a runner next to me lost his balance and tripped under my feet. Luckily, I avoided treading on him. I was wearing trainers with nails and we both fell. When I got up, the race was done but we agreed that medals weren't the most important."[12]

Cheung Yan-lung also had several children with Dolly Chan Shuk-ching. Up until 1975, men in Hong Kong were able to keep concubines as a second wife, and Chan was spouse #2. Their second child together, Haywood Tak-Hei (born 1952), took the lead from his father and pursued a career in business. He accompanied Cheung to different events as a little boy which allowed him the opportunity to meet high-ranking British officials in person, and learn English and etiquette.

"These are the pluses. In these occasions, I learnt from my father that I should treat others sincerely," he stated in an interview.[13]

Like Alex, Haywood wanted to have his own career and not rely on his family's power and influence. He felt helping his family was both a responsibility but also a burden and wanted to take accountability for his own growth. Looking back at his upbringing, Haywood felt his father was strict but open and commented,

"He never forced us to get the highest mark in exams because the top student was usually a bookworm and the last one was a troublemaker. He thought that the average one was the cleverest."[14]

Haywood went to Canada and focused on a degree in Science with a major in Geology from Concordia University, Montreal. After graduation, he traveled to the States and worked for a hotel. During that period, the economy of Hong Kong took off and he returned home to oversee the securities business for the family. Today, Haywood has over 30 years' experience in metal trading, securities, and futures brokerage as well as forex dealing in Hong Kong. He was formerly Chairman of Simsen, the brokerage firm his father started, from 1997 to 2011 and is currently the President of the Chinese Gold and Silver Exchange Society.

Haywood's brother, Stanley Tak-Kwai (born 1959), also has three decades of experience in banking, finance, securities and futures brokering, and forex dealing. During the 1990s, he set up the first ever Chinese finance news and data satellite system which covered the whole of mainland China. Stanley also served as Vice Chairman of the Pok Oi Hospital, Director of the Hong Kong Securities Association Limited, amongst others. He and his mother made unpleasant headlines in July 1994 when her immigration application to Canada was turned down by authorities in Hong Kong. According to visa officer Jean Paul Delisle's declaration of facts, the application was rejected because Delisle felt Chan and her son were members of an organization engaged in criminal activity; more specifically the Sun Yee On.

In later years, Cheung Yan-lung found himself a third consort, Yuk-Kow Hui, whom he met at an entertainment establishment. After marrying into the family, Yuk-Kow Hui ran a food manufacturing business. She also managed a property agency in Sai Kung with the help of her daughter, Christine Fong, who is a District Councilor of the Sai Kung district.

Over the years, Cheung held three chairing positions (Sheung Shui Rural Committee, Rural Council, and Regional Council) and owned properties valuing over five hundred million HKD. When the Hong Kong government started developing the New Territories in the 1970s & '80s, he was the Chairperson of the Heung Yee Kuk and acted as an arbitrator between the government and the inhabitants. Cheung shrewdly acquired vast tracts of farmland in Sheung Shui, Fanling, Sha Tau Kok, and Ta Kwu Ling thereby obtaining prodigious compensation from the government under the Land Exchange Entitlement Letter B arrangement. As his wealth accumulated, he ventured outside the property and construction business into the financial sector and established Cheung's Finance, in which many villagers started investing in gold and stocks.

In the 1990s, the elder Cheung slowed his pace and preferred to play Mahjong in Kowloon Tong with good friends, such as Chan Yat-sen. Dubbed the King of the New Territories, Chan's life story was another classic tale of the peasant boy who rose from rice to riches. Like Cheung, he developed close links with Kuomintang figures in Hong Kong and lead the Kuk for many years before dying in 2007. While Cheung distributed his fortune among his children many years ago, his family still retains a few properties in Shek Wu Hui for rental, including a building named after his late father. When Cheung's children were growing up he echoed to them a Chinese proverb: *"Diligence is a priceless treasure. Prudence a protective charm."*[15]

The auspicious timing and social connections of Shek Wu Hui brought fortune to Cheung and his family. He started with local capital, proceeded into politics, and filled gaps in the governing power during the colonial era. In a "Who's Who of British Hong Kong," Cheung Yan-lung's awards, honors, and achievements would fill multiple columns. His family, though, will forever be his greatest asset and absolute triumph.

---

[1] See Web and More, "Lineage and Urban Development in a New Territories Market Town," page 85.

[2] See Web and More, "Fu Sing & Yan Nei," page 16.

[3] Sheung Shui Land Investment Company (1932) was a venture partnership between the Liao and metropolitan capital interests from Kowloon and Hong Kong which controlled the new market at Stone Lake.

[4] See Web and More, "Lineage and Urban Development in a New Territories Market Town," page 88.

[5] See Web and More, "Decline of Cheung Yan-lung and the Heungs."

[6] See Web and More, "Fu Sing & Yan Nei," page 16.
[7] Ibid.
[8] Samuel Chan Che-chung and Hazel Chung. "From Reel to Real." Magazine of the School of Journalism and Communication, CUHK. May 2010, Issue 116.
[9] See Books, The Dragon Syndicates, page 200.
[10] See Web and More, "Fu Sing & Yan Nei," page 16.
[11] See Web and More, "Partners in Crime."
[12] Hong Kong Movie News Dec. 1978: 36-37.
[13] See Web and More, "Haywood Cheung Loves Adventure and Is Not Afraid of Failure."
[14] Ibid.
[15] Ibid.

3

The Shaw Brothers

Fu Sheng was the least scholarly among his siblings in the Cheung household. While his brothers hold university degrees, Alex only completed Secondary 4.[1] In those days, there was a major public examination for Secondary 5 (11th grade) students and those who held good grades advanced to matriculation classes (Form 6 and 7) to prepare for college. Secondary 5 was considered the minimum qualification that one needed to be eligible for white-collared work. Despite his disinterest in academia, Alex didn't suffer from low self-esteem and graciously admired the achievements of his siblings. A friend who attended junior high with Alex recalled the soon-to-be rising star as quite the mischief-maker. The former classmate said Alex refused to listen to the instructor during class and was generally restless. To pass the time, he'd attempt to get others to distract the teacher's lectures. He mimicked Alex's teasing,

"You sing. Sing like a bird. Sing now or I will keep poking you."[2]

The young Fu Sheng had a movie star's look at an early age but was also ridiculed on occasion. Alex looked like a Western kid when he was a pre-teen and his peers called him gweizai; version of gweilo for boys. During exams, Alex continually handed in his papers with questions unanswered. When his peers laughed at him, he accused them of cheating and said a real man would rather hand his paper in blank than cheat. Alex's lack of interest in education eventually came to a head when he and Cheung Yan-lung had a major quarrel.

"When I was fifteen, I was not getting along with my father. After a fight, I ran away from home briefly and went to work as a construction worker in my uncle's property development company."[3]

Alex spent the following months pouring concrete, hauling mud, and balancing 20-foot-long rebars on his back. Rebars were heavy and difficult to control, so he'd bounce them while walking to maintain his balance.

The daily wage was only 15 dollars but his perseverance and stamina earned him the nickname of Superman. When Alex wasn't on the job site, he enjoyed spending his free time at the Kowloon Tong Club with family and friends. His parents owned a large property on Boundary Street which was a few minutes away from the posh tennis club.

Just up the block from the resort was a residence with the address of 41 Cumberland Road. Martial arts fans worldwide are familiar with this location as being the final home of the late Bruce Lee. For years, it has been rumored that Alex purchased this property late in life and was even residing there when he passed. A childhood friend of Alex, who frequented the Kowloon Tong Club with him, debunked this myth of Fu Sheng ever owning the legendary fighter's home.

"There was no connection to Bruce Lee's house. Bruce's house sat behind Kowloon Tong Club and was five minutes from Alex's home. We used to see Bruce jog and would roll down the window and scream at him. Always got a thumb up. Alex own the property? Fan made fantasy."

Over the summer of 1971, Alex had no desire to return to school and his construction job only provided him extra pocket change. He was biding his time and had his eyes set on a different academy of learning. Alex expressed when he attended public school that he felt lethargic whenever entering a classroom. This subsequent campus though was novel. A local motion picture studio announced they were launching a new training facility and seeking background actors. What Alex did not realize was that this job change set in motion a series of events that provided him with more wealth and happiness than he would ever know. But for now, he was content just to get a raise as his acting salary was 30 dollars per day.

"I could earn money and have fun from acting, which was much better than staring at the books or wandering on the street."[4]

Enter the Shaw Brothers of Hong Kong. Of all the production companies to come out of the colony, one stands above the rest despite the fact its beginnings were in Shanghai. The Shaw line started during the Ming Dynasty (A.D. 1368-1644) when they relocated from the Yangzhou Prefecture in Shandong to the Zhejiang province. The family assumed the name of Tu but changed it to pay tribute to the name of the Ningbo neighborhood, Shaw, where they resided.

Three centuries later, Yuh Hsuen Shaw (1867-1920) ventured out of Ningbo to pursue a career in the Shanghai textile industry where he built up a prosperous business. His eldest son, Shao Renjie aka Runje Shaw, had a successful career in law but his passion lied in the arts. Runje procured a theater in 1923 as he deemed it was a persuasive method of conveying information to the masses. He expanded a few years later with two more theaters but took note of the stage's shortcomings stating it was,

"...seriously inhibited by its lack of freedom to present time and space. But film can bring to life on screen everything presented on stage."[5]

Runje foresaw the financial rewards this new medium could bring and established the Tianyi Film Co. aka Unique Film in 1925 with younger siblings, Runde Shaw and Runme Shaw. Tianyi went on to create highly successful genre films, including swordplay, and was among the first Asian moviemakers to take the leap from silent to sound. They produced *Swordswoman Li Feifei (1925),* regarded by many as the earliest Chinese martial arts film, and the first Cantonese talkie, *White Gold Dragon (1933),* which was a commercial success in Southern China.

Despite its creative and fiscal growth, Runje branched out from the mainland after a Shanghai based amalgamation, Lianhua Film, put a stranglehold on the local distribution circuit. A suspicious fire in 1936 crippled their Tianyi Studio in Hong Kong and the company reorganized into Nanyang Productions. Some years later, it was further renamed as Shaw & Sons, Ltd. Control of the Hong Kong operations was passed onto Runde while Runme, along with baby brother Run Run Shaw, had ventured to Singapore to facilitate the distribution and exhibition of their movies. Despite occasional setbacks, the Shaw empire expanded, and by 1939 included 110 theaters and nine amusement parks in British Malaya, Borneo, Java, and Thailand.

War then broke out and with it came the Japanese occupation of Southeast Asia. Runme and Run Run planned to escape to Australia but a delay in their travels turned out to be a blessing in disguise as the ship was sunk by a Japanese torpedo. They opted to stay in Singapore where their theaters were stripped and film equipment confiscated for propaganda productions. While much was lost, the brothers salvaged a good chunk of their fortune by hiding four million dollars of gold, currency, and jewels in their garden. The buried treasure kept the Shaw family alive during the war and helped them restart their business after the Japanese surrender. Recalled Run Run,

"The pearls were a little brown, the watches rusty, the bank notes mildewed, but the gold was nice and yellow. The diamonds, sapphires and emeralds were in excellent form. We were still rich."[6]

More than a decade later, the Shaws made their most audacious move yet. By the late 50s, Runde had lost interest in the film industry and focused more on real estate. In 1957, Run Run left Singapore for the colony with an aggressive agenda. He broke ties with the waning Shaw & Sons, Ltd. and purchased forty-six acres of a remote parcel from the government near Clear Water Bay. The hilly property was acquired for the trifling sum of forty-five cents per square foot due to its proximity to the communist border and 650,000 square feet of land was initially cleared for six sound stages. This was the birth of Shaw Brothers (HK) Ltd. with Run Run and Runme as principal shareholders. Upon its completion, Shaw Brothers Studio would become the largest privately-owned film production facility, not just in Hong Kong, but in the entire world.

Shaw Brothers Studio officially opened December 6, 1961 and was fashioned after the traditional Hollywood system with a staff of creative talent under exclusive contracts. Run Run and Runme adopted the Fordism industrial mode of vertical integration for their new studio which combines production, distribution, and exhibition under one roof.[7] Run Run recruited university educated professionals like Raymond Chow, Leonard Ho, and Chua Lam to help bolster his management team.

Between 1961 and 1964, Shaw Brothers Studio made 13-18 films per year and set a record in 1965 with a total of 26, which averages out to one every other week. Further land was cleared for an additional six sound stages, and by decade's end, Movietown (as it was known locally) occupied 850,000 square feet of ground. There were five blocks of administrative buildings, 12 sound stages, 16 permanent outdoor sets, an editing and sound recording studio, and four staff dormitories for its workforce of 1500 plus.

"In its heyday, Shaw Studios worked around the clock in three eight-hour shifts, producing an average of 40 films a year on a budget of HK

$2.5 million each. Most of the 1000 films Shaw produced were low budget, formulaic musicals and melodramas, although martial arts films became the staple diet later..."[8]

Among the studio's unique characteristics was the Shawscope logo that heralded each film accompanied by high tempo trumpet fanfare. This opening credit sequence quickly became one of the most memorable in Asian cinema and an advantageous marketing tool. Another distinctive attribute was the studio's ability to groom future stars for their stable. Ivy Ling Po, Linda Lin Dai, Betty Loh Ti, Jimmy Wang Yu, Li Ching, and Lo Lieh were just a few of the many talented actors loyal to the Shaw banner. While the glamour of being on the silver screen appealed to many, the monetary gains were quite minuscule. Initially, everyone signed multi-year contracts which included room and board. Lo Lieh joined the studio in 1962 and spoke of his early days there,

"At the time, the price of a Shaw Brothers contract was very low. You could not buy a car, a house. After you signed the contract, they paid you $200 a month. If you made a picture, they paid you $700. You couldn't really afford to live on this, so you had to find other ways to make money."[9]

Run Run Shaw was extremely proactive in perfecting the talent of his performers, so an in-house film school was established in the summer of '61 to both improve veterans' drama skills and instruct up-and-coming actors and actresses. This school was known initially as the Southern Drama Group but later renamed The Shaw Films Training Centre. The following decade, it was further revamped as the Shaw HK TVB Training Centre under a joint management.[10] The new training facility launched August 8, 1971, and its first group of novice actors began a rigorous one-year course of study that incorporated both theory and practical studies.

The initial classes were full day sessions and the curriculum divided into two parts. The first half of the year focused on absorbing fundamentals needed for performing in front of the camera, as well as, behind-the-scenes concepts. Courses included performance, photography, dialogue, screenwriting, dance, makeup, fashion, hairstyling, and martial arts. As explained by one of Shaw's top talents at the time, many students weren't versed in the fighting arts but proper training made them appear they were.

"You have to know how to hold your hands, where to kick to, how to

give out all your energy and avoid hurting your partner. If you do not know the martial arts you end up looking very ugly," recanted Chiang Da-Wei.[11]

The second half of the year was devoted to internships in the field as background talent and bit roles. Graduates then entered full time employment with either Shaw Brothers Studio or TVB, and on September 28, 1972, Run Run presented the initial 45 certificates. First year alumni included Tony Wong Yuen-San, Michelle Yim, Meg Lam Kin-Ming, Gracy Tong Ka-Lai, and Danny Lee Sau-Yin.

These early grads came up in an era when Shaw actors enjoyed the cloistered protection from the outside world. It was a utopian environment where they honed their skills without interference of the harsh media frenzy that surrounded show business. Movietown for them was the real world and unlike the stars of today, who seek fame and fortune, they were content in their own reality. Writer Tony Page described the place as if lost in a time warp with centuries old citadel ships and tiled roof temples mixed amongst the grid-like maze of modern studios and administrative buildings.[12]

"Even when we were not on a shoot we'd see completely dolled-up actors going by on horseback. And when you wandered onto a soundstage, you'd see people beating the hell out of each other. It's not something young actors today could be part of," commented Lee Sau-Yin.[13]

Another graduate of this maiden class that autumn was the fresh faced, seventeen-year-old Cheung Fu-Sheng who favored his English name of Alexander. School was now out and Alex was eager to break from the pack and show the world what he had learned.

---

[1] One of the most reiterated pieces of misinformation on Fu Sheng is that he lived in Hawaii as a teenager and attended (some even say, graduated) high school there. The author has confirmed from various sources, including Alex's family, that Fu Sheng never attended high school (or lived) in Hawaii.
[2] Southern Screen Aug 1979: 28-29.
[3] See Web and More, "Fu Sing & Yan Nei," page 16.
[4] Southern Screen May 1981: 46-47.
[5] See Web and More, "1925: The Start of a Legendary Studio."
[6] See Books, The Legend of Bruce Lee, page 61.
[7] See Web and More, "Moguls of the Cinema."
[8] See Books, The Asian Film Industry, page 99.
[9] See Books, Hong Kong Action Cinema, page 15. (Author note: Unless otherwise noted,

all $ figures are in Hong Kong dollars.)

[10] In 1967, Run Run Shaw founded TVB (Television Broadcasts Limited) which not only became a breeding ground for new talent but also morphed into the world's largest supplier of Chinese language programming. The Shaw HK TVB Training Centre encompassed talent from both TVB and Movietown.

[11] See Books, Kung Fu: Cinema of Vengeance, page 20.

[12] See Web and More, "The Men Who Make Celluloid Dreams."

[13] See Web and More, "Take Two."

4

Chang Cheh

Yin and Yang. This is the Chinese concept in which contrary forces are complementary and interconnected. They are the starting point for change. In Taoism, the pairs are poles such as ascending and descending, whereas in Western thinking, they're equated with good and evil. Whether it was fate or fluke, the beginning and ending of Alexander Fu Sheng's career is interlinked by two films that ominously echoed this philosophical pairing.

In 1970, Shaw Brothers Studio embarked on an audacious production titled *The 14 Amazons (1972)*. The project was an extravagant tale of patriotism, gallantry, and sacrifice that featured an impressive ensemble of Shaw's most popular superstars. Using the folklore *Generals of the Yang Family* as their source material, producer Run Run Shaw and directors Tung Shao-Yung and Cheng Gang featured a predominantly female cast which included Ivy Ling Po, Li Ching, Lily Ho, as well as, Yueh Hua, and Lo Lieh.

Generals of the Yang Family is an anthology of Chinese novels and plays about a military family from the early years of the Song Dynasty (A.D. 960-1279). The story of the Yang, particularly its female generals, was an enduring favorite on the Chinese stage. In bringing the celebrated tale to the screen, the Shaw's undertaking encompassed 140,000 feet of celluloid, 200 working days, and a staggering cost of $4 million.

The 14 Amazons wrapped production in February 1972, and when released that summer, it set box office records in Hong Kong, Taiwan, and Singapore. The film secured four Golden Horse Awards including Best Director for Cheng and Honorable Mention for Best Feature Film. At the 19th Asian Film Festival, the picture won first prize for Best Screenplay (also written by Cheng) and Lily Ho was honored as Best Actress for her portrayal as the "son," Yang Wen Kuan.

Fu Sheng made his debut in this epic as a Hsia soldier, but is lost in a sea of extras as Run Run Shaw employed an enormous cast.[1] Unbeknownst to Alex and lead actress Lily Ho, the pair would share a common link. Ho's character was the grandson of Yang Yanzhao who, in the *Generals of the Yang Family*, was the 6th son of Yang Ye. Yanzhao was the lone warrior to return home from the Chenjiagu battlefield, after the Yangs were betrayed by their countrymen. Yanzhao aka Yang 6th brother became the character that Alex eventually portrayed over a decade later. It was a role he would not complete due to his own untimely death.

When looking back at *The 14 Amazons*, Alex didn't share the same exhilaration many enjoyed. Besides the low wages, these bit players worked without any union representation, insurance or medical benefits, brown-bagged their lunch, and provided their own transportation to location shoots. Despite it being his first time on a set, Alex considered it as one of the low periods in his career and recalled only those miserable moments working as an extra.

The next project the budding actor partook in was an anti-Japanese film that slipped into obscurity until it was remastered and released by Celestial Pictures nearly three decades later. *The Thunderbolt Fist (1972)* was directed by Korean filmmaker, Jang Il-Ho, who made ten films for Movietown in the early '70s. Some of his more popular efforts included *The Deadly Knives (1972)* with Ching Li and Lily Li, *The Iron Man (1974)* featuring Jimmy Wang Yu, and *Devil Bride (1975)* starring Lo Lieh and Ku Feng.

Released December 30 1972, *The Thunderbolt Fist* was a tale of revenge and innocence lost which focused on the Chinese struggle against the heavy-handed Japanese. This theme was widespread at the time, as depicted in several films including the highly popular *Fist of Fury (1972)*. Unlike Bruce Lee's movie, the martial arts in *The Thunderbolt Fist* took to the backburner, with the melodrama being the focal point, and the film struggled at the box office. Coincidentally, *The Thunderbolt Fist* featured roughly twenty of the same cast members who appeared in the record setting *King Boxer (1972)*. Some speculate that *King Boxer* director Jeong Chang-Hwa may have assisted his compatriot with a few of the directorial duties on *The Thunderbolt Fist* but remains uncredited.

The Thunderbolt Fist's lead, Taiwanese actor Chuen Yuen, received a mixed bag of comments for his role as Fang Tie Wa, whereas his younger co-star, Shih Szu, garnered the more positive reviews. Shih Szu was also from Taiwan and collected numerous dancing trophies as a child when she was known as Lei Qiu-Si. The teen actress, accompanied by her mother, moved into the Shaw dormitories when she was only 16, and quickly became a staple of Movietown. Reviewers at Hong Kong Movie Database dote on Shih Szu's portrayal as one *"who lights up the screen with a devil may care attitude"* and *"...she's petite with a pixie-cute smile."*[2] The *Thunderbolt Fist* would be the first of a half dozen productions that Shih Szu appeared in with Fu Sheng during the course of the '70s decade.

Alex's appearance in this movie is a blink-and-you-miss cameo. Around the 15:00 mark, there is a cave scene where a group of Chinese have taken refuge. Jang Il-Ho's camera slowly pans across the crowd of men in which we finally lay our eyes on Alexander Cheung Fu Sheng. This picture was Alex's final project before beginning a long-term relationship with one of the studio's most illustrious filmmakers.

Chang Cheh's career was surging at the turn of the decade with an abundance of impressive hits beginning with his best-known film, *One-Armed Swordsman (1967)*.[3] The director cranked out nearly twenty titles within the next five years that included box office gold such as *Return of the One-Armed Swordsman (1969)*, *The Heroic Ones (1970)*, and *The Anonymous Heroes (1971)*. The following year, Chang set his eyes on the Korean peninsula for his next endeavor, *Four Riders (1972)*, and spent the Chinese New Year scouting locations in the frigid climate.

The story of *Four Riders* was purely fictional although inspired by the first-hand account of an actor who took part in the war between the two Koreas. Production began mid-April, and besides being Alex's initial film with Chang, it was also his first under the guidance of martial arts choreographers Lau Kar-Leung and Tong Gai. Lead actor Chiang Da-Wei was good friends with the Cheung family, and according to Robert Tai Chi-Hsien, was the one who introduced Fu Sheng to the director.

"Fu Sheng's dad was Chiang Da-Wei's adopted father. Cheung Yan-lung asked Chiang to bring Fu Sheng to Director Chang. Fu Sheng went to the studio all the time to watch filming, so the director asked him one

day to put on a costume and play a soldier," Tai commented.[4]

The Korean War setting seemed a good fit for the director as military lines were in his blood. Born January 17, 1924, in Qingtian County (Zhejiang), Chang Cheh was originally named Zhang Yiyang (Chang Yee-young).[5] According to his memoirs, his early life wasn't favorable due to his complicated family background. The relationship with his parents was sadly a distant one and he did not delight in the parental love that a child deserves. This left an emotional scar for Chang and thus never reared any children of his own.

When the Second Sino-Japanese War aka War of Resistance broke out in 1937, Chang left his Shanghai home to participate in the anti-Japanese war efforts. He finished his high school education in Sichuan, and thanks to his father's military background, was accepted to Central University of Chongqing to study politics. He returned to Shanghai after the fighting subsided, where the executive party member of the Kuomintang (KMT) took a shine to Chang and appointed him as commissioner of Shanghai's Cultural Movement Committee (CMC). This position suited Chang's educational background as he took on several challenges which included the overseeing of a KMT-controlled theatre. It was during this time he befriended a young martial arts novelist, Louis Cha Leung-yung aka Jin Yong, who would become the inspiration for many of his future films.

Chang Cheh also became closely associated with many left-wing intellectuals and artists. During the Japanese occupation of Shanghai (1937-1945), Chinese filmmakers were forced to make propaganda projects under the Japanese run China United Film Company. Once the war was over, China United folded and those filmmakers were now regarded as Japanese collaborators. They pleaded with Chang who, with the backing of the Shanghai CMC, was able to exonerate the men. This was a big break for Chang as it secured him some powerful and lasting relationships. One of the individuals pardoned was the boss of the Guotai Company which financed Chang's directorial debut, *Happenings in Alishan (1949)* aka *Wind and Storm Over Alishan*.

Chang Cheh was twenty-six-years old when he first went to Taiwan. By 1948-49, members of the KMT were slowly jumping ship to join the

Communist Party and he knew the CMC was on its way out. In Taiwan, he befriended Chiang Ching-kuo, the son of Chiang Kai-shek, and forged a close alliance but Chang soon became frustrated with the political infighting. He had yet to consider film as a career but knew neither Taiwan nor the mainland was ideal. Chang soon set his eyes on Hong Kong and thus began his stalwart career.

In 1957, Chang moved to Hong Kong at the invitation of actress Helen Li Mei to direct her next film, *Wild Fire (1958)*. Chang's involvement was cut short by Motion Picture & General Investment Co. (MP&GI) after rumors surfaced of his involvement with Li Mei. While this could have been a crushing blow for the novice filmmaker, Chang didn't let it dissuade him and shifted gears by immersing himself in writing articles under the pen names of He Guan and Shen Si. His pseudonym writings caught the attention of Run Run Shaw and, strangely enough, MP&GI. Despite his prior history, he opted to sign a one-year contract with MP&GI but detested the company's favoritism toward its female artists while their male counterparts remained in the shadows. When his contract was fulfilled in 1961, he immediately jumped ship for Shaw Brothers Studio where his directorial career took off by leaps and bounds.

"...his yanggang (staunch masculinity) style was so overwhelmingly powerful that it simply uprooted the foundation of local cinema and established the supremacy of the male action star for years to come." wrote film critic, Sek Kei.[6]

The late 1960s and early '70s witnessed an avalanche of violent and masculine films by the auteur which coincided with the counter culture movements sweeping Hong Kong and beyond. Young audiences flocked to Chang's movies like moths to a fire. His heroes embodied uncertain times and they regarded this *"new trend towards violence as a purging of repressed emotions."*[7] Yanggang and the martial arts movie became the manifesto for the new generation in which Chang drew his inspirations from the blood-soaked blockbusters of chambara that Jeff Yang summarized as a *"genre where heads and limbs flew with abandon."*[8]

Chang Cheh's *The Assassin (1967)*, *Golden Swallow (1968)*, and *Vengeance! (1970)* were all commercial and popular successes. As acclaimed as they were, these films were branded "violent and bloody" to which Chang took offense, stating it was a shallow assessment of his work. Some critics went even further condemning him as a blatant, unabashed purveyor of the most brutal and degrading screen violence, a mass corruptor of public morals, and the man indirectly responsible for rising crimes in Hong Kong.

"I refuse to accept that screen violence will lead to moral decay," scoffed Chang. *"If we have to deplore all violence then we must deplore war which is the ultimate violence. But, governments wage it."*[9]

Chang's anti-war picture, *Four Riders,* was a testament to his belief that the 20th century was plagued by governmental war mongering.[10] The film was Fu Sheng's earliest collaboration with a group of actors whom were instrumental in his early years of development. Ti Lung, Chiang Da-Wei, Chen Kuan-tai, and Wong Chung starred as the four battle fatigued soldiers who have escaped the Korean frontlines only to discover that even civilization is a raging zone of conflict and horror.

"We went to Seoul and shot for about two weeks and then returned to the studio for the bulk of the shooting. I recall Chang wanted to use Four Riders to promote Wong Chung as he had hopes of making him the next new star of Shaw." Chen Kuan-tai recalled in a 2013 interview.[11]

The movie's opening sequence evoked haunting images of Ingmar Bergman's *The Seventh Seal (1957)* as four indistinct figures crossed a snow-clad landscape. These characters were meant to be loosely based on the Four Horsemen of the Apocalypse, Book of Revelation in the New Testament. One reviewer interpreted *Four Riders* as a cleaning scourge against the evils and corruption of the modern world with a Chang twist.

"In Chang's more dystopian version, the impression is of futility of heroism in the face of an all-powerful, deadly state machinery – one that in spite of its might is nonetheless irrational, absurd and incapable of providing for human happiness or justice."[12]

Alex was born one year after the Korean Armistice Agreement brought hostilities to an end. Being over 1000 miles from the battlefield, most would think the conflict had little or no bearing on his family. In actuality, many individuals in the New Territories benefited from the war as the UN trade embargo of China created a lucrative black market for goods smuggled into the mainland. Alex's father and grandfather took full advantage of the situation by running contraband all along the border from Mirs Bay in the east to Deep Bay in the west. Everything from food and medicine to fuel and engines for airplanes was smuggled into China. Cheung Yan-lung recanted,

"On a dark, moonless night the beach at Kat O often resembled how I imagine a smugglers' cove in eighteenth-century England would have looked, with small boats, men with lanterns, and piles of goods! The length of the border meant it was almost impossible to police it effectively."[13]

Four Riders was one of three Chang Cheh films released in 1972 that secured over one million in box office receipts. Screening for a mere eight days in local theaters, this maiden Chang/Fu Sheng collaboration cracked the seven-figure mark and was 18th overall that year. Though Alex was relegated to mise-en-scène, his association with Chang eventually went well beyond a director/actor relationship. As a close family member stated, *"Chang Cheh treated Fu Sheng like a son."*[14]

Chang Cheh's next production, *Young People (1972)*, actually began principal photography a month earlier than *Four Riders* but was the second occasion that the cinema "father & son" worked together. Alex again had neither dialogue, nor a character name. However, he participated in various sequences and demonstrated his interests in music, playing a drummer in the finale, and the martial arts. As the title reflects, this was one of several films in which Chang tackled the youth genre. The three leads (Ti Lung, Chiang Da-Wei, and Chen Kuan-tai) were featured in the critically successful Shaw Greek tragedy, *The Blood Brothers (1973)*, but *Young People* embraced a more carefree narrative. This was a non-action movie about competitive but fun-loving college coeds.

"Director Chang wanted to make a film to help the younger generation become better people, better citizens. After the riots of '67 and all the social discord, Hong Kong audiences needed a break from reality. They needed to escape to a place where life was fun again and not so detrimental," recalled Chen who played martial artist, Ho Tai.[15]

In creating this picture Chang did more than that. He constructed an inadvertent time capsule of early 1970s Hong Kong with its free spirit fashions, quirky music sequences, and exaggerated product placements. Initially titled *Days of Youth* during its early filming, the project was partially shot on location in Sha Tin District, in the New Territories. Using the spacious Chung Chi College in Ma Liu Shui as the backdrop, the film provided the viewing audience a breath of fresh air from their claustrophobic urban decay. To help promote the project, a Grand Prix go-cart race was held for three days during Easter weekend 1972. The event took place in Shek Kong, attracting thousands of spectators, and was featured in the movie's thrilling finale.

Making her debut in *Young People* was 16-year-old Agnes Chan Mei-Ling who embarked on a singing career two years prior. She already established herself as up-and-coming despite being nearly a year younger than Alex. Her first song, "The Circle Game," sold the most singles in Hong Kong's pop music history and she rose to teen idol stardom after debuting in Japan with another hit single, "Hinageshi no Hana." Chan also starred in her own weekly primetime broadcast show at RTV before joining elder sister, actress Irene Chen Yi-Ling, at Shaw Brothers Studio.[16] Neither Run Run Shaw nor Chang Cheh were overly concerned with Chan's lack of acting abilities; just including the pop star was good enough to bolster box office revenue.

Young People released on July 7, 1972. Ironically, Alex's favorite month was July and he considered seven his lucky number. He accurately predicted this was a good sign for things to come as the picture finished in the top ten with returns slightly over $1.2 million. The movie also proved lucky for Alex in a personal way, for it was the start of a thirteen-film collaboration with Ti Lung. A fixture in many of Chang Cheh's blood-curdling martial tragedies, Ti Lung's acting prowess proved advantageous for Alex's career and the two men established an off-screen friendship that would last a lifetime.

---

[1] Fu Sheng appears on the left side of screen at 00:04:26 with Wang Hsieh.
[2] See Film Reviews and Interviews, "The Thunderbolt Fist (1972)."
[3] While One-Armed Swordsman (1967) was the first Shaw film to pull in one million dollars in receipts, the first Hong Kong film to surpass the one-million-dollar box office was The Golden Eagle/Jinying (1964) directed by Chan Ching-Po and produced by Feng Huang (Phoenix) Motion Picture Co.
[4] "Q & A with Robert Tai." Personal interview. 12 Nov. 2013.
[5] Erroneously listed on the net as 10 Feb. 1923 (possibly originating from an April 1976. Taiwanese article) amongst other incorrect dates. His actual birth date of 17 Jan. 1924 is

based upon the director's memoirs (page 50), Shaw Screen, and author confirmation at Chang's burial site in 2010.

[6] See Books, Chang Cheh: A Memoir, page 11. (Author note: The slogan "yanggang" was initially coined by Chang in his film column "My Views on Cinema.")

[7] See Books, Hong Kong Cinema: The Extra Dimensions, page 100.

[8] See Books, Once upon a Time in China, page 50.

[9] Leslie Fong, "Director Who Gave Asia Men Movies." The Straits Times [Singapore] 20 May 1973: 4.

[10] In the States, it was titled as Hellfighters of the East.

[11] "Chen Kuan Tai Returns to South Florida." Personal interview. 4 Aug. 2013.

[12] See Film Reviews and Interviews, "Kung Fu with Braudel."

[13] See Books, Hong Kong Remembers, page 38.

[14] Facebook post.

[15] "Chen Kuan Tai Returns to South Florida." Personal interview. 4 Aug. 2013.

[16] Rediffusion Television was the first television station in Hong Kong (1959). Its pay cable service would come under heavy competition after TVB made its first free-to-air broadcast in 1967. On 24 September 1982, it was renamed as Asia Television or ATV.

5

Ti Lung and Chiang Da-Wei

Ti Lung was born Tan Furong (Tam Fu-Wing) in 1946 in the Xinhui District of Guangdong. He described himself as a thin and feeble young man who attended Eton, Hong Kong's elite boarding school, which has its origins dating back to Henry VI of England. Unfortunately, his family lived in poverty and he abandoned his studies at age eleven to start work. He labored as a tailor shop trainee and ultimately brought in $2000 per month as a designer. While this was a respectable wage, the twenty-one-year-old gave it all up after noticing an advertisement in the local paper. Tan Furong had grown up watching Jimmy Wang Yu films and when he saw that Shaw was recruiting actors, he decided to take the plunge and was among five chosen from over 2000 applicants.

"I think the main reason for my selection was that I had been taking part in gymnastics exercises for more than five years, which gives me an advantage in swordsman films," he remarked.[1]

Before Tan Furong entered the Shaw Brothers organization in 1968, he also trained in Wing Chun (Yong Chun) under Sifu Jiu Wan, a respected elder of the southern based system. Jiu Wan learned the style from his cousin, Jiu Tong, who was in the same martial arts lineage as Wing Chun Master Yip Man (Bruce Lee's teacher). At Shaw's in-house Nanguo Acting Training Class, the new actor was introduced to Karate, Thai boxing, Taekwondo, Judo, and Mantis Style kung fu. Tan admitted that attending the Shaw school was quite exhausting but he would still find the time to take in a show at the local movie house. A personal favorite of Tan's was French actor Alain Delon. *"Dark, dynamic, and magnetic"* is how the Shaw actor described Delon, and he desired to have a screen name with Delon's characteristics in mind.

"Delon has an attractive look, full of mystery. The appearance of a tough guy but at other times seductive. All the girls can fall in love with

him, he's an international star . . . and I admired him so much."[2]

After his six-months of training, Tan appeared on screen in the period swordplay *Return of the One-Armed Swordsman* but was credited as Tam Wing. Soon after, he adopted the screen name of Ti (lucky) Lung (dragon) after a production secretary suggested the nom de plume was a fitting match. Now known as "Ti Lung," the actor remarked on entering the industry, he would emulate Wang Yu's posture and heroic stance as if *"you're holding back 10,000 soldiers"* but found it difficult to mimic the proper reactions to the fight sequences.[3] The novice praised his instructors on how they helped him learn the art of cinematic deception and Ti Lung got his big break when selected to play the lead in Chang Cheh's action drama *Dead End (1969)*.

Subsequently, Ti Lung received ongoing roles as the majestic hero in blood splattered operatic brawls but it was his performance in *The Blood Brothers,* as the treacherous Officer Ma, which captivated the viewing audience. He was bestowed the Special Jury Prize in 1973, at both the Golden Horse Awards and the Asia-Pacific Film Festival, for his efforts. His accomplished character acting secured him years of praise from fans and critics alike until his relationship with Movietown concluded in the summer of 1985. After a brief lull, the megastar began the next phase of his career. This time it was not Chang Cheh but his former assistant, John Woo, at the reigns.

Woo cast Ti Lung in the brutally violent crime thriller, *A Better Tomorrow (1986),* which emulated the same spirit of tragic heroism that Chang championed in his own martial arts films. Ti Lung acknowledged that he used his relationship with Alex for his character's motivation in both this movie and its 1987 sequel. Both films were a tremendous success, revolutionizing Hong-Kong cinema, and providing a new lease on life to Ti Lung's career. He remains as one of the best known and revered figures to both the old aficionados and new supporters of Hong Kong cinema.

Fu Sheng's next film in 1972 was on the heels of one of Chang Cheh's biggest hits. During the second week of February, Shaw Brothers Studio unleashed the kung fu basher, *Boxer from Shantung*, to the euphoria of Hong Kong audiences. Co-starring established stars Chiang Da-Wei and

Ku Feng, this early Republic film told the tale of real-life Shanghainese boxer Ma Yongzhen and made a superstar of martial arts expert Chen Kuan-tai. As described in an on-line review, Chen is a *"force of resolute, badass charm throughout the film, exuding star power and raw energy."*[4] Taking in over two million at the box office, Chang captured lightning in a bottle and was quick to capitalize on his success by creating a continuation of sorts with the film *Man of Iron (1972)*.

More a companion piece than sequel, the new film was set twenty years after the original. Chen now portrayed anti-hero Chow Yun-Wan who was a one man wrecking machine. While it was Chang's in concept and script, this latter basher exhibited a discrete touch that was not completely his own. In Chang's memoirs, he wrote that Pao Hsueh-Li was truly the executing director despite credited as an associate. Pao was a capable cinematographer who added some fine-tuning to his collaborative works with Chang Cheh.

Man of Iron proved to be a milestone in Fu Sheng's bourgeoning career as he was finally awarded his first words of dialogue. The scene was rather short in which a teenaged Alex (no screen name) approached Chow Yun-Wan and warned him that he was walking into an ambush. Chen Kuan-tai relived the scene in an interview with the author.

"I recall the first time we worked together. He had been in one or two previous productions but just as a background player. An extra."[5]

Chen Kuan-tai studied the DVD as it played. On the screen, a young man rides his Raleigh bicycle into a dapper looking Chow Yun-Wan.

"Alex was hanging around the studio like he always would. He was young. Just a teenager. A baby (laughter). Chang took an immediate liking to Fu Sheng. I think this was late spring or early summer in '72. Hard to believe it's been forty years. Wow. Anyway, the director put him into this scene which began our wonderful relationship and his career."[6]

Man of Iron would not be the only *Boxer from Shantung* spin-off as several films have been attributed to this tale. The initial screen adaptation was *Shandong Ma Yongzhen (1927)* by Zhang Shi-Chuan and released to mesmerized audiences at the Palace Theater in Shanghai. This silent picture was an early hit in Chinese martial arts movie history and featured Zhang Huichong aka "China's Valentino."[7] The film's adrenaline-charged climax occurs in a teahouse with the hero battling to the death an overwhelming number of machete-wielding assassins. His demise is avenged by his sister; however, in the 1972 rendering, the vengeance story was presented in a sequel titled *The Avenger (1972)* aka *The Queen Boxer*.

Even before Fong Ming Motion Picture Co. released *The Avenger*, the Taiwanese film industry jumped on the bandwagon. Doris Lung portrayed the avenging sister in *A Brave Girl-Boxer in Shanghai (1972)*. If that wasn't enough, another spin-off titled *Queen of Fist (1973)* aka *Kung Fu Mama* focused on the family matriarch. As for *Man of Iron*, Chan's version released in October '72, eight months after *Boxer from Shantung*, and claimed slightly over one million dollars in receipts. *The Avenger* made $300,000 less placing it 29th for the year, nine spots lower than *Man of Iron*.

Fu Sheng continued his studies that summer of '72 and took on one additional film project before his upcoming graduation. The new picture, *The Generation Gap (1973),* provided him more dialogue and Alex was assigned his first screen name. While things seemed to be progressing nicely on the set, his days at the Shaw school weren't always filled with moments he savored. The young actor often found himself at odds with the appointed leaders of his class. Wong Yuen-San was the class president while Danny Lee Sau-Yin was the vice president. Alex begrudgingly looked back and remarked,

"Yuen-san was the leader and everyone obeyed him. He was nicknamed 'OK Boy' but I still debated him. I was younger and didn't talk back too much. I stopped myself short, and this is a bit embarrassing, but I kind of wept a little. It was difficult as I did not cry much."[8]

Coincidentally for Alex, director Chang again tackled the difficulties of youth in *The Generation Gap* which conveyed a much darker tone from the prior year's contemporary youth escapades. Chiang Da-Wei and Agnes Chan star as a love-strewn couple who find themselves at odds with the older generation and societal norms.[9] *The Generation Gap*, working title *The Rebel,* was one of four Shaw entries that secured major awards at the 19th Asian Film Festival held in Singapore. Chiang was quite the rogue teenager himself, but fortunately for his worldwide fan base, he did not wind up like his character in this film.

Chiang Da-Wei's small bones and ordinary features were quite contrasting to the majestic Ti Lung whom he played opposite of in thirty plus films. Some people kidded Chiang early on because he was slim and short which procured him the nickname, "Shrunken King." His wiry frame made him stand out from others onscreen and yielded him a refined nimbleness in scenes of ferocious confrontation. Chiang possessed a wily smile which made him appear as if he was contemplating something, though one never knew exactly what. His introverted quality allowed him to appear effete and romantic but it also made him unpredictable. Chiang's characters could go on a rampage or undermine his opponent with subtle discreteness. One critic wrote,

"Chiang Da-Wei is dangerous not because you will love him, but when you fall in love with him, you may only get the cold-shoulder."[10]

Chiang Wei-Nien (birth name) was born to a thespian family in 1947. Both his father, Yim Fa, and mother, Hung Wei, were popular actors in old Shanghai but sadly his dad passed away when he was only four. The family of seven, along with an uncle and his grandmother, lived in the impoverished Kowloon Walled City and relied on Hung Wei to do voice-overs and films to survive. Chiang recalled his poverty-stricken youth.

"I tried looking everywhere at home but still couldn't find a single dollar. One dollar was enough to buy bean sprouts and beef, but only those unwanted parts. To put it bluntly, it was the meat for dogs."[11]

Hung Wei eventually remarried and the family welcomed a little brother, Derek Yee Tung-Sing, into the home. During the 1950s and early '60s, Chiang appeared as a child actor in various films for Shaw, including *A Mellow Spring (1957)* and *The Kingdom and the Beauty (1959)*. Like Alex, Chiang didn't like studying and he repeated a year in both primary and secondary school. His mother wanted him to finish his education but he refused and ran away from home. Chiang landed a job as an office boy and later in an antique shop. Neither job lasted very long. It was then his elder brother, actor Paul Chun Pui, invited him to participate in the Hollywood production, *The Sand Pebbles (1966)* starring Steve McQueen, which was filming locally in the Sai Kung District.[12]

In 1966, Chiang and family relocated to Taiwan when his step-father started up a satellite company for Union Film. The nineteen-year-old would only stay for ten months before returning to the colony with aspirations of landing further employment in the cinema. Upon a chance encounter with action choreographer Tong Gai, he was invited to do some stunt work for Chang Cheh's *Golden Swallow* featuring Jimmy Wang Yu and Cheng Pei-Pei. Chang didn't know the young stuntman; however, he did know Yim Fa from when he played the lead in an early screenplay of his.[13] The director kept a close eye on the beginner, and after a few more films, approached him with a five-year studio contract. Chiang agreed but only for three years. Surprisingly, this reduced deal was approved after Chang sold the idea to Run Run Shaw that any signing was advantageous for all parties involved.

After appearing in *Dead End* with Ti Lung, Chiang Da-Wei was honored with the Best Actor Award at the 16th Asian Film Festival for his role in *Vengeance!* The following year, he starred in the remake *The New One-Armed Swordsman (1971)* which solidified his status as one of Shaw's leading men. Over the decades, Chiang has retained close ties with the Cheungs and is the godson of Cheung Yan-lung and wife. A few years after Chiang introduced son number nine to director Chang, Alex would repay the favor with a goodwill gesture of his own.

The Generation Gap landed in theaters in April 1973 but failed to crack the top 20 with a less-than-stellar box office return. That didn't prevent Chiang from picking up the Most Contemporary Award for his efforts though he was having second thoughts in how martial arts were portrayed for the screen. While Chiang became a part of Shaw's highest paid actors, making roughly a half-million dollars a year for four films, he confessed he presented the wrong picture of the arts to the silver screen.

"Today, all we see of kung fu is violence. And that it is ugly."[14]

He put the blame squarely on film producers for over-dramatizing for the audience. Though not as fanatical as his good friend Bruce Lee, Chiang was still passionate about the martial arts and its true spirit, and looked to the future when he could direct and produce his own films.

As for Fu Sheng, he too was looking forward to brighter prospects. Alex and his fellow classmates graduated from the Shaw HK TVB Training Centre on the final Thursday of September 1972. No longer a trainee, the enthusiastic seventeen-year-old wasted no time as he immediately jumped into his first official film.

---

[1] Vincent Wong, "Film Team-up Here to Stay." South China Morning Post [Hong Kong] 11 October 1970: 7.
[2] See Film Reviews and Interviews, "Meeting a Shaw Brothers Legend."
[3] See Books, The Making of Martial Arts Films: As Told by Filmmakers and Stars, page 60.
[4] See Film Reviews and Interviews, The Boxer from Shantung (1972).
[5] "Chen Kuan Tai Returns to South Florida." Personal interview. 4 Aug. 2013.
[6] Ibid.
[7] See Web and More, Shandong Ma Yongzhen (1927).
[8] Southern Screen May 1981: 46-47.
[9] See Web and More, "Pop Star with a PhD."
[10] See Film Reviews and Interviews, "Seventy Years of the Shrunken King: Chiang Da-Wai."
[11] Ibid.
[12] According to Lau Kar-wing, stunt coordinator Loren Janes provided a three-week training course, in the spring of 1966, to about 20 HK martial artists at the local YMCA which revolutionized the way action was shot in future HK films.
[13] Chang's first screenplay was a nonmusical drama entitled A Girl's Mask (1947) aka Jia Mian Nülang which was adapted from part of the French novel series "La Comédie humaine" by Honoré de Balzac. The film was directed by Fang Pei-Lin (1908–1948) who perished in a plane crash the year after the film was released.
[14] Florence Chong, "Why kung fu films make David Chiang so sad." The Straits Times [Singapore] 4 November 1973: 13.

6

Alex the Actor

Cameras rolled September 22, 1972 on Chang Cheh's *Police Force* becoming one of Hong Kong's first major crime films set in a contemporary setting. The production value was greatly enhanced thanks to the cooperation of the Royal Hong Kong Police who provided extras, vehicles, and training. Less than a week after production began, Alex had his diploma in hand and was fast at work on the set for multiple scenes. He was a huge motorcycle enthusiast, and in this "introduction" film, he literally rolled into frame on a Honda CB175K6 from the background into a medium shot.[1]

Alex's first action sequence was a karate competition where he put his martial arts flairs on display against several adversaries. In the final round, he's pitted against Lau Kar-wing who was the real-life brother of action choreographer Lau Kar-Leung. In a later segment, Alex would again show off his fighting prowess by fending off two knife-wielding thugs — while his hands were tied behind his back! Even though his character was killed off early in the film, it was just enough to whet the audiences' appetite for things to come. A reviewer commented,

"Within these 15 minutes of screen time, Fu Sheng is so electric that his charm and energy leaps off the screen with incredible force. This was his first substantial role and he absolutely kills it. There's no way to watch this movie and not think he wouldn't star in future films. Star power is something certain people have, and Fu Sheng has it in spades."[2]

Alex celebrated his 18th birthday during the production and roughly a month later signed his first contract with Shaw Brothers Studio. It was a five-year deal in which he earned just $650 per month.[3] While a paltry sum, it was enough to provide him true economic freedom from his family. He enjoyed steady pay increases as his star power rose, and unbeknownst to anyone at the time, Alex would eventually belong to Shaw's highest paid performers.

The lead actor in *Police Force* was relatively unknown outside of the studio and the latest promoted by director Chang. Wong Chung was tan with a solid build and sported a pair of thick lips. He was a circus acrobat prior to entering the industry in which his mother, Chung-ying Wong, was the leader. She followed her father into the business and started The Wong Circus which performed in Shanghai and Hong Kong. Chung and younger brother, Shaw bad boy Wong Ching, underwent strenuous training starting as toddlers that eventually evolved into tightrope and aerial performances. On why he changed careers, Chung commented,

"It's hard for a circus to survive in Hong Kong because the place is too small and the expense of a circus is huge. The States and Shanghai are different. Those places are larger, which can support a tour, and so it's a huge business. But it's impossible for Hong Kong."[4]

Wong Chung left the circus life and took work as a film extra in the late 1960s. Two dozen film credits later, Chung got his official introduction in *Have Sword, Will Travel (1969),* in which he portrayed a mute killer, but went virtually unnoticed until *The Water Margin (1972).* It was after this film that Chang Cheh commenced work on *The Delinquent (1973)* aka *Street Gangs of Hong Kong* which was Chung's first major role. Due to that film's success, the director offered him the lead as Inspector Huang Gao Tung in *Police Force.* Chung was both elated and concerned as he knew the success of the project balanced on his shoulders.

"As the leading actor, the audience, director, and even myself, have a higher expectation. To do a great job, it will be very demanding. I have been reading the script closely to understand the characters, which isn't easy, but I feel fairly confident."[5]

As Chang Cheh was juggling multiple productions, he employed co-director Ulysses Au-Yeung Jun, who started his cinema career managing a movie theater in the small town of Shuangxi, Taiwan. Au-Yeung found work in the industry as a script supervisor, screenwriter, and eventually an actor under the stage name "Yang-Ming." His performance in Lin Fu-Di's *Golden Demon (1964)* was a major hit and over the next seven years appeared in numerous films.

After shooting the successful *Prodigal Boxer (1972),* Au-Yeung was contracted by Shaw Brothers Studio but found work difficult in Hong Kong. He returned to his native land, now using the alias Ouyang Chun, and continued making films that included *The Ming Patriots (1976)* and *The Secret of the Shaolin Poles (1977)*. Au-Yeung's career reached an apex with the release of *Gangland Odyssey (1988)* in which his lead and former Shaw actor, Alex Man Chi-Leung, won Best Actor at that year's Golden Horse Awards. Co-starring was Tien Niu who appeared opposite of Alex in *The Brave Archer (1977)*. *Police Force* was Au-Yeung's one and only film for the Shaws before breaking his pact with them.

Principal photography on *Police Force* shot over the course of the 1972/73 winter and wrapped on the first day of spring. The picture released three months later, and while it didn't face any stiff competition, the film brought in only $657,000 during its seven-day run. Nevertheless, Chang Cheh and Fu Sheng were already hard at work on two new projects that January and had no time to dwell on lackluster results.[6] The first film was of the same mold as *Young People* and *The Generation Gap*. Tentatively titled *The Friend* and later renamed simply as *Friends (1974)*, it was the director's last venture into the genre of contemporary youth drama.

In *Friends*, Chiang Da-Wei starred as a destitute painter and the quasi leader of a rag-tag group of adolescents who dreamed of better days. Lily Li played his girlfriend, a bar maid in debt to loan sharks, while newcomer Alex was cast as the son of a wealthy businessman who preferred slumming with the local gang. Filming took place between January and June 1973, shot in several locations throughout the colony, but was ultimately held up for a year before its theatrical release.

This was the first movie in which Alex appeared throughout the production and he held his own in both acting and combative scenes. Critics agreed when nearly 400 performers, directors, and producers converged on the Taiwanese capital for the 20th Asian Film Festival. For his role of Du Jia-Ji in *Friends*, Alex was bestowed with the Best Young Newcomer Award. Despite his recognition at the festival, this picture holds a low point in Alex's resume. The movie suffered from uninspiring receipts, not even surpassing the half million-dollar mark, making it the smallest box office for any Fu Sheng film. Regrettably, a far greater spectre plagued this production concerning a fellow cast member.

Actor Chen Wo-Fu, a native of Kaiping but raised in Hong Kong, was the third child of six and began training in Tai Chi Chuan as a teenager. Chen signed a five-year regular/basic actor contract with Shaw in 1972 and was among the most promoted kung fu stars. After appearing with Chen Kuan-tai and Danny Lee Sau-Yin in the short, *A Register/Book of Heroes,* Chen Wo-Fu found himself vying for the role of Ma Yongzhen in Chang's *Boxer from Shantung*.[7] Although he wasn't chosen, his skills and agile moves received high regard.

In early 1973, Shaw Brothers Studio was making plans for *The Shadow Boxer (1974)* which some believe was a response to Golden Harvest's breakout hit, *The Big Boss (1971)*. Director Pao Hsueh-Li recognized the potential in Chen Wo-Fu and selected him to be the film's leading actor. Chen's master, Cheng Tin-Hung, was so delighted that he took on the role of action director in hopes of making his student famous overnight. The filming of *The Shadow Boxer* went smoothly and was completed over the summer. Chen also appeared in two other Chang Cheh films and was part of Chiang Da-Wei's crew in *Friends* before it all unraveled for the promising superstar.

On January 31, 1974, a tragic incident transpired in Movietown's Dormitory #4. Chen was preparing to go out with his girlfriend and was using the bathroom for a longer than normal amount of time. His roommate Ah Shen grew concerned when he didn't hear any noise coming from the shower other than the sound of water hitting the floor. He knocked on the bathroom door but received no response. Ah Shen and another colleague broke down the door and found Chen's naked body sprawled out on the floor. An in-house nurse attempted to revive Chen before being rushed to Queen Elizabeth Hospital where the actor was pronounced dead.

Chen Wo-Fu's cause of death was officially listed as a suicide. Authorities stated he asphyxiated himself from carbon monoxide poisoning when he inhaled the gas from the bathroom's water boiler. The news of his death came as a shock. Chen was a steadfast, gentle, and reserved young man who intended to open his own school in Tsuen Wan. Run Run Shaw reflected in an interview,

"There have been a number of suicides and such-like over the years.

There is a great problem in that you get ordinary people, and suddenly, they're famous. Fans hound them, they become larger than life, and they sometimes lose their balance."[8]

Chen's sudden death was noted by many on the Shaw lot, including Alex, who realized the emotional strain involved in changing from a nobody into a celebrity. He was mindful of the 19th century British writer Arthur Helps who said *"Keep your feet on the ground but let your heart soar as high as it will."* Good advice because, in less than a week after production commenced on *Friends*, director Chang took on another project that placed Alex in his first ever starring role. This character would initiate a reoccurring theme for him as the mischievous, yet empathetic man-child who blundered about and found himself in one predicament after another.

On January 22, 1973 cameras went into action on *Na Cha the Great (1974)*, a story set during the Shang Dynasty (1600-1046 B.C.) in which a mortal turned deity championed the cause of the common people. While the legend of Na Cha is a household tale amongst the Chinese, Chang Cheh made some changes to his version, such as incorporating Fu Sheng's temperament inside the character of Na Cha. Chiang Tao was cast as Ao Guang and played Alex's nemesis.

"He gave Na Cha a modern look which was different from before. The previous ones were boring but this one was more fashionable. This film was the first time Chang used special effects. Action films usually use wires but Na Cha had a lot of gadgets," Tao commented.[9]

The origin of Nezha [Na Cha] is based on Nalakubar, a deity from Hindu mythology, whose status spread throughout China during the Ming Dynasty. According to folklore, Nezha's mother gave birth to a ball of flesh after being pregnant for over three years. His father was the commander of a military fortress at Chentang Pass, and believing the ball was an evil spirit, split it with his sword. The ball broke in half and Nezha emerged, not as an infant, but as a young boy.

Some years later, Nezha killed a son of Ao Guang aka Dragon King of the East Sea. The furious father confronted Nezha, threatening to flood Chentang Pass with a tidal wave, and report him to the ruler of Heaven. To save his family from ruin, Nezha took his own life by disemboweling himself in a sacrificial ritual. Chiang Tao reminisced on working with Alex in their second of nine films together at Shaw.

"We were enemies in the film but got along well. He was friendly and worked well with everyone. Fu Sheng would retake the shot for perfection. He acted very seriously. But he was also rather funny behind the camera and would give comments even if he wasn't in the scene."[10]

In the folklore, Nezha was brought back to life by his teacher, Taiyi Zhenren, using a lotus to construct a human body for his soul. He was armed with two formidable weapons, Wind Fire Wheels and a Fire-tipped Spear, which he used to free the people from the oppressive Ao Guang. In the film, Chang Cheh employed a variety of special effects to display Na Cha's powers. While some seemed second-rate, such as a giant fish tank serving as a rear projection, or back projection as the Hongkongers used to call it, one must recognize that the film was shot four years before *Star Wars (1977)* revolutionized the SFX industry.

"We shot inside a sealed area in a small studio. The 'Wind Fire Wheel' was exceedingly hot, and as there was no ventilation, we would have to take a break after just one shot."[11]

The figure of Nezha is indeed a complex one but also contradictory. In some versions of the legend, he waged battle against his father after his rebirth. It is not far-fetched to consider Nezha as a prototype for defiant youth or the rebel without a cause. The adolescent on the cusp of adulthood or what director Chang labeled "xiaozi" aka little brat or boxing punk.

Na Cha the Great maintained a longer than normal production schedule (15 months), and like *Friends,* wasn't distributed until the second half of 1974.[12] The picture would have to wait for the release of Chang's first three Shaolin monastery inspired films before it made its way into theaters. Mark Pollard, former webmaster and host of the popular Kung Fu Fandom forum, reviewed the movie on kungfucinema.com.

"This is not a great film, but an interesting example of classic Chinese fantasy in cinema. The kung fu action is fanciful and features a thrashing of rubber dragons. But Fu Sheng is the film's saving grace thanks to his light-hearted antics and solid action performance."[13]

---

[1] Alex owned the motorcycle that appeared in the film.

[2] See Film Reviews and Interviews, Police Force (1973).
[3] Alex's original five-year deal was further extended by the three years he was contracted with Changgong (1973-76) making his contract with Shaw expire in 1980.
[4] Hong Kong Movie News Aug 1972: 32-33.
[5] Ibid.
[6] The six Chang films released in 1973 were Blood Brothers $1,283,896, The Delinquent $840,570, The Pirate $762,460, The Generation Gap $698,166, Police Force $657,076, and Iron Bodyguard $446,474.
[7] Southern Screen Feb 1974: 68-69.
[8] See Books, The Legend of Bruce Lee, page 65. (Author note: There was an outbreak of suicides amongst Hong Kong leading actresses from 1964-1969.)
[9] Na Cha the Great (1974). Dir. Chang Cheh. 2003. DVD. Region 3 IVL.
[10] Ibid.
[11] Ibid.
[12] According to Lawrence Wong Ka Hee, Director of Film-Physical Production at Shaw Movie City HK Ltd., beginning and ending production dates were based on the remuneration pay dates. Though several of Fu Sheng's films experienced hiatuses, only the start and finish dates were provided to the author. While the start day provided for Na Cha the Great was January 22, 1973 at Shaw Studios, it is believed that the majority of the production was more likely lensed at Changgong (in HK), possibly during late '73/ early '74, with production finalizing on May 5, 1974.
[13] See Film Reviews and Interviews, Na Cha the Great (1974).

Cinema father and son

Chang Cheh and Fu Sheng

Cheung siblings
Alex (far right)
David (seated left)

Taiwan 1974

Fu Sheng
Chiang Da-Wei
Ti Lung

Alexander Fu Sheng: Biography of the Chinatown Kid

The Fake Ghost Catchers with Lily Li, 1982

Newlyweds, 1977

Ti Lung, Fu Sheng, Chang Cheh, Chen Kuan-tai, Chiang Da-Wei: 1974

Amy Tao and Ti Lung, 1980

left: Wits of the Brats

Fu Sheng's brothers celebrate new master, Lau Kar-wing

Alexander Fu Sheng: Biography of the Chinatown Kid

top: Fu Sheng with
Chi Kuan-chun, Bruce Tong,
Kwok Chun-Fung (seated)

middle: Alex, 2 siblings,
the Lau Brothers, and
stuntmen enjoy a meal
1982/83

Alex's Dressing Room H

**Ti Lung and Sun Chung
Avenging Eagle**

7

Chang's Film Company

The spring of 1973 proved quite historic for Alex's burgeoning career. While Asian audiences were acquainted with martial arts films, they were relatively unknown to the Western world. With ten soundstages, two dozen directors, 140 contract players, and a recruiting program for new talent, the Shaw Brothers were ready to explore the overseas film market. They owned a chain of cinemas in North America and optimistic of the growing worldwide interest in Chinese culture and traditions.

On the 21st of March, *King Boxer* starring Lo Lieh released in U.S. theaters, under the retitled *Five Fingers of Death*. It raked in US$696,000 by week's end, placing it as the number one movie in America.[1] Other Asian films followed, and according to Variety's box-office chart ending on May 16, 1973, the top three films in the States were of the martial arts genre: *Fist of Fury, Deep Thrust,* and *Five Fingers of Death.*

"*Dubbed into English, French, Italian, and German, the Hong Kong produced action films proved instant hits with moviegoers in Europe, the Mideast, and the United States. One kung fu spectacle called Five Fingers of Death has already grossed $7.5 million playing in a four-month run in some 500 American cities.*"[2]

The month of June proved to be the high-point for wuxia dominance at the U.S. box-office as five Hong Kong kung fu movies emerged in the Top 50. Joining the earlier mentioned films were *Kung Fu, the Invincible Fist* and the Shaw produced, *Duel of the Iron Fist,* featuring Ti Lung and Chiang Da-Wei. Others that premiered were *Shanghai Killers, Fearless Fighters,* and *The Hammer of God* aka *The Chinese Boxer*. On August 16, 1973, the Loews State Theater on Broadway at 45th Street premiered the recently deceased international sensation Bruce Lee's *Enter the Dragon (1973)* which grossed US$25 million.[3] Martial arts cinema would never be the same. Thanks to these films and others, a legion of worldwide disciples were inducted that spring/summer, many of whom would become faithful followers of Shaw Brothers Studio and Alexander Fu Sheng.

One of the first Westerners to interview Alex was British born journalist Vaughan Savidge who worked for RTHK (Radio Television Hong Kong) as well as dubbed kung fu films, including *One-Armed Swordsman*.[4] In the early summer of '73, Savidge drove out to Clear Water Bay and sat down with the rising star.

"He was a charming man. Extremely easy to speak to. Always smiling. He had a dog with him; bull terrier called Popeye. I remember Alex telling me Popeye was a bit crazy and didn't understand mirrors."[5]

Vaughan commented that his interview was held in Alex's dressing room which was totally mirrored from waist height up. When Alex lifted Popeye, for the terrier to see his reflection, sure enough the dog went bonkers barking and carrying on. Vaughn laughed and continued,

"He lived with his father in a big gated house off Prince Edward Road. He struck me as down to earth; a normal young man who happened to be a movie star. I'm not sure he saw movies as the be all and end all in his life. It was just something he was doing that was fun."[6]

Alex enjoyed a carefree spirit. He took pleasure in many hobbies, including dogs, kung fu, hunting, traveling, ball games, and reading adventure stories. The actor had subscribed to the Reader's Digest since he was in school and read it from beginning to end. Alex and friends went to all his premiers in the early part of his career. They also caught midnight showings of Western films at the Gala Theatre and Royal Theatre in Mongkok and the Majestic Theatre on Nathan Road where Alex practiced learning English. When he was 14, Alex had a high school crush on a girl named Elaine, and after seeing *The Graduate (1967)*, he parroted Dustin Hoffman's obsessive cries of "Elaine;" much to the chagrin of his friends.

Another passion Fu Sheng relished was cars. If a person mentioned a specific model, Alex enthusiastically discussed the features, price, factory, and so on. Hearing his infatuation when talking about automobiles, one might believe they were speaking with a car salesman. Alex also commented that he took delight in speed driving and made an alarming statement that crashing was an experience.

Fu Sheng's film career was fast-tracked in 1973 when Chang Cheh announced a new endeavor called Changgong aka Chang's Film Company. The director was planning a slew of Shaolin-themed productions and intended to heavily promote the rising star. Chang's apparent departure from Movietown though generated frenzy within the rumor mill. A few years prior, Shaw executives Raymond Chow and Leonard Ho quit to start rival Golden Harvest and this was assumed to be another defection.[7] When Chow left Shaw Brothers Studio, he invited Chang to join him with an offer to be his own boss but Chang declined, commenting he had no interest in the business side of the industry and would rather focus on the art of filmmaking.

The rumors came to rest when Chang Cheh explained that he had no intentions of leaving Shaw. Runme and Run Run had accumulated a sizable amount of capital by distributing films in Taiwan and profits were not allowed to leave the country because of the Nationalist government's monetary controls. Run Run approached Chang with the idea of a new enterprise to use up these assets. Enter Changgong. In setting up an indie company in Taiwan, Chang could now withdraw these funds from the blocked account to create new movies that would then distribute in Hong Kong. The filmmaker realized this would be a losing venture but it permitted him a greater level of autonomy.[8] He was able to sign his favored actors, freeing them temporarily from their pact with Shaw, to work with him in Taiwan.

Chang Cheh though was not ready to leave Hong Kong just yet. His plan was to shoot a series of titles in Movietown under the Changgong banner. Wuxia novelist and longtime friend Louis Cha came up with the name of Changgong, which was a play on words and meant long bow. This is the basis for the archer in the company's trailers, portrayed by Chi Kuan Chun, and for all of Chang's Film Company's output. Changgong set up their new offices at 79 Waterloo Road in Kowloon and rented out workspace at Wader (Wa Daat) Studio. Chang decided the first film to officially inaugurate the company would be *Heroes Two (1974)*. This film would initiate Chang's lauded series known as "The Shaolin Cycle."[9] Linn Haynes, martial arts film historian, described the origins of the film's title on Media Blaster's *Heroes Two* commentary track.

"In the case of 'Heroes Two,' the title was changed a couple of times.

Up until the last minute the Shaw Brothers were unsure if they would stay with 'Fang Shih-yu and Hung Hsi Kuan' for international distribution. Luckily, someone at the Shaws realized it was unlikely such a title with two names, largely unknown outside of Asia, would strike much of a cord. The title 'Two Heroes of Shaolin' was thought of, then 'Two Heroes,' and finally 'Heroes Two' was decided on."[10]

On June 6, 1973, principal photography for *Heroes Two* kicked off which would make Fu Sheng a full-fledged movie star. With a reputation for being personable, Alex earned the nickname Chatty Boy on the set. Whoever's ear was within reach of his voice became his next victim and those who worked with him were never lonely. Of course, when cameras were rolling, Alex undeniably dominated the screen. He possessed an effective concoction of boundless skill and animated charm as he wandered the countryside armed with a nonchalant manner and a white cooling fan. Alex had high expectations for *Heroes Two*, in addition to, the upcoming Changgong projects and was ever ready to defend his staunch relationship with the filmmaker.

"Director Chang and I are just like father & son. Sometimes he worked in the factory house despite having a serious fever or other ailment. Though there were no filming sessions for me, I would still go to the set to see him. His working attitude deserves respect from all the actors and filming crews. I believe no one in this industry can work like him."[11]

Heroes Two's narrative centered on two champions of the Shaolin monastery who, due to a case of mistaken identity, find themselves at odds with each other. Chen Kuan-tai was the legendary Hung Hsi Kuan while Alex portrayed Fang Shih-yu; a role he reprised in three other movies. In the film, Alex's boyish good looks and cheeky grin were merely a foil as his sprightly fighting skills dismissed his opponents as if they were an afterthought. While his interpretation of the folk hero was certainly entertaining, what was the real Fang Shih-yu like?

The legend goes that a man named Fang De ran a silk emporium in Nanjing. During a storm, an aged salt smuggler by the name of Miu Hin requested shelter in his shop. Fang De was originally from Guangdong and noticed the wanderer also possessed a Guangdong accent. Over the ensuing weeks, they became friends and in time Miu Hin betrothed his daughter to Fang De. Her name was Miu Tsui Fa (Miao Cuihua) and she was a highly-skilled martial artist under the tutelage of Ng Mui. As it turned out, Miu Hin was more than he led on and actually a member of the legendary Five Elders of Shaolin like Ng Mui. Miu Hin was an "unshaved" (lay) disciple who assisted in the development of Wing Chun kung fu. According to the late Qing Dynasty (A.D. 1644-1911) martial arts novel, *Evergreen*, he requested Miu Tsui Fa bathe her new grandson, Fang Shih-yu, in herbal oil and then swath the infant in successive layers of,

"...bamboo strips, wooden rods, and iron bars so that his muscles, bones, and joints became as hard as metal. At age three, he was already training with an iron helmet and iron boots. At age seven, he started learning various forms of fist and footwork. By the age of fourteen, his versatility extended to all kinds of weaponry. Endowed with exceptional strength, his body was all but invulnerable."[12]

Fang Shih-yu became an unrelenting champion of the oppressed but his Achilles' heel was his temper. One summer, he traveled with his father on a business trip to Hangzhou where they encountered a military official from the north, Lei Laohou aka Lei the Tiger, who erected an elevated fighting arena (lèi tái) for any southern fighter who dare challenge him. The teen Shih-yu was enraged by this degrading contest and not only defeated but killed Lei. This event stoked a feud between Shaolin and Wudang as Lei was the son-in-law of Li Bashan of the Wudang school.

Over the next decade, Fang Shih-yu continued to win favor with locals but also drew the ire of the Manchus for his anti-Qing activities. According to popular legend, Fang Shih-yu was murdered in his early twenties by the notorious turncoat Bak Mei in a battle of vengeance for the killing of Lei. Another speculation states he was accidentally slain by Ng Mui which would mean he was killed by his own mother's Sifu.

The earliest record of this folk hero on screen is believed to be *The Adventures of Fang Shih-yu (1938)* directed by Hung Chung-ho, grandfather of modern kung fu star Sammo Hung, which led to a sequel the following year. After the Second World War ended, Hung Chung-ho recruited a Cantonese opera performer to take on the role in *Fang Shih-yu and Misao Cuihua (1948)*. Actor Sek Yin-Tsi soon became synonymous with the legend as he reprised the role in at least eighteen films between 1948 and 1955.

Heroes Two was the fourth time that Alex and Chen Kuan-tai would perform in a film together. Nearly ten years Alex's senior, Chen was born in Guangdong but raised by his paternal grandfather who was an affluent landlord living in Hong Kong. Each year, he dispatched one of his sons to the mainland on business. In 1949, Chen's father was chosen to go but the Chinese War of Liberation intensified. Chiang Kai-shek and upwards of two million Nationalist Chinese retreated from mainland China to the island of Taiwan after the loss of Sichuan. Mao Zedong's Communist Party now controlled the mainland, stranding Chen's father behind ideological lines who was unable to return to his son.

The fatherless four-year-old was placed in a Chinese run school by his grandfather, inciting him to develop a rebellious personality. Chen began studying martial arts at age seven, and over the next decade, trained in various combat skills that included Karate, Judo, and Muay Thai. When he was 23, his Sifu Chan Sau Chung aka the Monkey King sent the young fighter to represent their school at the Southeast Asian Chinese Martial Arts Tournament held in Singapore. All the competitions were full contact and Chen achieved five straight victories, including a few knockouts, and was crowned the light heavyweight champion. He reflected,

"In those days, we didn't have gloves. You were put in an arena and told to fight whomever, regardless of style and technique; rather like in the old days of Fang Shih-yu."[13]

During this period, Chen Kuan-tai was working for the Hong Kong Fire Services Department but quit during the 1967 Riots. Some friends in the film industry thought Chen might like making movies and introduced him to Lau Kar-Leung and Tong Gai. They admired his skills and offered him the opportunity to work on some of their projects. Chen agreed and gained multiple cameos on a variety of turn-of-the-decade films that included *The Chinese Boxer (1970)*, *The Duel (1971)* and *Vengeance!* His later role as Ma Yongzhen made him a bona fide star.

"I earned the role for The Boxer from Shantung because of my martial arts tournament victories. I was selected from over one thousand candidates to play the part of Ma."[14]

Chen Kuan-tai initially signed a three-year pact with Shaw, and during the making of *The Boxer from Shantung*, signed another three-year deal. Chen was a workhorse for the studio and found himself on three different film sets per day with minimal sleep before rethinking his contract with the company. He felt there was a contradiction in terms of how many films he was required to make and how long he must exclusively work for them. Chen decided to break his contract in 1976 and embarked on an expensive legal battle with the studio head. Ultimately, the suit settled out of court but it cost Chen much of his fortune.

A positive outcome of his legal battle was that he was at liberty to work on his directorial project, *Iron Monkey (1977)*, which showcased Chen's exemplary monkey style kung fu.[15] The actor eventually returned to Movietown for Chang Cheh's *Crippled Avengers (1978)* which initiated his second career with the Shaws. He stayed with the studio until it closed and has racked up 150+ acting credits in a career still going strong. As for *Heroes Two*, this movie also put him on the radar with many Western fans for his portrayal of the stoic warrior Hung Hsi Kuan.

The cinema Hung Hsi Kuan, which has multiple alternate spellings that include Hong Xiguan and Hung Hei Goon, was first introduced in *Hong Xiguan's Big Brawl at Liu Village (1949)*. The following year, Hung and Fang Shih-yu appeared together in *Seven Shaolin Heroes' Five Ventures into Mount Emei (1950)*. They would be pitted against each other in *Duel between Fang Shih-yu and Hung Hsi Kuan (1952)* due to a case of miscommunication; similar to what we observe in *Heroes Two*.

The real-life Hung Hsi Kuan is renowned for being the father of the Hung Gar Kuen system which is ranked among the most widely used and respected styles of martial arts in the world. As with most Chinese systems, the origins of Hung Gar Kuen are chock full of folk tales and inconsistencies. The earliest accounts, before the well documented career of Master Wong Fei-hung, are rather ambiguous because much of this history was passed down orally. A more widely accepted version is that Hung Gar Kuen originated in the 17th century when China was under the rule of the Manchus (Qing Dynasty).

Hung Hsi Kuan was a tea merchant by trade but abhorred the Manchus and spent most of his life fighting to restore the Ming Dynasty. He hailed from Hua County in Guangdong and there are rumors of distant royal ancestry. His real surname was Jyu but changed it to Hung to avoid persecution from the Qing authorities as well as to pay tribute to the founder and first emperor of the Ming Dynasty. Hung Hsi Kuan took refuge at the Shaolin Temple, becoming a top student of Ji Sin Sim Si, and stayed there until the Manchus sacked it. According to one version, Hung survived the catastrophe by hiding in the Red Junks where he continued his revolutionary activities. After his first wife died, he remarried a crane stylist named Fang Yongchun who was the niece of Fang Shih-yu.

How Hung Hsi Kuan died is an even bigger mystery. Legend has it that he lived to the age of 93 when taken unaware in a match by a young fighter who used the Phoenix Eye Fist maneuver against him. In the Lau directed film, *Executioners from Shaolin* (1977), Chen Kuan-tai starred as Hung Hsi Kuan once again but succumbed to the hands of the nefarious Bak Mei in which his son would extract his vengeance.

Fu Sheng and Chen Kuan-tai reprised their roles in *Men from the Monastery (1974)*, which one reviewer called a *"fast-paced scattershot tale of martial heroism"* due to its unorthodox and disjointed format.[16] The unusual narrative, presented in four separate chapters, documented the battles fought between the various Ming loyalists and their heinous Manchu oppressors. Alex and Chen's characters were featured in single episodes while newcomer Chi Kuan-Chun completed the triangle as he portrayed the real-life character Hu Hui-Chien (Hu Hui Gan). The final segment brought all three patriots together in a crowning skirmish against the vile Manchus. With Lar Kar-Leung and Tong Gai choreographing, the audience knew they were getting to revel in authentic Chinese kung fu. Sifu Lau had already begun training Alex in the arts of his forefathers and was impressed by the relative ease he grasped the movements. Sifu Frank Bolte, who learned the Lau family hung boxing, broke down the action into several examples.

"Right after the Shaw intro are movements from Hung Gar Kuen. Here Lau Sifu used bits and pieces from the fist sets called Mui Fa Kuen, Gung Gee Fook Fu Kuen, and a few Choy Li Fut movements."[17]

In Alex's opening sequence, his character endures the daunting task of fighting through the Wooden Men Alley to escape from the temple. Fang Shih-yu must engage multiple opponents before the task is complete.

"When he fights the first two opponents, he uses Geng Sao, Bong Sao, and Gung Gee Fook Fu Kuen. The next two opponents, a lot of Gwa Choi (falling backfist strikes) and against the following two [using butterfly knives], lots of blocks, double buddha palm strikes (seong fat cheong). Against the two opponents with staffs, Fu Sheng does the opening of the Gung Gee handset. Against the double dagger opponent, he uses the tiger tale kick from Gung Gee and crescent jump kick from Mui Fa Kuen."[18]

Alex was only beginning to display his fighting potential on screen; however, it was the new man on the block, Chi Kuan-Chun, who was possibly the greatest natural martial arts fighter Chang Cheh ever directed. *Men from the Monastery* was the first of a multi-film partnership for Alex and the mainland native, who was born as Wu Dong-wai in the Panyu District of Guangzhou. Chi left the mainland at an early age when his family moved to Hong Kong and started learning martial arts under Master Chiu Wai.[19]

After several years of training, a film agent approached Chi Kuan-Chun with a job offer as an extra in a Hollywood funded production. Chi soon enrolled with Cathay's film studio actors school to further explore this new career. His teacher there was Han Ying-Chieh *(The Big Boss)*, an actor who cut his teeth as a performer in a Beijing opera troupe.

The Singapore-based Cathay Organization was Shaw Brothers Studio's primary competitors in the 1960s. Cathay formed in 1935 and was the parent company of MP&GI but went into a downward spiral after the General Manger left the studio in 1962. Two years later, founder Dato Loke Wan Tho would die in a horrific plane crash that killed all 57 aboard. An attempted merger of Cathay and Shaw took place in 1968 but talks fizzled after Run Run was unable to secure 51% control. When Raymond Chow quit Shaw, and bought up Cathay's studio premises, the company had a final resurgence with the release of *From the Highway (1970)* but their production facilities shuttered within a few years. Luckily for Chi Kuan-Chun, he was just beginning his film career and Cathay's demise did not discourage him.

On January 4, 1973, Chi was amid twenty selected martial artists to participate in a strong man competition sponsored by local media outlets. The event was held at the Queen Elizabeth II Youth Centre and MC'd by

Wei Pin-Ao.[20] A crowd of 2000 were in attendance and judges included the director and cast from *Smugglers (1973)* which starred veteran actor Jason Pai Piao; Alex's future co-star in *Heroes Shed No Tears (1980)*. Eight of eleven judges cast their vote for Chi Kuan-Chun which left the normally reserved actor so elated he was unable to sleep that evening. He and the two runner-ups were offered the opportunity to work with the Chiangjiang Film Co. in Korea with Pai Piao to perform in a new production by director Suen Ga-Man.[21]

Always one to keep his eyes open for new talent, Chang Cheh was so impressed with Chi Kuan-Chun that he offered him a basic monthly salary of $2000 plus bonus pay when filming. This contract was four times the norm and the 23-year-old was more than eager to accept. During the filming of *Men from the Monastery*, Chi fought fast and strong and often practiced with background martial artists when the cameras weren't rolling. His spirit of never admitting he was weary and his dedication to the arts quickly earned him respect amongst his peers. When he wasn't coaching others, he was looking for instruction. Chen Kuan-tai had been teaching Alex a serial chain lock kick and Chi Kuan-Chun wanted to learn this kick as well. Initially, Chen said he didn't have anything to show him but Chi was smart and joked,

"You are Hung Hsi Kuan and I am Hu Hui-Chien. Hung Hsi Kuan is the eldest disciple of Southern Shaolin and has passed the test of Shaolin Wooden Men Alley while Hu Hui-Chien must sneak out from a ditch to avenge the death of his father. Apparently, his martial arts are not good, so the senior should really teach him."[22]

Chen and Alex had a hearty laugh and Chi was then invited to train with them. The story of Chi's character is a popular tale amongst the anti-Ching patriots. Hu Hui-Chien was born in Xuihui in Guangdong and his father owned a shop near the Alliance of Weavers headquarters. One day his father was beaten to death by the union members and Hu Hui-Chien was powerless to defend his family's honor. Hu was saved by Fang Shih-yu who introduced him to the Jiulian Shan Monastery where he trained with great fervor, but decided to leave the abbey before completing his instruction. Hu Hui-Chien knew he was unable to fight his way through the Wooden Men Alley and made his escape through a drain instead. On reaching his hometown, he smashed the weavers' HQ and killed several. One slain was purportedly a second-generation student of master Feng Daode of Wudang which also fueled the animosity between Shaolin and Wudang schools.

Chi Kuan-Chun reprised the role in two more of Chang's Shaolin Cycle films in addition to the Taiwanese flick, *Showdown at the Cotton Mill (1978)*, which was a loose sequel to Chang's *The Shaolin Avengers (1976)*.[23] He appeared in a total of eleven films with Fu Sheng and typically his characters were the composed counterpart to Alex's happy-go-lucky persona. Theirs was a delightful balancing act on screen. One U.S. fan, who saw many of these movies at the Great Star Theater in San Francisco, commented Fu Sheng and Chi Kuan-Chun were an *"Abbot and Costello, straight-guy-and-clown — but in a different setting."* Chi commented on his working relationship with Alex in 1986.

"The collaboration in front of the camera worked like a charm. We had an excellent director and a great crew, who managed to make even him, who didn't really know much about martial arts, always look good. But he was a really good comedian and he could easily adjust."[24]

Over the years, there's been speculation and debate amongst fans on the order in which *Heroes Two* and *Men from the Monastery* were produced. Some believe this latter film began earlier but then held back to allow *Heroes Two* to hit theaters first. The possible confusion may have stemmed from a short intro *(Three Ways of the Hung Fist)* attached to the opening of *Heroes Two*. This seven-minute demonstration featuring Chen Kuan-tai, Fu Sheng, and Chi Kuan-Chun was comprised of three parts. The first segment displayed Chen's "Crouching Tiger Fist," the second highlighted Alex performing "Tiger-Crane Duet Fist," and last was Chi executing the "Five Animals/ Five Elements set." Chi though never appeared in the main film itself but made his introduction in the later *Men from the Monastery*.

The fact of the matter is *Heroes Two* was not only the first released but also the first produced. *Men from the Monastery* started production on July 10, 1973 (five weeks after *Heroes Two* began) and both movies filmed concurrently. Production ended for *Heroes Two* in November while *Men from the Monastery* ended in December. *Heroes Two* proved itself in theaters as a small victory for Chang Cheh with over $1.3 million in revenue; Alex's largest return to date. The film's faithfulness to real martial arts choreographed by Lau Kar-Leung and Tong Gai made this production a bridge between the early basher movies and the shapes films that dominated the latter half of the 1970s. Looking back at these two projects, Chen Kuan-tai observed,

"In China, people were familiar with these heroes hence its success at the box office. Chang had a knack on finding people and knowing how to mold them into becoming star material. He used this movie and my popularity at the time to make Fu Sheng the next star of the Shaw Studios. I think he succeeded."[25]

---

[1] 50 Top-Grossing Films; Week Ending March 28. Variety, 1973.
[2] Ray Cranbourne, "What Makes Run Run Run?" Newsweek, 16 July 1973.
[3] Chang Cheh saw Bruce Lee's early Cantonese films and realized his potential. Lee contacted the director some years later and Chang recommended him to Shaw but negotiations broke down, so Lee signed with Golden Harvest. In Jan. 1973, according to The Nanyang Commercial Press, Mona Fong chose Chang to direct Lee's first film at Shaw Bros., "Nien Geng-Yau."
[4] Savidge said that his favorite dubbed line he wrote for Jimmy Wang in OAS was, "I'm going to kill you with my own two hands."
[5] "Vaughan Savidge meets Fu Sheng." Personal interview. 1 Nov. 2013.
[6] Ibid.
[7] The cause of this mutiny was the admission of Mong Fong into Shaw's management team in 1969. She initially met Run Run in Singapore in 1952 and they formally married in Las Vegas on 6 May 1997. Over the years, Mona worked her way up the ranks to become the Deputy Chairman and General Manager of Shaw Brothers Studio and TVB.
[8] Chang exhausted all of Shaw's capital in Taiwan in making Five Shaolin Masters (1975) and it was a Taiwanese film distributor, Lin Chongfeng, that helped bolster Changgong's working capital. See Books, Chang Cheh: A Memoir, 67-73.
[9] "Best Order to Watch the SHAOLIN TEMPLE Series aka Shaolin Cycle?" Kung Fu Fandom. 22 June 2012.
[10] Heroes Two (1974). Dir. Chang Cheh. 2008. DVD. Region 1 Media Blasters.
[11] See Web and More, "A Letter Written by Alex."
[12] See Books, Kung Fu Cult Masters, page 57.
[13] See Film Reviews and Interviews, "Chen Kuan-Tai - The Real Iron Monkey."
[14] "Chen Kuan Tai Returns to South Florida." Personal interview. 4 Aug. 2013.
[15] The Iron Monkey (1977) was released for only one day on 18 Nov. 1977, before Run Run Shaw's lawsuit ban was enforced. The ban lifted on 11 Jan. 1979. (For more on this lawsuit, refer to Chapter 12 end notes.)
[16] See Film Reviews and Interviews, Men From the Monastery (1974).
[17] "Shaolin Films of Shaw Brothers." Kung Fu Fandom. 02 July 2008.
[18] Ibid.

[19] Chiu Wai's Dai Sigung / Si-Tai-Gung (aka Great Grandmaster) was Wong Fei Hung.
[20] Best known for playing cunning interpreters in Bruce Lee's 1972 films: Fist of Fury and Way of the Dragon. His first credited role was in Chang Cheh's Happenings in Alishan (1949).
[21] This (unproduced?) film could not be located. Suen Ga-Man appears to have only directed five films. The only one with Jason Pai Piao being Smugglers (1973).
[22] Chinese newspaper article from Chi Kuan-Chun's now defunct site.
[23] Showdown at the Cotton Mill (1978) was written for Chang Cheh during his Shaolin period but it was never produced. It floated around Movietown for some years until Wu Ma decided to make the film on his own. Wu was inevitably black balled for his efforts and the film got snatched off the market by the Shaw Brothers.
[24] See Film Reviews and Interviews, "Interview with Chi Kuan-Chun."
[25] "Chen Kuan Tai Returns to South Florida." Personal interview. 4 Aug. 2013.

8

The Shaolin Monastery

The Shaolin Monastery's extensive history is filled with fables, speculations, and half-truths. While many recollections are consistently repeated, even more will never make it into the official histories. While the chronicles of the temple's fifteen centuries could easily fill a second book, and many have been written, this chapter only scratches the surface of this renowned holy place.

The Shaolin Temple is presumed to have been spread across five primary locations, not all active at the same time; however, smaller monasteries also followed their doctrine. While the Shaolin Temple is certainly the most famous, it was not the first Buddhist monastery in China. It is widely recognized that the Baima Temple aka White Horse Temple in Luoyang, Henan Province has that honor. Founded in A.D. 68, Emperor Ming of the Eastern Han Dynasty (A.D. 25-220) commissioned the Baima Temple after two Indian monks brought the first Buddhist scriptures into the region.

Some four centuries later, an Indian monk named Buddhabhadra was traveling through China in search of enlightenment. This monk had a generous heart and imparted guidance to anyone who sought his assistance. As repayment for Buddhabhadra's many virtuous deeds, the Emperor Xiaowen of Northern Wei (A.D. 386-534) offered him a plot of land at Henan in the Sacred Mountains on the side of Shao Shi (mountain). Together, they chose a spot in an area of Lin (young or new trees) for this new temple.

Near the end of the Northern & Southern Dynasties (A.D. 420-589), Emperor Wu Di called for the abolishment of Buddhism. He was concerned that those from the temple had become too prosperous, and confiscated their land. This edict reversed around A.D. 621 when the fighting monks supported the Prince of Qin in a military campaign which consequently established the reputation of Shaolin's monks as court loyalists. They would be called upon time and again to defend the country's coastlines and borders from outside aggression.

During this same period, pirates in the Fujian Province threatened stability in Southern China. The Tang Emperor dispatched 500 warrior monks from Shaolin to contend with the outlaws. According to recent research by three nonpartisan government historical parties, some monks stayed in the south and erected a new sanctuary to memorialize their fallen comrades. However, it should not come as a surprise that other experts suggest there never was a Southern Shaolin Temple, leaving most in a state of confusion between the legends and current historical findings.

The Song Dynasty reunited most of inner China or China proper, as it was later coined. Its founders established an effective centralized bureaucracy staffed with scholars as officials. Moreover, some writings suggest the founder of the Song was a Shaolin layman who felt the arts were a form of health-giving exercise. It was at this time that many kung fu systems came into existence and the animal styles began to flourish.

Although there aren't any surviving records of Shaolin's resistance to the invading Mongol Tribes during the Yuan Era, their reputation began to spread to other Asian countries such as Japan and Korea. Once the Ming Dynasty established, the Shaolin Temple(s) experienced its greatest growth, flourishing into a breeding ground of mathematics, poetry, philosophy, history, and martial arts. People from all walks of life, such as fighters, healers, teachers, and philosophers, sought entrance to the monastery and shared their knowledge in return for instruction and sanctuary. These were indeed the best of times for Shaolin — though it would not last.

When the Qing Dynasty came to power, Shaolin did not resist but in fact assisted the court to defeat the invading forces from Xilu.[1] The victorious monks were exalted for their valor but refused any government favors. Over the next half-century, their martial prowess matured much to the chagrin of the resentful Manchus. Once the new dynasty subdued the remaining areas of resistance, they turned their eyes to the temple as a thorn that needed removal. The most widely known tale of the temple's history is its destruction at the hands of the Manchus for anti-Qing activities which is the starting point for the film, *Men from the Monastery*.

Released on April 3, 1974, *Men from the Monastery* grossed a little over $822,000 putting it at the bottom of all the Shaolin Cycle films. Meanwhile, another Shaolin-themed movie commenced the previous autumn and was set in an undisclosed period when Fang Shih-yu and Hung Hsi Kuan were long gone. *Shaolin Martial Arts (1974)* began production on November 5, 1973 and was a superior third entry in Chang's series which expanded on the folklore. Joining Fu Sheng and Chi Kuan-Chun were three noteworthy newcomers: Leung Kar-Yan, Johnny Wang Lung-Wei, and Gordon Lau Kar-fai. Nicknamed "Beardy," "The Mayor," and "The Master Killer" respectively by their fan base, this trio of actors would work with Alex on multiple future productions.

"Fu Sheng? He was a friend and a mentor. I was so nervous during filming because it was the first time I acted and totally without any experience. He was always willing to help others," Wang commented.[2]

While new to acting, Wang Lung-Wei exhibited a decade's worth of martial arts training which helped him land his role in *Shaolin Martial Arts*. He began studying when he was 15-years-old and initially learned some kung fu styles, such as Hong Quan, but decided they were not the type of martial arts he was looking for. Under the influence of the British made 007 movies, Wang decided to learn karate but that was just the start.

"Afterward, when I first knew about Muay Thai, I was overwhelmed by its powerful skills. I think it is the most powerful martial art of the world. Even the late Bruce Lee acknowledged that Muay Thai is the best bare-handed fighting style among all."[3]

As a teenager, Wang found himself in reoccurring scrapes with his classmates and subsequently transferred from one school to another. He wound up getting into a fistfight a month before graduating from Secondary 5 and was dismissed by the dean. His mother couldn't deter his fighting ways, so she purchased him an acoustic guitar hoping he would change under the influence of music. Wang realized he couldn't adapt to the monotonous chores of office work and decided to sign up with a band.

At age 25, Wang Lung-Wei was working as a professional guitarist in a few Wanchai bars and taught karate part-time.[4] He was a greenbelt in 1973 and a karate free-fighting champion. One summer's day, he came across an advertisement that Chang Cheh was recruiting for new kung fu actors. The mustached powerhouse put in his application on a whim not realizing he would ultimately become one of Shaw's most ruthless villains. Wang personified all that was evil on screen with his brutish performances yet he captured the hearts of the audience who silently cheered him on.

Shaolin Martial Arts became a leading Shaw production to popularize the master/student training sequence which became a staple of the genre through the 1970s. Chang Cheh peppered the film with an assortment of unique instructing scenes that depicted pupils smashing fingers through wooden boards and capturing fish with their bare hands. The most famous of these old masters was played by Simon Yuen Siu-Tin whom Alex's character must charm to learn his advanced Tiger Crane techniques. The curmudgeon hermit became the catalyst for the character most commonly associated with Simon Yuen. A few years later, Yuen further developed the role when he paired up with Jackie Chan in *Snake in the Eagle's Shadow (1978)*.[5]

Production on *Shaolin Martial Arts* completed in March 1974 and released that summer. The picture made a respectable $1.28 million at the box office placing it 15th for the year. While it was an exceptional movie in its own right, Chang and Alex's next effort garnered them their greatest box office success. It proved to be the only film in their long collaboration that surpassed the two-million-dollar barrier. That project was *Disciples of Shaolin (1975)* which kicked off principal photography on April 12, 1974 in Hong Kong but finished up in neighboring Taiwan. Chang's rental contract with Wa Daat Studio was nearing an end and the owner wished to take back the premises after the lease expired. According to the filmmaker, *Disciples of Shaolin* was to begin shooting in Taiwan, but on short notice, Chang opted to lens the film's ending sequences in Hong Kong before the rental agreement concluded.

The director had recently leased two studios in Taiwan in preparation of moving his base of operations though he retained Changgong's office in the colony. The production houses were the former locations of Grand Motion Pictures and the China National Film Studio. Grand maintained a permanent street set construction for ancient costume films that was originally designed by Li Han-Hsiang who, like Run Run Shaw, modeled his studio after the Hollywood system. Chang also rented an office on Quan Zhou Jie, the former site for China National, and a dormitory for his staff and actors. He anticipated the move as strictly short-term and planned on making four or five films there, a half year at most, before returning to Hong Kong. However, this overseas relocation forced him to split up the fight choreography team that he had worked with for the last decade. Tong Gai didn't wish to go to Taiwan, so Chang approached Lau Kar-Leung who recalled his conversation with the director.

"*[Chang] told me, 'Without you, I won't be able to go through with it.' He asked me how to rescue martial arts movies. I said that fight scenes must be truer, like those in Bruce Lee movies. We must portray heroes who really existed and revive the kung fu the way they practiced it.*"[6]

The two men came to an agreement and Chang was ready to move forward. While he made all the necessary preparations for the relocation, the one matter that concerned him most was Taiwan's stricter screening and censorship standards. The filmmaker was known for shooting combat movies which were easy targets to be suppressed. If the projects weren't approved, or negatives confiscated, they wouldn't be allowed to export them which meant a sizeable financial loss. One such film under fire was *Disciples of Shaolin* which was initially rejected.

The film's working title of *Invincible Shaolin* [lit. Fighting to Power with Hung Boxing] was scrutinized by the Taiwanese Information Dept. which contended that the words "hung and red" were homophones and that the Chinese character for "fist" resembled the character "army." Basically, the film translated into "Red Guard Takes the World!" which shocked the anti-communist nation. The displeased Chang voiced his complaints to the authorities, arguing there was nothing immoral in the plot, and contended that Hung Boxing was only the name of a Chinese martial arts. In the end, the officials gave in but the director decided to abandon his original idea and used the title *Disciples of Shaolin*.

The film's cast and crew managed a break in the action while working on the closing sequence as Chang, even though facing a stiff timeline, acknowledged some things in life were more important than business. On the 20th of May, Chang's protégé and Alex's best friend, Chiang Da-Wei, exchanged vows with actress girlfriend, Maggie Li Lin-Lin, at St.

Theresa's Church on Prince Edward Road. Chiang and Li opted for a small ceremony attended by approximately three dozen family members and colleagues. Among them were Ti Lung, Wang Chung, and of course Alex who was quite possibly the orchestrator for this blessed union.

A few years' prior, Maggie Li Lin-Lin was a bridesmaid at a wedding for another Shaw actress, that Chiang Da-Wei also attended. The celebrants went out dancing afterwards and Chiang found himself quickly enamored with Li. She was dating actor Chan Ho at the time but that still did not deter the wannabe suitor.

Dauntless, Chiang visited her house a few days later to ask Li on a date but she wasn't home. Li's domestic helper was rather protective of her employer's daughter and did not allow him to wait inside. Several hours passed while Chiang waited outside her residence in the hot, humid Hong Kong sun like a warrior wishing to enter Shaolin. Li finally appeared and was so impressed with his devotedness that she agreed to see him. They dated for the next three years, but in 1973, split up as neither side was willing to compromise. The couple stopped seeing each other and had no contact for several months. Despite their separation, they still retained their feelings for one another but neither wanted to lose face.

Near the end of the year, Chiang and Li crossed paths in Taiwan, though they still refused to speak. Alex knew they enjoyed mahjong, so he invited the pair to play and had them sit at the same table. Later that evening, Chiang and Li's relationship rekindled thanks to the orchestration of Alex the matchmaker. The budding superstar felt he had now paid back his debt to Chiang for introducing him to Chang Cheh but little did Alex realize that he too would be the recipient of some future matchmaking.

---

[1] The historical identity of the Xi Lu is debatable. Some believe it was a kingdom of Tibet whereas others say Russia.
[2] "Johnny Wang talks with Teako." Personal interview. 14 Jan. 2003.
[3] Ibid.
[4] Playboy Bar on Hennessy Road and Neptune Bar on Lockhart Road. The legendary tattoo artist Pinky Yun had his tattoo shop above the Neptune Bar.
[5] See Chapter 19 notes.
[6] See Film Reviews and Interviews, "Interview with Lau Kar Leung: The Last Shaolin."

9

Along Comes Jenny

February 20, 1953. The mercury dipped to a crisp 46°F for the Portuguese port city of Macau. The low temperature tied for the coldest day of the year but that didn't deter an Austrian father and his Hong Kong bride from welcoming their new ray of sunshine into the world. Zhen Shushi aka Yan Suk Si, born that Friday morning, eventually became known as Yan Lei or Jenny Tseng. Her father, a retired civil engineer, divorced Jenny's mother when Jenny was still young but her mom would later remarry a Cantonese man and relocate the family to Hong Kong.

Little Jenny was a natural beauty, good natured, and considerate. Her mother and stepfather adored her. As a young adolescent, music was far more interesting to Jenny than books, and as she grew older, spent a good bit of her free time at a local music shop. In spite of her less-than-stellar academic record, Jenny was extremely popular amongst the boys and her good looks made many fall head over heels.

When Jenny was in high school, her family moved again to Taiwan. As usual, wannabe suitors were always eager to carry her books home. One day, Jenny was chatting it up with a few boys while on her bike and she accidently fell into a ditch. The boys all laughed heartily until the beauty showed her feisty side and chased them with a knife in hand.

Jenny developed an interest in Beijing Opera as a teen but her teacher thought it inappropriate, stating that Jenny had the face of a foreigner.[1] After graduating from Taiwan No.4 Girl's School, Jenny gave up the idea and decided to major in television production while supporting herself as a singer. She attended Shih Hsin University in Taipei, renowned for training professional journalists, but fell out of favor with the school's president and transferred to the Chinese Culture University (CCU). This move proved to be a blessing in disguise as Jenny was later discovered by a casting agent while attending CCU.

In 1971, Jenny's first album *Xin Hu* (Heart Lake) released. Over the next several years, she collaborated with Taiwanese musician Liu Jia Chang to produce theme songs for a variety of Mandarin films. It was publicized that the Taiwanese music market was divided amongst Jenny Tseng and artists Teresa Teng, and Feng Fei Fei. This talented trio's influence was felt throughout Southeast Asia and well beyond.

Jenny's growing fame derived from her use of clear, resounding, stirring vocals in live concerts. Due to her wide vocal range, the Hong Kong lyricist James Wong dubbed her "music's giant lung." Jenny's singing was like fine wine, mellowing with time, and with maturity came true richness. Jenny continued to perform for the next four decades, enthralling a world-wide fanbase, and becoming pop music royalty with a total of 130 albums and collections exceeding ten million sales. Many have hailed Jenny Tseng among Chinese music's most enduring artists, but in 1974, she was just another girl. A girl who caught Alex's eye.

"We started dating since June but before that he had been seducing me. Man-ming Tiu and I are close friends, and little Sheng and Ah Lung hung out together, so we knew each other for a while," Jenny recalled.[2]

When Jenny first met Alex the year prior (1973), she thought he was a bit aloof. When in larger groups, he simply sat there without saying a word. Things changed nevertheless when they reunited the following summer in Taiwan.

"...he behaved strangely a lot which attracted my attention. Once I invited a group of friends to my home and I was wearing shorts. Little Sheng kept staring and kidded. 'Jenny! Your legs . . . they are beautiful.'"[3]

Alex was slightly less reserved when he spoke of their first encounters. He admitted his shyness was something he was unaccustomed to when it came to matters of courting. Alex likened it to a training sequence in his films where he had to overcome great odds. Three weeks after he met Jenny, Alex confessed he still couldn't reach for her hand.

"Before that? Ha! Soon after I met a girl I can walk with my hand on her shoulders. Girls were at my beck and call! After I met her, everything became different and I had a hard time. I didn't believe in love at first sight until I met Jenny. Once I held her hand, I never let go of it."[4]

Jenny was the first of a two-part whirlwind that Alex experienced in the summer of '74. The other occurred on the 6th of June at the old airport in Kowloon City. Kai Tak was infamous for being one of the world's extreme airports. Located on the west side of Kowloon Bay, it was flanked by craggy mountains, the Walled City, and the pungent smelling inlet. The landscape was dotted with high-rise buildings in which planes made their low approach over the rooftops before a dramatic last-minute turn, coined the "Kai Tak Heart Attack," to align themselves with the runway.

On this early June day, Chang Cheh called for a news conference to officially announce details of his own sensational move in which he was shifting Changgong's base of operations to Taipei. Some of Shaw's top talents joined him that Thursday morning which included Ti Lung, Chiang Da-Wei, Lau Kar-Leung, Fu Sheng, and soon-to-be rising star, Lau Kar-fai who is best known today as Gordon Liu. Born with the Chinese name of Xian Qi-xi (Sin Kam-hei), Kar-fai became world famous for his landmark role in *The 36th Chamber of Shaolin (1978)* portraying real-life monk San Te. He acquired his Western name (Gordon) at the Roman Catholic Salesian English School; however, his surname of Lau (Liu) came about after becoming godson to the widow of master Lau Jaam.[5]

Another member of Chang's team was Jamie Luk Kim-Ming who had signed on the previous July and was in Alex's inner circle of friends.

"In Taiwan, the first few months were difficult for me. We were not staying in hotels. It was not luxurious. Studios were designed to house the new comedians and choreographers. We were closeted there for work on site because we did not know any area in Taiwan. We felt lost out there. One actor terminated his contract after only two months in Taipei."[6]

Actor Fung Hak-On worked on nearly forty films with director Chang and recalled the transition to the island nation. He said ten Hong Kong martial artists traveled with them but the company needed to recruit additional Taiwanese practitioners. He recalled that it initially didn't go too well, as Lau Kar-Leung wanted to separate the newcomers into top, middle, and low skill levels and test them.[7] The indoctrination of these Taiwanese stunt men into the Chang camp eventually led to the rise of several prominent individuals. Chen Julu (Kwok Chun-Fung), Chu Chi-Hsueh (Lu Feng), Zhao Gang Sheng (Chiang Sheng), Yu Tai-Ping, Li Yi-Min, and Robert Tai Chi-Hsien would be featured in an assortment of films alongside Alex from the mid-70s onward. These performers brought to the table a unique acrobatic flamboyance that helped create a fusion of operatic aesthetics with shapes and bashers.

The commencing of Changgong's inaugural film in Taiwan, *Five Shaolin Masters (1974)*, got underway on June 12. The lensing ceremony was minor and only involved lighting firecrackers along with the cheering and applause by the actors and some staff. The outdoor temperature was hovering near 100°F and the mercury-vapor lamps made it even more unbearable. Director Chang joked to his crew that any job was fine but if a friend wants to work in the film industry, better tell them to find something else to do. Lead actor Chiang Da-Wei couldn't agree more.

"Film production is a hobby. Although when we shoot movies we do tend to suffer a bit. How good would it be if we needed to shoot a raining scene under this kind of weather?"[8]

Minutes after he verbalized this, the skies responded with a thunderous cloudburst that brought production to an unexpected halt. Chang was familiar with the adverse weather on the island nation as his first directorial project didn't have a single scene shot in Alishan Township itself due to the uncooperative climate conditions. Chang shrugged his shoulders and lit up a stogie as he looked to the sky. Ti Lung and Alex though were unable to restrain themselves from enjoying Nature's response to their co-star's comment and broke out in laughter as the crew scurried off to get out of the downpour.

This commencement project revolved around the lore of five legendary masters who escaped the burning of Shaolin. As one online reviewer wrote, *Five Shaolin Masters* had the grandiose appeal of *"an '80s comic book cross-over"* in which a quintet of heroes was pitted against similar but overwhelming adversaries.[9] Accounts of these martial artists are varied, and to get a clearer picture, there are two points one must recognize.

First, there were two sets of masters: The Five Ancestors and The Five Elders. These two distinct groups can be occasionally mistaken as one in the same. The Five Ancestors were Hu De Di, Tsai De-Zhong, Ma Chao-Hsing, Li Shi-Kai, and Fang Da-Hong, while the Five Elders were Ji Sin Sim Si, Ng Mui, Fung Dou Dak, Bak Mei, and Miu Hin. There are also varying spellings of these names which can add to the confusion. For example, the Hong Kong Movie Database has Ti Lung listed as Tsai Te-Chung in *Five Shaolin Masters* but named Cai De Zhong in *Shaolin Temple (1976)*. Both characters are in fact the same; also known as Tsai De-Zhong.

Second, the burning of Shaolin was not a one-and-done incident. History has shown that multiple temples endured assorted attacks, including destruction by fire, which initiated numerous restorations. Records of these incidents are sketchy and contradictory, especially when the topic of the Northern vs. Southern monasteries is discussed.

According to the author's research, the first destruction of Shaolin allegedly occurred in the mid-6th century during the Northern Zhou (A.D. 557-581). It's certainly a subject of debate on whether the temple was incinerated or merely shuttered. During the early years of the Tang Dynasty (A.D. 618-907), the temple again closed [burned?] but soon restored. In the 14th century, the monastery was attacked during the Red Turban Rebellion and purportedly razed with many monks being killed or driven out. During the 17th and 18th centuries, there were several incidents recorded. In 1641, the rebel leader Li Zicheng sacked the temple, and in 1674, it was torched by a group of government officials. Some years later, Yongzheng Emperor (reigned 1722-1735) of the Qing Dynasty was believed to have cleansed the temple, and in 1760, the Manchu army was sent in and burned down the grounds.

Possibly the temple's most well-known monk is Ji Sin Sim Si. He was thought to have survived the monastery's destruction by the Qing army yet the stories disagree as to whether he was a survivor of the original incident in Henan or of the southern one in Fujian. Many assume the group known as The Five Elders left the northern location, after it was razed, to start up the southern site. According to Sifu Wong Kiew Kit, sixth generation successor of Ji Sin Sim Si, this statement is inaccurate. He is of the belief that two southern temples existed and that the one known southern temple was not started by Ji Sin. As he explained,

"One, the southern Shaolin Monastery was at Quanzhou and not at the Jiulian Mountain. Two, historical records show that this southern Shaolin Monastery at Quanzhou was built by imperial decree during the

Ming Dynasty and not by Ji Sin Sim Si during the Qing Dynasty."[10]

Based on this statement, Wong believes some of the Five Elders of Shaolin escaped from the first southern monastery at Quanzhou (a port city in Fujian). Legend has it that a Manchurian prince named Yong Cheng infiltrated the temple as a kung fu monk, and after becoming the Qing emperor, leveled it to the ground with the assistance of Lama fighters from Tibet. Ji Sin was one of the numerous monks to escape the destruction of the temple, and instead of abandoning the Shaolin life, he constructed a new southern site in Jiulian Shan. Temple survivors Bak Mei and Fung Dou Dak now sided with the Qing government and it was Bak Mei who led the Qing army to raze this second southern temple. Of course, since no archeological evidence has been uncovered for the second location, it only further fuels the flames that are legend.

The mid-1990s discovery of the first southern site unearthed coins and artifacts from different dynasties. This proved the temple was rebuilt multiple times but does not pinpoint where these masters truly originated. Some even say the stories of The Five Elders may have no basis in historical fact at all. They may have been merely fictional characters created from wuxia novels, *Wan Nian Qing* for example, or personifications created by anti-Qing organizations such as the Heaven and Earth Society. If all this wasn't confusing enough, Chang Cheh added his own artistic license to provide a revisionist history.

The director told a reporter in 1977 that his Shaolin Cycle films focused on the southern temple in Quanzhou but oddly admitted he wasn't sure if the southern temple(s) ever existed. Chang mentioned in his memoirs he didn't care if his films were historically inaccurate and *Five Shaolin Masters* is a perfect example. If this film was about The Five Elders, it would have been more plausible as they (based on Sifu Wong's argument) were based in the southern region. However, the characters portrayed here are actually the much earlier group, The Five Ancestors. According to the respected martial arts film historian and critic, Dr. Craig Reid, The Five Ancestors were the group who survived the burning of the northern temple in Henan.

Chang Cheh was well versed in the lore of the Shaolin heroes but admitted the truth was forever lost in time. He stated that he wished to do them justice by creating a stirring illustration rather than a lackluster biopic. While most fans were pleased with the outcome, some were quick to note that Chen Kuan-tai didn't join his band of brothers. Chen explained, in a 2013 interview, the director's motive was to provide other performers with more exposure. But that was only the half of it.

During his conversation with the author, the monkey stylist took bites of his breakfast and glanced over *Five Shaolin Masters* lobby cards. Chen picked up one and studied it. The card featured the martial arts quintet posing with their signature secret hand code. Chen then turned his attention to the film's trailer playing on the laptop and commented,

"Lot of politics at the Shaw Studios. That explains why you don't see me in this production. I was officially under contract at Shaw, so Chang would have to make a special request for me to go to Taiwan."[11]

Chen Kuan-tai's replacement was Meng Fei.[12] He was born Yeung Un Tong in 1951 and raised on the mainland by his mother and stepfather who were both medical doctors under Mao Zedong's reign. From the 1950s through the 1970s, thousands of mainlanders dove into the deep and polluted Shenzhen Bay to find sanctuary in the British colony. According to his former wife, a teenaged Meng was determined not to stay trapped in the communist country and successfully made the hazardous 2.5-mile swim to freedom. *Five Shaolin Masters* was Meng Fei's only collaboration with director Chang, but over the course of his career, appeared in more than 50 productions. A few of his better-known films include *The Unique Lama (1978), Green Jade Statuette (1978),* and *Invincible Kung Fu Trio (1978)* where he played Fang Shih-yu.

In *Five Shaolin Masters,* Alex wouldn't reprise his role of Fang Shih-yu but instead portrayed Ma Chao-Hsing who, of the five experts, was the least resolved. He moved about the countryside with a carefree nature fighting the Manchus with his primary adversary being Wang Lung-Wei's Ma Fu-Yi (the traitorous monk). Wang's character also sauntered through the film as the man with the fan, accompanied by the beats of composer Frankie Chan Fan-Kei and recordist Wang Yung-Hau.

Though Alex's character was one of the five masters in the movie, he had to endure junior status amongst his comrades, who associated him with being predisposed to adolescent flaws. This perception remedied itself after he's trapped by the devious Ma Fu-Yi and didn't cave into his threats of torture but instead mocked the very idea. The unseasoned youth now schemed with a mature deftness to hoodwink his captor using exaggerated hand signs. This strategy bought his colleagues enough time to overtake the stronghold and turn the tide against the Manchus.

Throughout the movie, a series of covert hand signals and codes are used amongst the Shaolin patriots. The most often seen was three fingers up and one down. This hand gesture signified the passing of the last Ming Emperor who died on the 19th day of the third moon (3-1-9). Others, though, saw it quite differently. Some years after the film's release, actor and longtime martial arts film fan, Toby Russell, met up with action choreographer Lau Kar-Leung for an interview in a Kowloon restaurant. When Russell saw Lau, he made the "three fingers up and one down" hand sign to greet the master but Lau became promptly frantic stating,

"No, don't do that. No No!! Making gangster signs isn't a smart thing to do in the middle of Hong Kong where some people are affiliated."[13]

This deceptively benign hand sign used by the five masters was in fact rooted in Triad lore. Unlike the criminal organizations of the modern era, these clandestine orders of yesteryear maintained more commendable objectives. These groups had a long tradition of self-preservation through unity and patriotism and date back as far as the Zhou Dynasty (1046-256 B.C.). It is theorized the first recorded society was known as the Red Eyebrows who painted their brows to appear more terrifying. Hailing from the Shandong province, this brotherhood supported the regional government to assassinate a usurper which led to the establishment of the Eastern Han Dynasty. Regrettably for them, they soon found themselves a target by the new régime and were eventually wiped out.

Over the centuries, these fraternities strived to exist and changed names to avoid infiltration or discovery. In 1344, the White Lotus society was revived and its army revolted against the Mongols to help establish the Ming Dynasty.[14] For nearly three-hundred years of Ming rule, the White Lotus remained politically detached. This changed in 1662 when the second Qing Emperor issued an edict that banned all such outlaws and many monasteries were destroyed. The White Lotus went underground where they forged alliances with other sects and established mutual rituals, secret signs, and passwords. The White Lotus eventually transmuted into a new organization called the Sam Hop Wui or Three United Society. They saw the world as a tripartite (Heaven, Earth, and Man) and their early flags bore a triangle to denote this unity of the three forces of nature. Both the name and this three-fold symbol were the foundation of the modern Chinese secret society, commonly known today as the Triads.

The Triads underground movement grew in the following years as they enticed a wide-ranging membership of those who were disenchanted with the presiding government. By the mid-1800s, the Triads had evolved into a massive subculture that addressed imperial injustices. After the failure of the Red Turban revolt in 1854, many affiliates felt the best way to survive was to get away from the Qing's iron grip and head south to Hong Kong. In less than a century, they established an impressive footprint in the colony and were well integrated into the fabric of Hong Kong's elite. The Triads were in their strongest position after the Second World War thanks partially to little or no police interference. They took over the black market that flourished during the war years, and by 1949, Hong Kong was on the verge of becoming the biggest criminal city on the planet.

Today's membership is rumored to be much smaller, and the Triads are not as prevalent as they were in decades past. Starting in the late 1970s, Beijing began to secure ties with the underground organization, quite shocking to many considering the Triad's past allegiance to Taiwan. In 1997, the former deputy secretary-general of Xinhua admitted Beijing befriended Triad bosses and came to an agreement that the mainland would turn a blind eye to the Triad's illegal activities if they kept the peace after the handover.[15] As they've done in the past, the Triads adapt to social and political change and today have become invisible to the point of almost being forgotten. However, that's the facade they create. The loose networks of Sun Yee On, 14K, Wo Shing Wo, and other less significant gangs are believed to have tens of thousands of members. They are ever mutating and adept in self-preservation. They have not become weakened but in fact have grown stronger thanks to Beijing's embrace.

---

[1] In a 2000 interview, a reporter questioned her Eurasian looks to which Jenny jested, "You can say I am 100% Chinese or you can say I am half this and half that. I don't even

know myself because my mother once said she picked me up from the street when I was still a baby."
[2] See Web and More, "Fu Sing & Yan Nei," page 11.
[3] Ibid.
[4] Ibid.
[5] As a teen, Lau Kar-fai secretly trained at Liu Jaam Gymnastics Academy in Sheung Wan. When he was training, Lau Jaam had already passed (1963) and Lau Kar-Leung was rarely around due to his film obligations but Jaam's widow took a liking to the young Gordon. In 1973, LKL invited Gordon to Macau to participate in the film Breakout from Oppression (1978) which launched Gordon's movie career.
[6] Five Shaolin Masters (1974). Dir. Chang Cheh. 2006. DVD. Region 2 Wild Side.
[7] See Books, A Tribute to Action Choreographers, page 132.
[8] Chinese newspaper article from Chi Kuan-Chun's now defunct site.
[9] See Film Reviews and Interviews, "Five Shaolin Masters aka 5 Masters of Death (1974)."
[10] See Web and More, "Answers to Readers' Questions and Answers - November 1999 Part 1."
[11] "Chen Kuan Tai Returns to South Florida." Personal interview. 4 Aug. 2013.
[12] Before Changgong established, it's alleged that Chang Cheh co-founded Nanhai [South Sea] Film Company with friend Cheung Ying and released 3 films featuring Meng: The King of Boxers (1972), Prodigal Boxer (1972), and The Young Tiger (1973). Cheung Ying would later become the general manager of Changgong. See Books, Chang Cheh: A Memoir, pages 76 and 103.
[13] "5 Shaolin Masters Hand Sign." Kung Fu Fandom. 02 Oct. 2011.
[14] The society was initially founded by a Buddhist teacher in the 4th century.
[15] Xinhua is the China news agency in Hong Kong.

10

The Boxer Rebellion

Chang Cheh mentioned in his memoirs that the restrictions on outdoor shooting, shortage of sound stages, and low standards of set construction in Taiwan hampered the making of *Five Shaolin Masters*. Location shots were lensed in the mountainous northern areas and around the Hsi-Lo Bridge which spanned the river Cho-Shui. The movie performed well at the box office, securing a lucrative Christmas release, putting it at the #5 spot for all Hong Kong films distributed in 1974. While extremely popular in the Western Hemisphere, the film did not come to American theaters until 1981 when it was released as *The 5 Masters of Death*. While the box office receipts were welcoming, production costs hovered around $2 million, which exhausted all the Shaw Brothers Studio's accrued capital in Taiwan

While shooting *Five Shaolin Masters*, the remainder of *Disciples of Shaolin* was filming concurrently. Alex is featured in the opening title sequence in which he performed the Tit Sin Kuen (Iron Wire Form). It is the most advanced and well-known internal set within the Hung Gar Kuen system. The iron rings Alex wore on his forearms were normally not incorporated into this routine as they would work counterproductive. Lau Kar-Leung realized Tit Sin Kuen is a special breathing exercise and meant for building up internal strength. To make it more visually engaging, he added the rings, some repetition was removed, and the end sequence was new. According to one of Alex's brothers, the actor learned this set in less than thirty minutes before filming it for the camera.

Disciples of Shaolin wrapped five weeks sooner than *Five Shaolin Masters*, but the movie was held back and didn't hit theaters until six months after *Five Shaolin Masters*. *Disciples of Shaolin* not only won big at the box office but also took awards at the 21st Asian Film Festival held in Jakarta, Indonesia. Chang Cheh gleefully remarked it *"...was an enormous success, indeed one of the best of my later works."*[1] The director boasted even higher praises for his star pupil, Alex, describing him as the embodiment of the xiaozi persona.

"...good looking, excellent physique, a delicate blend of rebelliousness and liveliness, a good comic sense who switched comfortably between literary and action roles. Jackie Chan undoubtedly outdid Fu in the martial arts and possessed a more mature image but its undeniable that Fu inspired the xiaozi character."[2]

Disciples of Shaolin won both the Mandela Award (Best Film in Praise of Nationalist Spirits) and the Best Music Award for composer Frankie Chan Fan-Kei. Chan composed the tracks on approximately 350 films that included numerous collaborations with director Chang. Cherished amongst Alex's fans, and even a personal favorite of Chi Kuan Chun, *Disciples of Shaolin* was fittingly assessed by a kung fu film reviewer who wrote that it was the end of an era, in which martial arts heroism became obsolete and replaced by the rise of a modern day, capitalistic society.

"It's not a Shaolin film but the specter haunts it. This is a world where the Temples, refuges of study and contemplation, have long been destroyed . . . even the productive political avenues of Ming Rebellion seem to have been snuffed out. What means are left for a martial-artist? Either you conceal it . . . or become a hired thug for the growing merchant class."[3]

With production on *Five Shaolin Masters* concluding in October, Chang wasted no time tackling his next epic. Six weeks later, on the 16th of November, cameras cranked up on *Boxer Rebellion*. This martial arts / historical drama was based on the uprising of Chinese patriots struggling to oust foreign occupiers at the onset of the 20th century. It was a lavish exhibition of considerable production value, historical inaccuracies, and a touching tale of romance between Alex and his off-screen love who were now settling into the role of a couple. Jenny remarked,

"For a love relationship, I like a more romantic one and I care more about atmosphere. I think Ah Sheng and I suit each other on this point."[4]

Whenever the twosome had some down time together, they avoided shop talk if possible. Periodically, Alex came home exhausted from a long day on set, but perked right up when he saw Jenny, and became the happy-go-lucky guy she fell in love with. Any concerns he had during the day were set aside as his attentiveness was now on the menu and what he could do to help her with the evening meal. Jenny commented,

"Ah Sheng won't bring troubles into our world. He's been working as an actor for so long, he never thinks of doing anything for himself or getting any advantages."[5]

Boxer Rebellion was the first of several productions the new lovers would appear in together. To commemorate the event, director Chang conceived a heartbreaking encounter with the enemy, in which Alex fought for his beloved's hand. It was just one of many films that Fu Sheng wouldn't survive. Some feel that his mortality created sympathy for his characters which made him more human in the eyes of his fans. A close friend of Alex's observed that, while top stars such as Bruce Lee and Jackie Chan played their roles skillfully, Fu Sheng was genuinely himself on screen, even in costume. Filmgoers took on a natural liking and association with Alex, whereas the others simply put on a good show.

Chang Cheh pulled out all the stops on *Boxer Rebellion*, but again while steeped in history, he was a man who didn't feel the need for historical faithfulness. One such inaccuracy was the inclusion of Alfred von Waldersee, who was portrayed by American actor Richard Harrison. In real life, the Prussian Field Marshal was more than twice the age of the thirty-eight-year old actor and didn't arrive in Beijing until the tail end of the rebellion. Waldersee was in charge of the pacification of the Boxers which he concluded to be neither rewarding nor necessary. The Prussian's association with Chinese courtesan Sai Jinhua, played by sex kitten Hu Chin, was believed factual though she publicly disputed any sexual relationship with him. Harrison recanted in a 2003 interview,

"I asked [Chang] if we could make my love scenes with the lead actress a little stronger. Everyone liked the scenes, but they were cut as it was considered appalling for a high-class Chinese woman to have an affair with a white man. Actually, we were really called barbarians."[6]

The Boxer uprising itself was more than just a reaction to the Western powers. In fact, it was a culmination of events. Flooding and harvest failures in the Shandong region, lack of competent local aristocratic leadership, and the expansion of martial arts rituals galvanized by popular religion all played a role. Shandong may be the birthplace of Confucius, but it also bred a reputation for rebellion and its martial arts tradition was to be reckoned with.

Hailing from the southwest section of this coastal province was the Big Sword Society which developed into a precursor to the Boxer Movement. The faction used an invulnerable technique known as the Armor of the Golden Bell (Jin-zhong zhao) and their initial intent was to protect people's lives and property. Their motives soon deviated as they initiated a campaign against the Christian communities and quickly fell out of favor with the local authorities.

Another group that surfaced at this time was the Spirit Boxers. The Spirit Boxers were a predominately impoverished peasant clique captivated with the notion of being part of a secret society. One crucial lure was their claim to be impenetrable to foreign weapons, but unlike the Big Sword, their power was said to come from divine possession. They asserted guaranteed victory as they had the support of spirit soldiers who came to the aid of any Boxer in time of need. Many of these deities were military figures borrowed from novels such as *The Water Margin* that were theatrically depicted in open-air performances. When the Boxers were possessed by these daemons, they played out their battles for justice and honor similar to the way the opera actors performed on stage.

Like the Big Sword, expansion of the Spirit Boxers was fueled by the 1898-99 droughts in Northern China. Their resentment towards the foreign occupiers now reached a boiling point, and taking to arms under the slogan "Fu-Qing mie-yang," they wiped out missionaries and slaughtered Chinese Christians.[7] The movement reached the Beijing area in June 1900 where they besieged the international Legation Quarter. Empress Dowager Cixi shifted her alliance from her Western guests and proclaimed a declaration of war on any nation with ambassadorial links in China. In an initial clash with the Boxers, an eyewitness spoke of the peasants' resolve:

"They came on us in a ragged line, advancing at the double . . . Not more than a couple hundred, armed with swords, spears, gingalls, and rifles; many of them being quite boys. It was an almost incredible sight, for there was no sign of fear of hesitation, and these were not fanatical braves or the trained soldiers of the Empress, but the quiet peace-loving

peasantry — the countryside in arms against the foreigner."[8]

Fifty thousand troops from the Eight-Nation Alliance arrived at the capital several weeks after the siege initiated. Empress Dowager fled under disguise and the rebellion was eventually put down with the signing of the Boxer Protocol.[9] It was a humiliating defeat for China as fighters and officials were imprisoned or executed and foreign delegations were permitted to post troops in Beijing. Other terms imposed included a two-year ban on arms imports and reparations of more than $330 million to the Allied Forces.

Chang Cheh expressed in an interview that the outside powers were merely a backdrop for his film. His focus was instead on the blind patriotism of the people. While he didn't sympathize with the Boxers, he did sanction the resistance movements initiated by folk heroes driven by their nationalistic beliefs. A local film distributor advanced one million dollars to Chang for the Taiwanese film rights, thus allowing him to lavishly spend on extras and personnel. Location shooting occurred in Hukou, Hsinchu in Northern Taiwan, and the Houli District in Northwestern Taichung City. The entire wardrobe was rented from Europe and Chang was able to coax Li Lihua, who played Empress Dowager, out of retirement to participate.

The director was quite upbeat about the production but its performance was decisively hampered by political interference. General Wang Sheng viewed Chang as a political ally of Chiang Kai Shek's son and pressured film censors to make substantial cuts before its release.[10] They deemed the picture offensive because Allied forces had invaded China and humiliated the population. The movie was well received, and even in its butchered form, box office receipts reached $2,650,000 in the first five days with near full house capacity for each showing.

When the film was presented to Hong Kong officials, it suffered a similar fate. The ruling British government did not wish to show a movie depicting resistance against the Western powers. They claimed it incited remnants of the Red Guard and their decade-long Cultural Revolution. The motion picture was banned in the colony but finally released, due to Run Run Shaw's persistence, as *Spiritual Fists*. This severely edited version performed poorly at the box office placing it #17 for 1976. Despite its censors, Chang was extremely proud of the picture and his protégée. He boasted in his memoirs that Fu Sheng was the vanguard of actors such as Jackie Chan, Stephen Chow, and Andy Lau.

"He's so full of character, handsome, and adept in both literary and action parts. It would be a memorable event if the full version of Fu's posthumous work, Boxer Rebellion, could be released."[11]

With the main production taking a little over three months to complete, the director decided it was time to return to Hong Kong for the Chinese New Year (February 11, 1975) and a well-deserved break. In less than a year, he completed four films: *Five Shaolin Masters, Disciples of Shaolin, Boxer Rebellion* and *The Fantastic Magic Baby (1975)*. Although this marked a big success for Changgong, his return sparked unfavorable rumors of prematurely shutting down the company's operation in Taiwan. Chang held a press conference to clarify his stance, stating he was misunderstood by some Taiwanese reporters and planning to return in a few weeks to prepare for a new movie. In the meantime, he wished to assist Chiang Da-Wei with his latest directorial effort, *The Condemned (1976)*, plus work on a few screenplays. At the time, Chang held three scripts in hand of which Alex was to appear. The first was a modern war tale featuring seven heroes of the Second Sino-Japanese War, the second placed several centuries earlier, while the third was quasi-experimental in nature titled *The Hell*.

Chang Cheh wasn't the only one setting reporters straight. Alex would also have to defend himself from misunderstandings in the press. His rising star and new singing girlfriend became fresh fodder for members of the media who started to hound the couple. Rumors circulated that Alex was more inclined to spend time with Jenny than performing in his movies to which he asserted,

"This is absurd! I came to Taiwan to work for Changgong. Except for when I was injured twice, I attended every filming session punctually. The fact that I went to accompany Jenny to her work was because there were no filming sessions for me. I was bored and that's why I chose to stay with Jenny. It's a very normal practice for couples."[12]

Jenny felt compelled to address the press as well but avoided emotions. She clarified they would be apart for weeks because of their work schedules and cherished any free time together. She recently signed a new contract and Alex initially didn't like that she went overseas alone. Despite the long-distance relationship, the lovebirds made sure they were in contact daily via phone. With Alex working in Taipei and Jenny in Hong Kong and elsewhere, they'd go Dutch on their long-distance calls. She joked with the press corps,

"He calculates the time thinking that I should be back and calls. 'So, you finished singing? Have you had dinner? No? Don't go out anyway. It's getting late. Call delivery!'"[13]

---

[1] See Books, Chang Cheh: A Memoir, page 96.
[2] Ibid.
[3] "Disciples of Shaolin (1975)." Kung Fu Fandom. 8 Feb. 2014.
[4] See Web and More, "Fu Sing & Yan Nei," page 11.
[5] Ibid.
[6] See Film Reviews and Interviews, "Richard Harrison: Shaw Bros to B-Movie Ninja Films."
[7] Support the Qing. Destroy the Foreign.
[8] See Books, The Boxer Rebellion: The Dramatic Story of China's War on Foreigners That Shook the World in the Summer of 1900, page 94.
[9] The eight nations were the Empire of Japan, the Russian Empire, the British Empire, the French Third Republic, the United States, the German Empire, the Kingdom of Italy and the Austro-Hungarian Empire.
[10] Further reading: http://www.wilsoncenter.org/publication/taiwans-cold-war-southeast-asia
[11] See Books, Chang Cheh: A Memoir, page 74.
[12] See Web and More, "A Letter Written by Alex."
[13] See Web and More, "Fu Sing & Yan Nei," page 11.

11

Lau Kar-Leung

The idea for Fu Sheng's next film came up when Richard Harrison was invited to take part in *Boxer Rebellion*. Chang Cheh had the international market in mind and selected the narrative of a Western explorer. When Harrison expressed interest as a co-producer, Chang became hesitant and voiced concerns of losing control over the picture if a difference in opinion arose. The two finally consented that this new venture was to be produced and financed solely by Changgong. Due to the film's lofty budget, they further agreed that locking up some international copyrights would alleviate risk. Harrison, who owned a business in Italy, proved advantageous to the negotiation of the European copyright while Run Run Shaw secured the U.S. copyright. Harrison described working on the project,

"Chang had a portable desk he sat behind with a bucket to spit into and he always smoked a large cigar. He would give orders for an hour or so, then nod off. When he woke up he would be in an angry mood and find someone to take his wrath out on; sometimes firing them."[1]

Harrison didn't wish to give a negative impression of the filmmaker and clarified by stating he worked well with Chang Cheh and respected the director. But there was another on the crew who made an even bigger impression on the actor.

"The one person who really impressed me was Lau Kar-Leung. He was an assistant director but staged the fight scenes. Lau was about half my size but a real Kung Fu expert. I honestly believe he could have kicked my head off."[2]

Lau Kar-Leung and crew went to work on *Marco Polo (1975)* on the last day of February 1975. The film starred Fu Sheng, Chi Kuan Chun, Bruce Tong, and Carter Wong Ka-Tat as four brothers-in-arms against an army of Mongol invaders. Chang's ancient interpretation is fittingly well-matched with its alternate title, *The Four Assassins,* given that Polo (played by Harrison) was more of a supporting player than the lead. The film didn't delve into the captivating tales of the Venetian explorer but instead kept him in the background as an impassive observer. Harrison lamented on his role,

"I really enjoyed doing the first film. The second film, Marco Polo, not as much. I called it Marco Polo watching Kung Fu."[3]

The real-life tale of the world-renowned explorer was chronicled in his book, *The Description of the World*, later known as *The Travels of Marco Polo*. Some critics have slammed the book as the construct of a man with a wild imagination, and the work eventually earned another title: *Il Milione* (The Million Lies). Polo's accountings of his travels to the Far East provided the Western world with its first clear picture of China's geography and ethnic customs. He befriended Kublai Khan who employed him as a special envoy and sent the Venetian into far-flung areas of Asia (Burma, India, Tibet) never explored by Europeans. When Polo returned to his native land, nearly a quarter-century later, he lost much of his acquired wealth to greedy Genoese officials in Turkey.

Just a few years after his return to Venice, he commanded a war vessel against the rival city of Genoa. Polo was ultimately captured and sentenced to a Genoese prison, where he met a fellow prisoner named Rustichello who assisted him to pen the now famous manuscript. After his 1299 release from incarceration, Polo returned to Venice where he married and raised three daughters. The traveler turned author passed away at his home in Venice on January 8, 1324. As he lay dying, friends and admirers paid their respects with some urging him to admit his work was fiction. Marco Polo though refused his critics stating, *"Non ho scritto la metà di quello che ho visto."*[4]

While the production of *Marco Polo* was in full swing, Alex saw two of the most influential people in his professional life go their separate ways. Chang Cheh and his long-associated choreographer, Lau Kar-Leung, ended their business relationship after working together on nearly four dozen films. It was a partnership that not only brought both men to the forefront but set the bar for future martial arts films. Lau stated he learned a great deal from Chang, as did many others who worked under the director, such as Tong Gai, Wu Ma, and John Woo. But problems persisted and so Lau made the difficult decision.

"*...I thought it best to go my own way and remain on good terms, rather than stay and argue.*"[5]

Sifu Lau had also been Alex's mentor for the past few years and the parting drove the actor to choose between the feuding duo. Alex owed much to both men, and with a heavy heart, opted to stay with his cinema father triggering friction between student and master. Lau had expectations of Alex starring in his directorial debut which was written specifically for him. Alex rejected the offer and even went so far as to criticize what Lau did during *Marco Polo* as morally wrong. The Hung Gar Kuen exponent, in turn, accused Alex of being a traitor as he was forced to cast nineteen-year-old Wong Yu (Wong Chi-kuen), who mirrored Fu Sheng's mischievous martial skills with boyish good looks. Over the following two years, the teacher avoided his student at all costs and pretended he didn't even see Alex when they crossed paths. In the Fall of '77, the martial arts master was admitted to St. Teresa's Hospital for gastric bleeding, and despite their cold relationship, Alex visited him at the hospital thus beginning the path to their reconciliation.

Lau Kar-Leung's past is steeped in martial arts tradition and he was highly regarded at Movietown. He was born in Guangzhou in 1937 and originally part of the Xinhui Clan.[6] Lau was the third eldest of six siblings, and as a young lad, lived on a houseboat with roughly thirty others. His mother came from a family of Chinese Opera performers and many on the boat were actors and musicians. She instructed her children to always hide on the boat whenever Japanese troops were in the vicinity. At six-years-old, Lau and a friend decided not to heed this rule. The two daring youngsters endeavored to steal a rubber raft from the soldiers as they ate their evening meal. Unexpectedly, the float punctured. The loud burst alerted the Japanese who believed it was an attack and returned fire. Luckily, Lau Kar-Leung went unscathed. His friend though paid the ultimate price with his life.

After two years, the family left the boat and returned to dry land. The opera troupe broke up, and the Lau members moved to Guangzhou where the father, Lau Jaam, taught martial arts to Japanese sympathizers. This led to rumors that he was a supporter of the conquering nation, and after the war, the Kuomintang arrested him. Subsequently, the family fled to Hong Kong after the 1949 Revolution, where Lau Jaam continued to teach.

Initially, Lau Kar-Leung wasn't a fan of boxing and lost every round in arranged fights. This is hard to fathom considering Lau Jaam was a student of Lam Sai Wing, aka the Magnificent Butcher, who in turn was a student of Wong Fei-hung. After he was observed losing a fight by his father's colleague, Lau Kar-Leung felt a bit ashamed so he began to take training seriously, and inside of two short months, started winning his boxing matches. Lau Jaam didn't push him into learning the arts but nurtured his son's new interest. His father introduced him to various elders who instructed the novice boxer with assorted styles.

Those early years in Hong Kong were lean times for the family. Lau Jaam previously owned his own martial arts studio and was a policeman in Guangzhou.[7] In Hong Kong, they lived in poverty, and the father took up work as a chiropractor. The family scraped by as he treated injuries and taught martial arts on the side. The elder Lau believed that work should come to them and not the other way around. Lau Kar-Leung said his father was a chivalrous, competitive man who believed in using martial arts and ethics to influence others. The teen recalled him winning matches and then prescribing medicine for the losers. Some of these men were so grateful that they became Lau Jaam's disciples. Lau Kar-Leung would incorporate this ideology into his own films many years later.

Lau Jaam also performed in Wong Fei-hung movies of the 1950s. He was brought into the industry by Lau Kwai-hong (1918-1955), one of the best-known comedy stars before World War II. Lau Jaam was cast in more than four dozen productions and many times appeared as his own Sifu, Lam Sai Wing. Lau Kar-Leung later joined him in the movie industry as an extra and played a pugilist in his first film under director Ku Wen Tsung.[8] Like Alexander, the young Kar-Leung was mischievous and enjoyed playing pranks on the set. A story goes that he once huddled in a coffin to escape the cold and then jumped out to shock his co-workers. But there were grave times as well. On one occasion, he was doubling for another actor when a mishap occurred and Kar-Leung nearly burned to death.

During the mid-50s, Lau Kar-Leung befriended fellow martial stuntman Tong Gai and the duo began a productive working relationship that revolutionized the genre. They worked on twenty or so productions when Yuet Ngee Motion Picture Production Co. approached them to choreograph the film *South Dragon, North Phoenix (1963)*. When Robert Wise's *The Sand Pebbles* came to Hong Kong in early Spring '66, they started up a stuntmen association dubbed No. 19.[9] However, it was their action direction on *The Jade Bow (1966)*, produced by Great Wall Movie Enterprise, that caught Run Run Shaw's eye. The mogul dispatched director Hsu Tseng-Hung to entice them to work on Shaw productions that ultimately became *Temple of the Red Lotus (1965)* and *The Thundering Sword (1967)*.

Shortly thereafter, Chang Cheh realized the potential of Lau Kar-Leung and Tong Gai, as the director was venturing into his own line of martial arts themed films. He recruited the twosome for *Magnificent Trio (1966)*, which was the first of nearly 50 projects featuring Chang as director and Lau as choreographer.

Lau Kar-Leung briefly addressed their notorious 1975 split in an interview many years later. When he returned to Hong Kong that spring, Lau intended to terminate his contract with Shaw Brothers Studio and teach kung fu in the States. Run Run didn't want to lose such a valuable asset, so Mona Fong proposed that Lau start directing his own films. Lau agreed but wanted to change the format. He believed martial arts films could be successful with an injection of comedy and that the villain needn't be destroyed in order for the hero to victor. Fong and Lau came to terms, and despite not having Fu Sheng star, he made *The Spiritual Boxer (1975)*. Chang commented that Lau had shown growing interest in directing and chose not to interfere with this undertaking. Rumors abounded for years about the friction between the Chang and Lau camps, but in 1989, the two men finally met publicly and put an end to such talk.[10]

Though Alex was deeply troubled by this course of events in 1975, he bore his own dissensions as well. While he and Jenny were discovering their comfort zone, Jenny's step-father didn't share the sentiment and her family judged Alex as someone far too immature for a serious relationship.

"He once came to my home and my father happened to be angry. So,

he pointed to him and said, 'Fu-sheng Chang, let me tell you. If I know you come to my home in future, don't blame me if I call someone to catch you like catching a thief!'"[11]

Jenny laughed when she reflected on the scene.

"It sounds funny when I talk about it now. Like catching a thief. Ah Sheng was so scared and sat down without saying a word. So, I told him, 'Go back to the hotel and I'll find you later.' After he was gone, I packed a suitcase and left as well."[12]

Jenny moved into the hotel with Alex for about a month before her parents finally conceded. Jenny's step-father saw how close they were and decided to not interfere in their relationship any longer. On March 23, with nearly a month's work of *Marco Polo* in the can, the couple briefly returned to Hong Kong for Ti Lung and Amy Tao Man-Ming's nuptials. Best men were Wong Chung and Danny Lee Sau-Yin, while the maids of honor were Lydia Shum Tin-Ha and Amy's younger sister, Tao Man-Fong. Groomsmen included Adam Cheng, Wong Yu, and Ling Fung and bridesmaids were Maggie Li, Lily Li, and Mei-Yi. The guest list was a "Who's Who of Shaw Brothers Studio" that included Run Run and his wife, Lily Wong Me-chun, Mr. & Mrs. Chang Cheh, Chiang Da-Wei, Ku Feng, Ivy Ling Po, Tien Ni, Wong Ching, Patrick Tse Yin, Li Ching, Chor Yuen, Yueh Hua, Ching Li, Wu Ma, Chan Wai-Man, Chen Kuan-tai, Pao Hsueh-Li, and a host of others.

That evening, at the Oceania Restaurant, a wedding banquet of sixty tables was reserved for the multitude of guests; however, reporters were quick to turn the spotlight on Alex and Jenny with their swirling romance. The couple was oblivious to all around when they were in each other's arms and kissed like kids chewing bubble gum. The twosome seemed inseparable and even the photos that Alex distributed to his fans included his beloved. This only fueled the paparazzi's meddlesome nature of when Alex and Jenny's big day would come. Alex didn't let the intruding questions spoil his good mood and bantered with the reporters,

"...why get married if you have no money?"[13]

While Alex and Jenny weren't willing to discuss marriage publicly, they conversed in private and saw it a strong possibility in the future. Though Jenny's family didn't oppose such a union, her step-father pointed out the career span of an artist was unpredictable, possibly a flash in the pan. He advised her to treasure their time together but also use the opportunity to build up their nest egg. Jenny heeded her elder's advice and decided not to rush matters. She confided in a friend,

"If we get married, he won't act and I won't sing. What's good in shooting movies? It's such a hard work and even your personal affairs often come out to the public. I sing, not because of money, but mainly I like singing. Little Sheng's father asked me not to sing too. The two of us will start a business overseas."[14]

In Chang Cheh's next project, the off-screen couple appeared together once more in the supernatural martial arts experiment simply titled *The Hell*. Divided into three parts, the episode known as Earth was written specifically for them with songs by Steven Liu Chia-Chang and lyrics by Chang Cheh. Alex acknowledged he wasn't as good a singer as Jenny but she provided him with some quick instruction. According to an older sibling, Alex was born with an incredible knack, similar to eidetic memory, in which he memorized popular Japanese songs after only a brief exposure. Some years earlier, Alex practiced singing by listening to English-Australian pop-rock band, The Bee Gees, and took up the drums but his escalating film schedule had taken over.[15]

"I stopped years ago. I haven't played guitar for a long time either. I just don't have the time. To be honest, I haven't taken a break since I started acting."[16]

Presumed inspired by the 1960 Japanese horror movie, *Jigoku* aka *The Sinners of Hell*, filming started on *The Hell* on the 24th of March though it wouldn't show up in theaters until 1980. Initially shot in Taiwan, the picture was shelved after only partial completion and two years would pass before Chang attempted a second go at this production. Later retitled as *Heaven and Hell (1980)*, this film ranked as the director's most curious work. As critic Pollard explained,

"Heaven and Hell marks Chang's most unusual film, one that unevenly presents fantastic and horrific imagery, musical numbers, outrageous costumes and weapons, and different martial arts styles in various periods. The film is a sprawling mini-epic that plays more like a highlight reel of Shaw Brothers movies than a single, cohesive picture."[17]

During its initial filming, Chiang Da-Wei and wife Maggie Li were engaged in a forbidden love affair in the Heaven segment while the Mortal World (Earth) adopted the form of a musical and featured Alex, Jenny, and Taiwanese singer Pan Jian. The third section, titled Hell, highlighted Alex and Taiwanese acrobat turned actor, Li Yi-Min, protecting Shih Szu in said inferno. And that's literally where most of the film wound up! Choreographer Robert Tai recalled that Run Run Shaw and Mona Fong burned the reels after viewing the footage. Chang Cheh was into a heavy experimental stage at the time, as one might note from elements in *The Fantastic Magic Baby* and *Na Cha the Great*. Snippets of the original film did find its way into the final cut, crafting this picture into a highly muddled cinematic potpourri.[18]

Alex and Jenny shot much of their parts in the spring of '75 for the Mortal World sequence which used minimal stylized sets and props that were more suitable for a stage play than a film set. Alex's character protects his on-screen lover from a color-coordinated gang of pirouetting hooligans in a *West Side Story* style fight sequence featuring no sound effects or visible contact. As one reviewer mentioned, it was a brave style choice which regrettably didn't pay off. In a 1976 interview, Chang attempted to explain his position and why the film failed,

"Using 'Child in Red' (Fantastic Magic Baby) for example, it was an attempt to fuse dancing together with traditional Chinese ping drama . . . This so-called failure is because the technique for doing so hasn't matured yet . . . For the case of 'The Hell,' the situation is similar. In terms of experimenting, 'The Hell' was even bolder in this regard..."[19]

As his on-screen character stood up against aggressors for his lover's hand, Alex's off-screen fate mirrored this same Pandora's box. The couple's careers were on the upswing but the closely followed relationship started to play havoc with the love-struck twenty-somethings. Alex ultimately reached his boiling point with the media and fired off a memo to a Hong Kong magazine on May 25, 1975 to address the insensitive tales of the gossip mill.

"In the last few months, I've heard many ridiculous rumors that have upset me a great deal. Sometimes, I could not eat or sleep for several days. I remained silent and was patient until today. I must make the following

declaration. A declaration that I've made with pain."[20]

Alex first came to Jenny's defense by telling those who hounded them that they were in wholesome relationship. They shared many common interests and goals and he deeply admired her wisdom, courage, and diligence. Jenny was always on the move due to her contractual obligations, so Alex followed her whenever she flew between Hong Kong and Taiwan. They were quite attached as family and fans would attest.

"...we began to be attacked. Many absurd rumors published in the papers and magazines. What's their motive here? To hurt our relationship? Everyone has their history and no one is perfect."[21]

The most unbearable scandal involved their families. An article came out stating that Cheung Yan-lung didn't wish Jenny to enter the Cheung household. Despite earlier differences with his father, Alex held him in high respect and maintained his parents never made any such comments on his relationship with Jenny. He chastised the press,

"She is a hard-working and successful artiste. She earns more money than I do and she will not get anything from our relationship. I think this rumor has hurt Jenny a great deal."[22]

Alex admitted he was a bit of a free-spirit before meeting Jenny. He didn't have any concept of saving and spent every dollar in hand. She helped him open a savings account which allowed him to be more prudent with his salary. Additional tales he disputed involved his cinema dad and claims that their relationship was a struggle. Alex contested such talk was nothing but media hogwash and they were as close as ever. The actor signed off his letter,

"I am not a writer, but to destroy these rumors, I have to write the truth. I hope those who created these lies are held responsible. Nonetheless, I'll take appropriate actions to protect myself and Jenny."[23]

---

[1] See Film Reviews and Interviews, "Richard Harrison: Shaw Bros to B-Movie Ninja Films."
[2] Ibid.
[3] Ibid.
[4] "I did not write half of what I saw."
[5] See Books, Hong Kong Action Cinema, page 46.
[6] Yung Jing-Jing clarified during his 2013 funeral that her late husband's birth date was incorrectly listed as September 3, 1936 on his identification card. 1937 was the correct

year. Master Lau reiterated this year in an interview with the HKFA. Lau commented that his mother said he was born in the Year of the Ox on the third of the Lunar September. When the author raised the question with Lau's daughter in 2017, she admitted that neither she nor her mother knew the actual date and Lau should have been older than stated at the time of his death; possibly 1934.

[7] His father's martial arts school in Guangzhou was known as Hu He School.

[8] The Battle Between a Brave Lad of Guangdong and the Girl Bodyguard (1950)

[9] While not the first HK Stuntmen's Association, Number 19 was a well reputed group started in 1966 by Lau and other Guangdong natives. It got its name from its location at 4/F, 19 Pak Hoi St., Yau Ma Te.

[10] When LKL left Taiwan, god-brother Lau Kar-fai was unable to leave with him as he had signed a three-year contract with Changgong. Gordon thought of breaking his contract and return to HK to work on Challenge of the Masters (1976) but supposedly Chang Cheh held the actors' passports, so they wouldn't abandon him. Chang finally agreed to end Gordon's contractual obligations with Changgong once he finished filming Seven Man Army (1976).

[11] See Web and More, "Fu Sing & Yan Nei," page 11.

[12] Ibid.

[13] Ibid, 29.

[14] Ibid, 11.

[15] Alex's favorite song was "I Started a Joke" that was originally recorded by the band in 1968. Alex could sing in both Chinese and English.

[16] See Web and More, "Fu Sing & Yan Nei," page 21.

[17] See Film Reviews and Interviews, Heaven and Hell (1980).

[18] Milky Way Pictorial July 1975: 42-43.

[19] See Film Reviews and Interviews, "Chang Cheh Talking about Chang Cheh."

[20] See Web and More, "A Letter Written by Alex."

[21] Ibid.

[22] Ibid.

[23] Ibid.

12

Changgong Goes to War

With *The Hell* going into hiatus that spring, Chang Cheh and Fu Sheng forged ahead with two new productions. The first, *Seven Man Army (1976),* began on June 7, 1975 and was a larger-than-life combat movie that centered on the last days of seven Chinese soldiers. This project consumed massive amounts of physical, human, and financial resources. It was a motion picture of such monumental scale that even Run Run Shaw and Mona Fong flew to Taichung that September to witness the shooting of the Second Sino-Japanese War spectacle.

The filming of the major battle sequences took place at Chenggong Ling, a military training base just south of the Taichung Airport in Central Taiwan. The military provided over 10,000 troops and dozens of tanks for the major combat sequence which took nearly six weeks to complete. Chang commented the tankers and artillery were free but he had to pay for ammunition and fuel as well as provide meals to the army division.

"Now I understand that the biggest expense on earth is war. It is not cheap even to forge a war for filming. It cost ten million Taiwan dollars for just a half month and the entire production will cost anything between twenty to thirty million Taiwan dollars."[1]

The script for the *Seven Man Army* was based on factual events and adapted from two books; *The History of the Second Division of the Republic Army* and *The History of Wars of the Imperial Japanese Army*. Alex played the role of Private He Hong Fa, and on June 26th, got his first dose of army life when the director ordered the cast to undergo military style haircuts. Fu Sheng's shoulder-length hair, valued only second to Jenny Tseng luxurious locks, was cut to below his ears. The mortified Alex stared at his hair on the floor and gritted his teeth,

"My heart seizes every time the scissors touched my hair! I feel like it wasn't the hair that was cut, but my own flesh!"[2]

Fu Sheng was joined by a stellar cast that included Ti Lung, Chiang Da-Wei, Li Yi-Min, Chi Kuan-Chun, Pai Ying, and the jubilant return of Chen Kuan-tai.[3] The seven men they portray are unknown figures to most, but were a vital component of the war effort against the Japanese invaders. To gain a deeper appreciation of these seven warriors of Pa Tou Lou Tzu, one needs to first understand how they came to be at this spot and why it's such a strategic position.

Beginning with the Qin Dynasty (221-206 B.C.), there were over 20 different feudal dynasties that participated in the construction of Wan-Li Qang-Qeng; i.e. the Great Wall of China. The colossal structure zigzagged across the countryside and stretched for over 13,000 miles. The sections on the edge of Beijing proper were erected during the Ming Dynasty and served as a vital defense in the capital's protection. Roughly 70 miles northeast of Beijing lies the town of Gubeikou. This seemingly inconsequential settlement has long been a location of military significance due to its passageway that links the northern and southern areas of the Yanshan Range. A fortification at Gubeikou was recorded as early as the Eastern Zhou Dynasty (770-221 B.C.) and continually reinforced over the next 1500 years. The key section of the Great Gubeikou Wall was built in the Ming Dynasty under the supervision of General Xu Da.

This 25-mile-long wall rises and falls along the rugged mountain ranges and consists of four sections: Wohushan aka "Crouching Tiger Mountain," Panlongshan aka "Coiled Dragon Mountain," Jinshanling, and Simatai. The wall has 143 beacon towers that vary in size with the largest accommodating a garrison of over 100 soldiers. South Heaven Gate at Gubeikou Pass is the name of the Nantianmen [gateway] at this specific section of the wall.[4] There were no man-made boundaries here as the mountain on the opposing sides served as a natural defense.

From the mid-1600s to mid-1800s, the ruling emperors rested here on their travels to the summer resort at Jehol and the imperial hunting grounds in Northern China. This Nantianmen is two and one-half miles south of Gubeikou, and while not as strategically important as the town, if Gubeikou were compromised, the relief army must build a last line of defense here. An invading army from the north would need to first pass through this Nantianmen in order to press southward to Beijing. If you travel west of the gateway, you would reach Pa Tou Lou Tzu. There are eight diaolous serving as watchtowers for the Great Wall and that's where Pa Tou Lou Tzu got its name.

In the first half of the 20th century, the Chinese combatted various acts of Japanese aggression before the Second Sino-Japanese War was officially declared. Japan's conquest of China's three northeastern provinces, which set up the puppet state of Manchukuo, allowed the massing of several divisions to initiate its push into China proper. The province of Jehol was annexed by the Imperial Japanese Army to act as a buffer between China and Japanese-controlled Manchukuo in Operation Nekka. The seizure of Jehol ultimately morphed into the crowning incident of the early '30s that poisoned relations between the two nations.

The events depicted in *Seven Man Army* took place in April of the 22nd year of the Republic (1933) at Pa Tou Lou Tzu near the Nantianmen of the Gubeikou Great Wall. The 25th Division of the Army, led by General Guan Linzheng, initially resisted the invading Japanese military. Linzheng's troops were later replaced by the Second Division headed by Division Commander Huang Chieh and Battalion Commander Liu Yuzhang. Despite their best efforts, the Nishiyoshi Japanese troops overran the region with unmatched ferocity as they pummeled Gubeikou and the Nantianmen with airpower, tanks, and cannons. The confrontation at Pa Tou Lou Tzu was the final skirmish as only seven soldiers were left to defend the outpost, and in *Seven Man Army,* we bear witness to their life and death struggles.

As he was observing the production, Run Run Shaw stated he never imagined a motion picture to be so true-to-life or witnessed a scene of such scale. He boasted that the battle sequences of *Seven Man Army* were on par with its Western counterparts. The mogul recognized that if Chinese films were to establish themselves in the international market, they must match the quality and quantity of the West.

When set construction of the Pa Tou Lou Tzu tower was completed, war veterans Huang Chieh and Liu Yuzhang paid a visit to the film location at Chenggong Ling. Amid the explosive volleys of cannon fire, Huang and Liu explained the specifics of the battle to the seven actors.

The veterans illustrated with diagrams of the terrain, using tree branches and rocks in the dirt, as they laid out the positions of the Chinese and Japanese troops. Of the seven soldiers, six were never identified. The only known combatant was Wu Chao Zheng, played by Ti Lung.

Wu Chao Zheng was born in 1905 and the son of Chinese medicine doctors. In 1924, he was admitted to the newly opened Whampoa Military Academy which produced many prestigious officers. Wu completed his military training at 17 and was a Battalion Commander at 26. When the Japanese troops invaded Northern China in 1933, he was ordered to the Gubeikou area. Wu was only 29-years-old when he died in action at Pa Tou Lou Tzu. More than a half century later, the Chinese government endorsed Wu Chao Zheng as a revolutionary martyr, and in 2005, the villagers of Gubeikou erected a monument made of granite in commemoration of the Seven Warriors of Gubeikou. On the backside of the stone, the tale of the seven was engraved which has an unfortunate twist. According to the inscription, the seven soldiers weren't left to defend the outpost per se but sent uphill as battalion sentries. When the Chinese Army retreated, the seven were cut off or simply forgotten. They continued to fortify their position as they hadn't received any new orders.

As the Japanese Army advanced, the invaders presumed there were at least 100 Chinese soldiers at the top of the mount. They used cannon fire and warplanes to no avail and could not get the men to surrender. After their artillery was depleted, the troops climbed the summit and fought with rifles, sabers, and hand-to-hand. The dust cleared after four days of intense fighting in which the Japanese came to realize they had devoted extensive resources against just seven soldiers. They were shamed. The Japanese regarded these men as a symbol of the spirit of the Chinese Army and bequeathed them the title "Shina Seven Warriors." To honor them, a makeshift monument was constructed before they moved on.

The Chinese soldiers were dubbed national heroes by Chen Kuan-tai but also commented, as time withers by, people begin to forget. This film, notably the last picture Chang and Chen made together before the actor severed his contract, helped a new generation discover the history of this vital battle and the men who fought for their nation. Chen recanted how they were required to attend a mini boot camp where they received special training in ordinance and military tactics but lamented,

"...Even a film about war has casualties. During the filming of a larger battle sequence at Chenggong Ling, one soldier participating in the film was struck by shrapnel from an explosion and died."[5]

Seven Man Army wrapped on October 4, 1975 and released April 16, 1976. Despite its substantial production budget and historical value, the film struggled at the box office finishing #37 for the year with total revenue slightly under $800K. Though the poorest showing at the box office for Chang and Alex since *Na Cha the Great*, the epic combat flick won the Outstanding Feature Award at the 13th Annual Golden Horse Awards. Beyond its financial gains and accolades, the film's genuine worth is the awareness it garnered for the valiant efforts of those seven lost souls now immortalized on celluloid.

The second production that "father & son" began that summer highlighted some of Alex's best on-screen fighting. *New Shaolin Boxers (1976)* got underway August 15, and despite its title, is far removed from the tragedy of the Shaolin Temple and not part of Chang's Shaolin Cycle films. If anything, this movie has been looked upon as the second episode of an unofficial Fu Sheng tragedy trilogy along with *Disciples of Shaolin* and *Chinatown Kid*. As in those films, Alex's character was righteous but green. He carried himself with a cocky swagger, championing the cause of the underlings, only to find he created more trouble than he solved. Once again director Chang included Alex's off-screen partner Jenny, and employed a new martial arts choreographer, Chen Jih-Liang.[6]

"I enjoyed working with Fu Sheng. He is a quick learner. I can show him a set a few times and he has it burned to memory. It's a unique gift and he makes my niece happy, so he lives a rather charmed life I must say," stated Chen who took Alex on as his indoor disciple.[7]

New Shaolin Boxers had a multitude of alternative titles including *The Choy Lay Fat Kid, Silly Kid,* and *Mad Boy*. This film moved away from the typical Hung Gar Kuen instruction seen prior and utilized a newer style (relatively speaking) called Choy Li Fut. It was considered a southern style but combined the north's agile footwork and circular twisting body movement with the south's long arm/hand techniques from the animal forms. While the stances are similar to Hung Gar Kuen, one pivotal difference was that CLF practitioners whipped their upper torsos to generate more power in their arm and fist techniques.

Instructor Chen was recruited to coach Alex, and the actor hurled himself into the fight sequences with conviction and competence. The Choy Li Fut style was primarily used at the end of the movie, after the obligatory training sequences, but Chang Cheh decided to mix it up. The director enhanced the viewer's experience as the final bout was intercut with the earlier training scenes to show how the style was taken from practice to application. This serious drama was indeed a different direction for the fun-loving Fu Sheng. Alex's grave performance against the villainous Wang Lung-Wei and his disemboweling claw weapon was one for the books. Alex commented on the change of course with this film.

"For me, as an actor, it wouldn't be satisfactory if I played the same kind of role over and over again. You can't develop yourself like that and the audience would soon grow tired of you."[8]

New Shaolin Boxers didn't wrap production until March 1976 and it was several more months (September) before released to theaters. The flick made a little over $900K placing it fourth of six Fu Sheng films released that year. Sibling David Cheung maintained that Alex's role epitomized his off-screen persona.

"I always felt he is a hero who loves to help the weak people. Maybe sometimes he's childish and impulsive. In particular, when he thinks he's right, he will fight for anything. But if you ask other working staff, they will say my brother is a good guy who always helps people."[9]

The end of 1975 was fast approaching, and on November 20, Jenny returned to Kowloon for the eighth anniversary ceremony of Hong Kong Television (TVB). Alex took a break from his filming schedule in Taiwan to join her and the paparazzi were ever persistent to fuel speculation the pair would soon announce their engagement. Some sources reported such to occur on the wedding anniversary of his godfather Cheh Chang.[10] Alex tried to brush off the hearsays, commenting he was too busy shooting and getting ready to travel with Jenny to entertain such speculative notions.

The reality was Alex still shouldered a wariness of the media and remained guarded in what he told them. For nearly a year, reports continued to circulate that Cheung Yan-lung was against their union but the elder Cheung echoed, as Jenny's father did prior, to allow a career to forge ahead and acquire more assets. He understood that marriage meant an individual was mature, independent, and ready to support a family. Cheung only had his son's best interests at heart and wasn't trying to manage his life.

When cornered by some journalists, Alex found himself on the defensive and brought up an incident that occurred after the TVB show to prove his father supported their relationship. Jenny had fallen ill with a stomach ailment during the ceremony and Alex rushed her to the hospital. Mr. and Mrs. Cheung not only visited Jenny while she was recovering, but unknown to the younger couple, Alex's parents fully paid all her hospital bills.

Fu Sheng soon found himself back in Taiwan. The first of December saw the start of a new production at Changgong, *The Shaolin Avengers,* in which he starred again opposite Chi Kuan-Chun. Alex revised his role of Fang Shih-yu and Chi returned as Hu Hui-Chien as Chang Cheh fleshed out the folk hero's origin depicted in the earlier *Men from the Monastery.* If one doesn't become lost in the narrative of flashbacks, and flashbacks within flashbacks, this quasi-remake delved deeper into the Fang Shih-yu legend and was loaded with blood-soaked kung fu carnage. Also included was an early appearance of Taiwanese actors Chiang Sheng and Lu Feng who put their talents on display in a comedic flashback fight sequence. The acrobatic duo, part of Chang's new Venoms team, would appear in over a dozen more films with Alex.

The Shaolin Avengers managed an incredibly short production period, lasting only 38 days, which was Fu Sheng's quickest film to date. Working with Alex always put a smile on Chang's face but some off-set friction caused the director's disposition to sour. Chi Kuan-Chun made a complaint about his salary and how he hadn't been offered a raise since joining Changgong.[11] Chang reasoned that everyone signed a contract and they must work accordingly. Granted, Chi's salary was not on par with Ti Lung or Chiang Da-Wei but the director asserted,

"How can you compare with them? Chiang and Ti put in years of hard time. They got even less in their early days."[12]

With Alex, it was a different tale. The recently turned 21-year-old just saw an increase in his pay to $750/month but made far less than Chi's $2000 monthly salary, not to mention $3000 bonus for starring in a film. Alex though was the favorite son of Chang and his position allowed certain perks. His cinema dad allotted him sizable amounts of pocket change in private each month. These allowances helped the grossly underpaid actor with his living expenses; however, if Chang treated everyone like he did Alex, he would probably have gone bankrupt.

Shooting at the same time with *The Shaolin Avengers* was another Fu Sheng/Chi Kuan-Chun pairing in *Magnificent Wanderers (1977)*. This latter film was set in the late 14th century when the Yuan Dynasty was on its way out and the Mings were establishing their own stronghold. Rounding out the leads were the old stalwart Chiang Da-Wei and growing star Li Yi-Min in his third outing with Alex and Chang. The pseudo-comedy was a film widely scoffed at as a low point in the director's repertoire. Some say Chang was experimenting with the cross-genre of chuckle-fu which captivated audiences in the last half of the '70s but sorely missed the mark. The movie does have its place nevertheless as Chang allocated even more screen time to Chiang Sheng, Lu Feng, and Kwok Chun-Fung who displayed their exemplary martial and acrobatic skills in the finale.

Magnificent Wanderers was the last complete Changgong film shot in Taiwan before the director returned to the shores of Clear Water Bay. The picture was held back for nearly 15 months, before releasing in May 1977, and struggled at the box office. The good news was that it would be the last film of Fu Sheng's career that failed to breach the one-million-dollar mark.

---

[1] Southern Screen Oct. 1975: 20-22.
[2] "Fu Sheng Has Become an Ace of Chang Cheh." The Kung Sheung Evening News [Hong Kong] 12 Aug. 1975: 3.
[3] The return was short-lived as Chen Kuan-tai began a two-year-long lawsuit with Run Run Shaw that summer. Chen had been financing independent projects, such as The Simple-Minded Fellow (1976) in which he invested over HK$400,000, through his Tai Shen Film Company. Shaw didn't object to these ventures until Chen opted to act in a non-Shaw Brothers production. Shaw claimed Chen was in breach of contract and demanded he withdraw from the project but Chen refused. The lawsuit finally settled in September 1978. (Author note: Some sources list Chen as director of The Simple-

Minded Fellow but that couldn't be confirmed due to lack of copy. Chen was quoted in a 2002 interview that he was a producer only).

[4] Nantianmen = southern gate of a defense wall. Beitianmen = northern gate of a defense wall.

[5] "Chen Kuan Tai Returns to South Florida." Personal interview. 4 Aug. 2013.

[6] Chen Jih-Liang was Jenny's uncle.

[7] Southern Screen Sept 1976: 52-53.

[8] See Web and More, South China Morning Post, Nov. 1976.

[9] Southern Screen Dec 1982: 50-51.

[10] November, 11 1969.

[11] Hong Kong Movie News Jul 1976: 28.

[12] In 1975, both Ti Lung and John Chiang were earning $20,000/ month plus a bonus of $90,000 per film. Chen Kuan-tai was receiving $3000/ month and $50,000 per film.

Fu Sheng with his two younger brothers

Pre-wedding photo

Alex's parents, 1960s

Alexander Fu Sheng: Biography of the Chinatown Kid

top: Lau Kar-wing
instructs Alex on the set

left: Marco Polo publicity photo

bottom: Seven Man Army
cast photo with director Chang

right: Shaolin Temple
      with Chang Cheh

middle: Lau Kar-Wing &
      Lau Kar-Leung with
      the Cheung Family

bottom: The Eight Diagram
      Pole Fighter

Fu Sheng and
Gordon Liu
September '82

left: The happy
couple on the set
Boxer Rebellion

below: Heroes Two
featuring
Chen Kuan-tai

Chiang Da-Wei
visits the set
Na Cha the Great

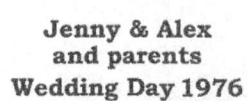

Jenny & Alex
and parents
Wedding Day 1976

Shih Szu
Chang Cheh
Fu Sheng
1975

13

Back to Movietown

The year 1976 brought sweeping changes to Alex's world. The first was the conclusion of Changgong's filming in Taiwan. Run Run Shaw was growing concerned of the partnership Chang Cheh was enjoying with his Taiwanese film distributor and how it might steer the director away from him. The mogul flew to Taiwan to convince Chang it was time to fold up his tents and return to Hong Kong. Chang heeded the boss' request and received a lucrative 25 picture contract with Shaw Brothers Studio totaling five million dollars over five years. Chang sensed the Taiwanese film industry was on the wane but still had one more film to make utilizing Taiwanese assistance. Nevertheless, he headed back to the Pearl to begin work on his last and most cohesive of the Shaolin Cycle films.

Production on *Shaolin Temple* was set in motion the first week of June in which the director finally focused his narrative on the monastery itself. The temple's reputation grew substantially over the centuries and appealed to many who sought to join the Shaolin tradition. To weed out the unworthy, the monks implemented a stringent process for choosing who became part of their community. Applicants were forced to wait outside the temple for many days, even weeks, before they were allowed entrance. Those who passed this initial trial gained admission only to find themselves not learning the coveted martial arts skills by legendary masters, but toiling at menial tasks such as kitchen or laundry duty.

Over the ensuing months and years, pupils fetched water, cooked and served meals, and maintained the estate. For their diligent service, these apprentices were cultured on a variety of subjects that included mathematics, calligraphy, history, poetry, and Buddhism. Those who completed this probationary period were assigned a mentor who took them under their wing to further their instruction.

The film, *Shaolin Temple,* dramatized how these students were worked to near exhaustion throughout their training. Grueling martial arts repetitions, Qigong movements, and endurance training were a way of life. This arduous regimen of mental and physical drilling played out each day and those who failed were politely asked to leave. Under the sweltering summer sun, many of Chang Cheh's actors endured similar physical and emotional challenges. Lengthy, sultry days of shooting didn't stifle Alex's demeanor even though he performed beneath the sun and oversized production lights. Sweat streamed down his face, making him squint as he practiced his lines, to which he confessed,

"I hate bright lights. Whether it's the flashing cameras or the sun, I just can't stand it and usually wear sunglasses when I go out. Those who don't know me think I'm arrogant but my eyes are really sensitive."[1]

After one shot, Alex took off his shirt as swift as he could. He dashed over to Chang's chair and slurped down his beverage without pause. Only bystanders felt it to be scandalous because of the dignity of the director, but for Fu Sheng, there was nothing unnatural about it.

"Having worked together for years, we're more than colleagues. We have a chemistry and I know what he likes or doesn't, so he trusts me."[2]

Chang Cheh was indeed the commander on the set and everyone labored to his expectations. The filmmaker was notorious for being hot-headed on occasion but the appearance of his favorite son always soothed Chang. The result was a welcoming calmness as all were in a better mood when Alex was near. Ti Lung was part of the all-star cast and watched the mischievous actor as he approached a few of the actor-monks. Alex jumped on their backs, rubbing each bald head, and the newly grown hair tickled his hand which made him giggle like a child. Ti Lung commented to a pair of reporters on the set,

"This is a person who has everything. He has fame, fortune, born with a silver spoon in his mouth, and now has a girlfriend. He has never met any obstacles in his life. Really, he does not know what a worry is."[3]

Alex then spied Ti Lung's presence from across the large set and hastened to his side, shrieking out his name over and over. The regal actor turned to the reporters and joked, *"He must be drunk."*[4]

While Alex seemed to be enjoying himself on stage, returning to Hong Kong meant Jenny was left behind in Taiwan as she had prior work commitments. Alex kept himself in good company though as each morning he brought his two dogs to the set and played with them during breaks in his air-conditioned dressing room. People who were close to him said there was a communication between Alex and the canines, like the way the actor and his cinema dad communicated.

"*Chang only needs to give me a glance, or I give him one, and we know what each other is thinking. We understand each other more than many fathers and sons.*"[5]

Only a few years in the industry and Alex had already experienced major changes both intellectually and emotionally. While he would attest that working with both his mentor (Chang) and his master (Lau) helped him mature, it was Jenny who was truly the most influential.

"*Since I was in school, I drank one and a half bottles of brandy each night. You don't believe that? You feel the most comfortable when you're a little drunk. After I get fully drunk, anything could happen.*"[6]

Now, circumstances had changed for the passionate youth and he gave much praise to Jenny for showing him a way out of this destructive behavior. He quit drinking and smoking, and to her credit, became more tolerant. While he enjoyed being the new Alex, there were still the tabloid rumors that irked his temper the most. He did his best to shun members of the press as he felt they were only interested in digging up dirt to sell their papers. On occasion, he would speak with a reporter but when the topic of recent gossip about Jenny was brought up, the fiery Alex cut to the quick.

"*—I don't care what the rumor said! I can tell you there's no basis for it. Jenny Tseng and I will not change because of any rumors. I was in Taiwan when I first heard it and swore, when I come back and leave the airport, I will hit whoever asks me about this!*"[7]

When speaking of these matters, the laid-back Alex couldn't sit tight or stand still. He became quite agitated and moved from sitting on a wooden stool to his dressing table. Alex rocked a chair back and forth with his legs looking for the words. He then blurted out,

"*Let me tell you. The more effort you pay to get something, the more you treasure it. I treat Jenny like this and I will marry her in this lifetime!*"[8]

The columnist was quick to change the subject and inquired about the possibility of him leaving Movietown. Alex had initially denied these reports but finally acknowledged that a representative from a Thai company was willing to pay him $300,000 for one film, while an Indonesian company offered $450,000. He admitted to entertaining the notion as the offers were rather tempting. Just starring in a handful of such films and he could easily retire before turning 30.

"Compared with such a big sum of money, the salary I get from Shaw is just a fraction though the most important thing is 'Yi.' Whatever we do, we must never forget our roots."[9]

While Alex remained steadfast in his loyalty to Chang Cheh and Shaw Brothers Studio, he confessed acting was simply a means to an end.

"I'm not particularly interested in acting. It's mainly because I am making a living. To be independent I chose shooting films, but this is temporary. I won't stay in the industry for the rest of my life."[10]

After principal photography on *Shaolin Temple* concluded, there was a two-month hiatus before the start on Alex's next project. *The Naval Commandos (1977)* was the third and final war extravaganza for Chang Cheh plus a temporary return to Taiwan. The filmmaker once more secured assistance from the military in which Admiral Tsou Chien, commander-in-chief of the Chinese Navy in Taipei, orchestrated the opening sequence. Pre-planning required an entire year while principal photography took place over 70 to 80 working days. The weary director slumped back in his chair and commented,

"The Taiwanese Navy kindly lent us their navy crew, battle ships and air fighters, but cost of fuel and ammunition already amounted to an astonishing figure, not to mention the large number of extras and many other inestimable expenses."[11]

Chang was highly optimistic that this rousing epic set in 1937 would set the bar for future Chinese naval war films. While the movie was based on historical events, the director did take his customary liberties with the actual accounts. In his version, Chinese patriots embark on a suicidal mission to sink the Japanese Navy's flagship. When their vessel is destroyed en route, they must rely on a local gangster (Chiang Da-Wei) and his hot-headed bodyguard (Fu Sheng) to fulfill their mission.

The flagship Izuma, as it was called in the film, was actually named the Izumo.[12] She was launched in 1899 and engaged in both the Russo-

Japanese War and World War I. The vessel saw action again at the onset of the Second Sino-Japanese War when she was targeted by the Chinese Air Force while anchored in the Huangpu River outside Shanghai. The CAF mistakenly bombed the British cruiser HMS Cumberland and dropped shells into Shanghai proper which killed more than 1700 civilians and wounded 1800 others.[13] Two days later, the Chinese torpedo boat No. 102 (helmed by Chi Kuan-Chun in the movie) sank after a failed attempt on the Izumo. The wife of the Admiral of No. 102 was still living in Taiwan in 1976, so Chang invited her and the survivors to his planning meetings where they became his production advisors.

As for the fate of the Izumo? Despite being boarded and sunk in the movie's finale, the real-life Japanese flagship endured for the war's duration. Just weeks before V-J Day, or the Victory of War of Resistance against Japan Day (China), she was strafed by two dozen Allied planes at the bombing of Kure. While the ship didn't sustain any direct hits, near misses caused severe underwater damage, and she took on a 15-degree list to port. An hour after, the Izumo capsized into the shallow waters. Two years passed before the ship was raised and sold for scrap at the Kure Naval Arsenal.[14]

In *The Naval Commandos,* Ti Lung commanded the Ning Ha. She was one of two Chinese cruisers built initially with assistance from Japan in the early '30s. In August 1937, the Chinese Nationalist Government sent the Ning Hai, and sister vessel, Ping Hai, down the Yangtze River to Jiangyin to help defend Nanking, the Nationalist's capital city. The following month, she was attacked by enemy forces and sunk upstream but the Japanese salvaged the ship and renamed her Mikura. The vessel underwent further reconstruction towards the end of the war and took on the new name of Isojima. She decisively met her demise on September 19, 1944 while on patrol in the Philippine Sea. The American sub USS Shad slammed three Mark-23 steam torpedoes into her hull sending the thrice-named vessel to its watery grave.

The Naval Commandos was the last time Alex worked on set with both Ti Lung and Chiang Da-Wei. The Iron Triangle collaboration on over two dozen films came to a peak with *Shaolin Temple*.[15] Interestingly enough, the two actors were cast in *The Naval Commandos,* but to the keen observer, they never appeared together on screen. The same situation went on for the next two decades, in which they mutually participated in several movies but never performed at the same time. Both actors played an integral part in Fu Sheng's early career, and like the separation of Chang Cheh and Lau Kar-Leung, this break up required Alex to further step out of his comfort zone. But this was only the beginning.

The Naval Commandos was also the last film that featured Alex the bachelor as he and his partner finally announced a date for their long-presumed union. Alex's mother purchased two six-carat diamond rings, worth $70,000 each, and presented them to the couple as an engagement present. Fu Sheng and Jenny Tseng were indisputably the hottest duet in the colony, and this betrothal triggered the power couple's popularity and marketability to soar, not just in Hong Kong, but in all Southeast Asia and beyond.

---

[1] Southern Screen Sept 1976: 44-45.
[2] Ibid.
[3] Hong Kong Movie News Jul 1976: 28.
[4] Ibid.
[5] See Web and More, "Fu Sing & Yan Nei," page 20.
[6] Ibid.
[7] Ibid.
[8] Ibid.
[9] Southern Screen Sept 1976: 44-45.
[10] Ibid.
[11] Southern Screen Apr 1977: 26-27.
[12] Not to be confused with the "Izumi" which was a Japanese cruiser scraped in 1912.
[13] August 14, 1937 is known as Bloody Saturday but these unintended atrocities are conspicuously absent from the film.
[14] The Japanese Navy resurrected the name Izumo in 2013 with a new helicopter carrier.
[15] Chang Cheh + David Chiang + Ti Lung = Iron Triangle. Many of their collaborations proved to be a recipe for box office gold as they cranked out 17 films between 1969-1972 (27 overall).

14

Wedding Bells

Ti Lung drove over to Alex's Kowloon Tong home the morning of December 4 as he had done many times prior. He and Alex enjoyed taking their dogs, Nancy and Ah King, down to the coastline where there were fewer prying eyes. Alex felt free there. A world away from his troubles. But this Saturday was far from a day at the beach as his best friend had a mission. Ti Lung was put in charge of picking up the bridegroom but found no one at home. While Alex epitomized the oh-so-cool persona of James Dean on screen, he was nothing of the kind that late autumn day and settled his pre-marital butterflies by taking a long drive through the New Territories. When Alex finally returned, there were some reporters hoping to get a few pictures of the groom, but he initially turned them away. Ever the diplomat, Ti Lung explained to him that this day was meant to be a joyous occasion and not to shun the spotlight. Always heeding big brother's advice, Alex dutifully smiled for the cameras before heading off.

The duo rounded up the remaining members of the best-men team: actors Wong Chung, Stephan Yip, and Jamie Luk. The group then proceeded to the Miramar Hotel to receive the bride, though it wouldn't be easy as Alex needed to first partake in an ancient custom known as the Chinese Wedding Door Game. This tradition originated in an era when the transportation network wasn't as developed, and if a new bride moved away with her spouse, she may never see the family again. Her kinsfolk frowned on the idea of losing a daughter forever, so they would attempt to block the groom at the door and quiz him about his would-be wife. The suitor had to prove his love for his new bride and negotiate with the bride's family with token money (Li Shi) in a red color envelope.

Jenny's entourage were all experienced bridesmaids and well prepared to engage the groomsmen team. Alex and company arrived earlier than expected so the sneaky actor decided to knock ever so softly.

A bridesmaid assumed it was just hotel staff and proceeded to unlock the door. Like the mighty warriors they portrayed on screen, the groomsmen all barged into the room and caught those inside off-guard. Alex swooped up Jenny and ushered her away without a fight or paying a single cent. He was rather pleased with himself.

Jenny always dreamt of designing her own wedding dress but it became an impossibility as the weeks drew closer to their big day. A famous wedding dress tailor, Ko Chung-ki, was called in and the idea of a classic gown was quickly dismissed. The designer expressed it would be an utter loss for such a superb figure to be concealed in an old-fashioned round dress and created an elegant gown to wow the crowds. Jenny was so delighted with the design she wore it to the Marriage Registry's office. Alex's mother was also pleased with the dress, not to mention her daughter-in-law's curvy figure.

"It's a figure for a mother. She will give birth to a lot of babies for the Cheung family," beamed Angela Liu Cheung.[1]

Alex and Jenny arrived at the San Po Kong Marriage Registry in the Wong Tai Sin District around noon. TVB sent a crew to film the wedding process, but despite their celebrity status, the couple didn't receive any preferential treatment from the court. There was a long queue outside the building and the additional media and crowds of fans made it extremely congested. Alex was already a bundle of nerves and with the air-conditioner not functioning, it only added to his anxiety. After the exchanging of vows and rings, he took a deep breath and hugged his mother. She looked at him perplexed and kidded,

"Silly boy! Why do you cry in the wedding?"[2]

Jenny's forehead was covered in perspiration from the humidity but was too busy to notice. After receiving the marriage certificate, she flashed a "V for victory" with two fingers, kidding with a big grin that Alex was now her man and he couldn't go anywhere without her. The throngs of waiting fans broke into cheers when the newly married couple reappeared. They waved to the crowds as they got into Run Run Shaw's Rolls Royce which was lent to them for their wedding day. Alex was appreciative of the gesture but was quick to comment to his new wife in private that the Rolls was just a bit slow for his taste.

The newlyweds returned to Alex's family home at Sheung Shui to carry out the traditional Chinese wedding tea ceremony. The way of the tea (cha dao) was an important part of Chinese tradition dating as far back as the Tang Dynasty. This practice demonstrated respect and gratitude to the parents for all their years of love and care. The tea was a symbol of purity, stability, and potency. The purity aspect signified their love was untainted. Stability stood for devotion. Potency represented that the wedded couple were to have many children. After serving the tea, the bride and groom received many luxurious gifts in which Cheung Yan-lung gave Jenny a diamond bracelet and new mother-in-law presented her with an exquisite pair of jade earrings. Later that evening, the happy couple returned to the Miramar Hotel where they received their guests. It was the first of three nights of banquets held in Hong Kong and Taiwan.

Inside the hotel ballroom, there were over 200 tables for the invitees. The set-your-watch punctual Run Run Shaw and Chang Cheh were delayed in traffic, but once they arrived, the movie mogul gave his opening speech to officially kick off the celebration. During the banquet, Alex and Jenny thanked their guests and toasted Amy Tao for introducing them. The ballroom was packed with family, friends and colleagues, as well as business associates of the Cheung patriarch, in which the festivities lasted into the early morning hours. While all in attendance had an enjoyable time celebrating the newlywed's future, there were two conspicuous absences; Lau Kar-Leung and Alex's old roommate, Chiang Da-Wei.

The following evening, the couple convened their second wedding party in the New Territories which consisted of more than 100 tables, and on the 12th of December, a third banquet of roughly 80 tables was held at the opulent Yuanshan Hotel in Taipei. Better known as The Grand Hotel, this famous landmark was built by Chiang Kai-shek in the early '50s. This venue has accommodated dignitaries from all over including three American presidents, a British Prime Minister, the Shah of Iran, King Hussein of Jordan, and now, Mr. and Mrs. Cheung Fu-Sheng.

The Hong Kong festivities also included a trip to the recently opened Ocean Park Hong Kong; an oceanarium and animal-themed amusement park. Unfortunately, a real honeymoon would have to wait as Alex's hectic schedule was taking him to San Francisco to shoot B-roll for his next

Chang directed production. Alex had intended to visit the States with Jenny the prior year, but due to the wedding, the trip was postponed. Now the couple had the opportunity for a working honeymoon, compliments of the studio, with free hotel and airfare.

During the first week of New Year 1977, Alex and Jenny accompanied Chang Cheh and a skeleton crew to the Bay Area. The filmmaker rapidly shot material throughout the city that he planned to intercut with the bulk of his next assignment titled *Chinatown Kid*. The team captured footage of the world-renowned Lombard Street in Russian Hill, the Golden Gate Bridge, Jackson Street, and at Dragon's Gate on Grant Street. They also shot around Ross Alley which is San Francisco's oldest backstreet and once notorious for its brothels and gambling.

Chinatown Kid was the motion picture that finally made Alexander Fu Sheng an action hero outside of Hong Kong and Taiwan. The original story was written by Chang, James Wong Jim, and Ni Kuang who collaborated with the filmmaker on over 70 movies.[3] The screenplay was initially penned in 1975 and Chang started production in Taiwan before he pulled his squad out of the country. Jenny spoke of the project in September '75, when she returned to the colony for a nightclub opening ceremony.

"Besides working on Seven Man Army, Alex also started working on a new film, Chinatown Kid. The script was written specially for us, but since I'm in Hong Kong, he will have his scenes shot first. This film is really spreading our love from real life onto the big screen."[4]

The assignment was put on the back burner for the next 15 months as Chang needed to focus on other productions. In early '77, his schedule finally freed up enough that he could pursue the project. He regarded this as a picture that needed making. The idea for the script came to Chang in 1974 while on vacation in the United States, where he encountered many residents complaining about the public security in Chinatown.

"When I found out it was the same in every Chinatown, I realized it was a social problem and this sparked a desire to make a film on this."[5]

Alex was cast as Tang Dong, an illegal refugee who finds himself at odds with a local Hong Kong gang. His grandfather ships him off to America where life should be better but Tang's problems inevitably follow him. His tale epitomizes what many fresh off the boat had to face. There was the monotonous toil in becoming a proper citizen or the lure of the easy path with the promise of riches. Modern Chinese youth in Chinatown had a different ideology from that of the older migrants and many didn't want to endure hardships like their forefathers. They failed to merge with the receiving society, and over time, became an isolated group within the Chinatown. These expats endeavored to create their own factions like the Italian mafia groups. While the Cosa Nostra maintained a well-defined structure with rigorous regulations, these wayward emigrants paid no respect to such. Chang Cheh continued,

"They're unsettled and fight for members and territories. They slay one another to vent their rage. The massacre in the Fall of '77 at the Golden Dragon Restaurant and its reprisal attacks is one such example."[6]

When Chang and Alex were filming in the States, the director felt a lurking danger in Chinatown and didn't want to draw too much attention to what he was shooting. His plan was to get in and out before any of the locals started questioning his intent. A bloodbath sequence had already been planned for the film, but in the final week of production, Chang reshot it to put the spotlight on the real-life tragedy.

"If they found out what I was going to film, I am afraid that the target in this massacre would have been me!"[7]

In 1977, the Golden Dragon Massacre was considered the worst mass slaying in San Francisco's history. At the time, there were two major factions in S.F. Chinatown's underworld: Wah Ching and Chung Ching Yee aka Joe Boys. The incident was in response to a summer confrontation in which several Joe Boy members were assaulted and Wah Ching leader, Michael 'Hotdog' Louie, was believed to be the orchestrator. Three months later, the Joe Boys were tipped off that Hotdog Louie was dining at the Golden Dragon Restaurant and decided it was payback time. In the early morning hours of September 4, 1977, three masked gunmen burst into the popular Chinatown eatery and sprayed gunfire from one end to the other. Of the 75 occupants, five people died and eleven wounded.

The San Francisco Police Department reported the restaurant's interior looked like the aftermath of a firefight in Vietnam. There was so much gunfire it required over one hundred pints of blood to save the wounded. Despite the carnage, the Wah Ching leader went unscathed, and a week later, Joe Boy Yee Michael Lee was slain in a reprisal strike. Because of the Golden Dragon tragedy, the Chinatown Squad was re-established into the Gang Task Force as a separate unit in the SFPD.

In *Chinatown Kid,* Fu Sheng's character would be the new arrival in town who opted for the path of gold and merged with the San Francisco underworld. Similar to Joe Boy Yee, his character paid a heavy price for his destructive path. While this production was a starring vehicle for Alex, it's also well recognized for prominently featuring members of Chang's Venoms team. One of the gang's leader was played by Kwok Chun-Fung, who appeared in 15 films with Fu Sheng.

Kwok was born three years before Alex in Northern Taiwan. His mother was an acrobat and unable to bring children with her as she toured with her troupe. She sent Kwok, age 7, to his grandmother's home in Hsinchu City and hoped that he could study well. However, the years there were hard as the stern matriarch would physically discipline him if he didn't complete his chores. Of the six years in Hsinchu, he missed school for three. At age 13, Kwok happily rejoined his mother in Taipei and soon after entered the Lu Kwan Peking Opera School. Some years later, he formed a circus with schoolmate Chiang Sheng and others but closed it down after only six months as they squandered the proceeds.

Kwok met his future wife during this time; however, her mother was disinclined as he didn't have a reliable job. His girlfriend persuaded him to get a trade, so he became a carpenter and blacksmith. Kwok had plans of opening a small factory but it didn't pan out due to lack of startup cash. Reluctantly, he went to Japan for an acrobatic performance and upon his return was in Changhua where they were filming *Boxer Rebellion.* The film's foreman announced they needed ten background martial artists and Kwok was one of the chosen. Chang Cheh liked what he saw and invited him back to audition for *The Fantastic Magic Baby.* Kwok felt his performance was poor but Lau Kar-Leung promised to be in touch for future projects, and some weeks after, he got the call for *Marco Polo.* Despite working on further projects, Kwok maintained self-doubts when cast in *Chinatown Kid.*

"I was green and just learning the craft. I had a kissing scene with

actress Shirley Yu and it was extremely difficult. Total pressure. I simply followed the instructions of the director: Smile. Don't. Move. Don't. He guided me through everything. Triads? What's a Triad? I knew nothing."[8]

Alex's co-star in this film was another soon-to-be Venom. Sun Chien, originally named Suen Chien-yuan, was a 22-year-old newcomer from Taiwan who just signed an eight-year contract with the studio. A Shaw staffer described him as, *"Quiet as a kid when he is gentle, but quick as a dragon when he is aggressive."*[9]

Sun Chien lost his parents in childhood and was raised by his two older siblings. Unable to attend a university after high school, he opted to serve with the Taiwanese Armed Forces. Sun returned to civilian life in September '76, and just days after hanging up his uniform, spotted an advertisement that Chang Cheh was again on the lookout for new talent. His sister persuaded him to give it a go as he did not have any job prospects. Sun submitted his application, not expecting to hear back, but to his surprise was one of the few chosen.

The filmmaker said he selected Sun because, in addition to knowing karate, he had just left school (military service) and his background was like that of the film's character. Director Chang deleted a word of his original name and left the two words "Sun Chien" as his stage name. In real life, the actor didn't wear glasses but Chang made him don the spectacles for the movie to emphasize his bookish air.[10]

"I like smart people, but smart people may not be energetic. Sun Chien is not stupid. He may look foolish but he is smart. He is a wolf in sheep's clothing," Chang observed.[11]

A journalist commented how fortunate Sun Chien was, by comparing his situation to Fu Sheng's early career. Just five years prior, Chang had taken Alex under his wing and now he was a superstar. She asked him what he thought of his prospects but Sun smiled, pushed his frames higher up on the bridge of his nose, and humbly responded,

"I am not as good as Fu Sheng."[12]

In the film, Fu Sheng and Sun Chien's characters shared a sleeping space above a restaurant's kitchen, whereas in real life, Sun's living quarters were not much better.[13] As a rookie to the studio, he wasn't eligible for the lavish air-conditioned dormitories allocated to its luminaries. His 100 square-foot living quarters reminded the visiting reporter of a prison cell with its sparse furnishings and gloomy outer corridor. This didn't dampen Sun's spirits though as he had his canine, Julie, for a roommate. The German Sheppard was raised by the novice actor since a pup and made a good companion for him, not to mention for Alex's dog "Ah King." Fu Sheng quipped,

"He is called Ah King because he eats five bowls of rice, three eggs, milk, and beef every day. He eats better than I do! Jenny would blame me if I don't treat Ah King well. She loves Ah King more than me."[14]

Coincidentally, as Alex was portraying a gangster for the silver screen, his own parents had a run in with the underworld. Cheung Yan-lung and wife were the unfortunate targets when a brazen trio of armed men and a woman broke into the family home. A man dressed as a traffic police officer came to their Kowloon residence in mid-March and forced his way in after the Cheung's amah opened the front door. Both Cheung and the amah sustained knife wounds as the four robbed the house of cash and jewelry valued at $30,000 before escaping in Cheung's vehicle.

Chinatown Kid wrapped production in September and released December 2, 1977.[15] It racked up over $1.5 million at the local box office but that was only the start. The picture made its way across the Pacific into U.S. theaters and then onto the small screen via the syndicated Black Belt Theater. Thanks to film distributor Mel Maron, World Northal Corporation, and Globe Films, Alex "the Chinatown Kid" now joined the ranks of '70s martial arts superstars Jackie Chan, Chuck Norris, and Bruce Lee. Those who personally knew Alex may have disagreed and said the unassuming actor didn't see himself on the same level as those screen idols. On some occasions, Alex even blurted out his dissatisfaction with the industry. Earlier in the summer he grumbled,

"I don't like shooting films at all. I haven't taken a break in a few years and I am sick and tired of it."[16]

---

[1] Ming Pao Weekly 421 1976: 1.
[2] Southern Screen Jan 1977: 22-23.
[3] Born Ni Cong, he fled to Hong Kong in 1957 and penned over 400 screenplays in the 1960s/70s, during the boom in martial arts films. Though an uncredited contributor to Fist of Fury (1972), it has been said he created the character of Chen Zhen made famous

by Bruce Lee.
[4] Southern Screen Oct 1975: 30-31.
[5] Ibid., Nov 1977: 26-27.
[6] Ibid.
[7] Ibid.
[8] The Five Venoms (1978). Dir. Chang Cheh. 2004. DVD. Region 2 Wild Side.
[9] Hong Kong Movie News Mar 1977: 40-41.
[10] Sadly, according to a report by Toby Russell, Sun Chien lost an eye in a fishing accident during the early 2000s.
[11] Hong Kong Movie News Mar 1977: 40-41.
[12] Ibid.
[13] Fu Sheng and Sun Chien's crammed living corners were similar to what Run Run Shaw once experienced. He joined his brothers in Singapore in 1926* where they lived in the back of the Shaw office in a four-story building. It was located in a congested part of the port city and Run Run would sleep wedged up against the film canisters after toiling all day. (Author note: *Shaw official website states he arrived in 1926 while other sources list his arrival as 1928 after the 'Liuhe Encirclement'.)
[14] Hong Kong Movie News Dec 1978: 36-37.
[15] When Celestial Pictures released the Chinatown Kid (1977) DVD in February 2004, fans were stunned as this remastered disc featured a different ending, previously not seen footage, as well as, missing footage (See Web, "Chinatown Lost"). The original ending with Fu Sheng dying was intended for international markets minus Southeast Asia. The alternate ending (Celestial) with Fu Sheng arrested was for countries with stricter censor boards (Singapore, Malaysia, Kuala Lumpur). Interesting though, Chang alludes to a possible third ending where Fu Sheng perishes in the sea after a police raid. Whether this was filmed or just a draft of the screenplay is unknown (See Books, Chang Cheh: A Memoir, page 211).
[16] Southern Screen Aug 1977: 34-35.

15

The Brave Archer

The growing weariness from continuous shoots was understandable. However, Alex was aware of his rising popularity and didn't intend to disappoint. His next project, *The Brave Archer*, was filmed concurrently with *Chinatown Kid* but was released four months earlier than the movie that garnered him worldwide fame. *The Brave Archer* would be completed in only half the time and get a coveted summer month's release.

Actress Hui Ying-hung was still a teenager when cast for these two films. She grew up in the squatter area known as Rennie's Mill (Tiu Keng Leng) and worked as a street hawker. During her bittersweet ten years as a street kid, her favorite pastime was hanging around the East Town Theatre in Wan Chai, showing Lin Dai and Li Ching's Yellow Plum operas. She was not there to watch the movies but to merely gaze at the photos in the lobby. Hui commented,

"Once there was a premiere and the crowd gathered taking photos. I saw that beautiful lead actress, and I thought this was one of the rich people. I said to myself that I had to become like her in the future."[1]

When Hui turned 14, she applied to the Miramar Dancing Group and studied classical Chinese dance under renowned instructor Chung Ho. The dance troupe allowed her to travel to Australia and Denmark for performances but her career altering opportunity arrived when a representative from Shaw Brothers Studio visited the Kowloon nightclub where she worked. The man brought news that Chang Cheh was making *The Brave Archer*, and Hui plus two others were selected to audition. Wu Ma was the assistant director and presided over their auditions, and while her two seniors passed, she had to return for another session.[2]

"My heart sank. At my second audition, I received a script and was told to play Huang Rong. I didn't know who she was, but the assistant director gave me notes and I followed what he said. On that day, Fu Sheng

came and played Guo Jing for my audition. I later learnt who Fu Sheng was and he was very handsome."[3]

Chang Cheh phoned Hui two days later and offered her a role. Since it was only one movie, she wasn't presented with a contract until after the film was complete. Hui's father was suffering from cancer and her mother refused to sign as it was less pay than she could make at the nightclub. The teenager realized this was the chance of a lifetime, so her older sibling, who played a background martial artist in *The Warlord (1972)*, went with her to the studio to authorize the contract instead. Hui reminisced working on *The Brave Archer* set,

"It took us three days to shoot the Duel for Marriage fight scene. Each day the temps continued to be over 30 degrees Celsius. We all had worn fur and thick clothes which gave me heatstroke. Chang Cheh was angry about this, and breaking his chair, said to his staff: 'As these actors work so hard, why cannot we give them a break and a comfortable work environment?' From then on, I had my own chair and an assistant."[4]

Noted *Wong Fei-hung* series director, Wu Pang, had initially brought this Louis Cha authored tale to the big screen with two films in the late 50s. However, it was the Ni Kuang scripted, Shaw produced film of 1977 that introduced the West to the popular serial. Cha was born the same year as Chang Cheh and the cinematic duo went hand-in-hand like popcorn and movies. Both men held each other in high regard and would enjoy a long history together.

Cha's birth name was Cha Leung-yung, and was the second child of seven from a family of scholars. When he was eight years old, he discovered the wuxia novel *Huangjiang Nyusia* by Gu Mingdao, and became an aficionado of knight-errant novels.[5] Cha enrolled in the Provincial Jiasing High School and published a book, at age 14, titled *Gei Toukao Chujhong Jhe*. During the Second Sino-Japanese War, he penned critical articles which caused his expulsion from the school. Near the war's end, Cha enrolled at the Central School of Political Affairs, aka National Chengchi University, in Chongqing but was once again expelled after a violent argument with the KMT administrator.

In 1947, Louis Cha joined Shanghai's newspaper Ta Kung Pao as a journalist and was later stationed in Hong Kong as a copy editor. A few years after, he published *The Romance of the Book and Sword* and began work as a scriptwriter for Great Wall Movie Enterprises and Phoenix Film Company. Cha adopted the pseudonym, Jin Yong, because when the Chinese characters Jin and Yong combined, it formed the last character of his real name.

In 1959, Cha co-founded the Hong Kong newspaper Ming Pao, where he served as its Editor-in-Chief and wrote both serialized novels and editorials. His commentaries became well regarded and Ming Pao gained a reputation as part of Hong Kong's highly rated dailies. Cha went on to pen another 14 novels before he decided to hang up his quill. All his novels have since been adapted into film, television, and radio throughout Hong Kong, Taiwan, and the Chinese mainland. Cha's books have sold over 300 million copies worldwide ranking him among the most distinguished wuxia writers with his deftly concocted tales of history and fiction that encompass ingenuity, plausibility, and richness.

The Legend of the Condor Heroes, the basis for the first three *Brave Archer* films, was embraced as the most acclaimed by Cha. It was initially published in 1957 in the Hong Kong Commercial Daily and is the first third of *The Condor Trilogy*.[6] The narrative takes place in the Song Dynasty at the onset of the Jurchen's invasion of Northern China and the first segment revolves around the friendship of two sworn brothers: Guo Xiaotian and Yang Tiexin. The novel's focal point was the trials and tribulations of their future sons following Xiaotian's death and Tiexin's disappearance. Guo Jing (Xiaotian's son) was raised in Mongolia under the care of Genghis Khan while Yang Kang (Tiexin's son) in the Jin Empire as the foster son of Prince Wanyan Honglie.

Alex played the role of Guo Jing. The orphan boy was mentored in the fighting arts by the Seven Freaks of Jiangnan but he proved to be a slow learner and only managed to master part of their skills. There was little mention of Guo's upbringing in Mongolia, other than a brief scene where Fu Sheng is in a Mongolian yurt, and the omission left out an important part of the storyline. Turned out, in the novel, Guo was one of the finest archers in Mongolia and trained in his early years by the legendary archer Jebe; a prominent general to Genghis Khan. The book describes Guo exploits:

"*Seeing two eagles flying one above the other, he turned, aimed for the neck and released his projectile. It was precisely, as the popular expression described it: 'The bow bent as the full moon, the arrow flashing like a meteor.' The first eagle didn't have the time to escape before the arrow pierced its neck, continuing its way and planting itself in the flank of the second bird! Only one arrow for two eagles, which fell like stones!*"[7]

This incident earned Guo Jing fame and the admiration of the Khan, although the only reference, in the movie, is the opening shot where Alex draws a bow. The film's core focused instead on Guo's adventures with his new love, Huang Rong, who benefited from keen observation skills and intelligence. Many of Louis Cha's characters possessed a flaw that made themselves vulnerable which, by crafting the hero more human, allowed their plight to be more agreeable for the audience. While Guo was faithful and upright, he was hindered by his lack of intellect and followed his love like a faithful puppy dog. Wang Lung-Wei (Western Poison Ouyang Fung) was cast as the couple's nemesis and recounted the duo's relationship off-screen.

"*Tien Niu liked to play jokes on people in the studio but was scared of Fu Sheng. He was much naughtier than her and he always needled her. When Alex was around she became a nice, quiet little girl.*"[8]

While the film barely scratched the surface of the source material, the novel expanded on how the Jin Empire was overthrown by the Mongols who then set their attention on the Song. Guo Jing was unwilling to assist Mongolia in conquering his native land and returned home to counter the invasion in the sequel volume. His sworn brother, Yang Kang, meets his demise and leaves behind his yet to be born son, Yang Guo, who becomes the focal point in the fourth film. Undeniably, *The Legend of the Condor Heroes* is an intricate folk tale with an abundance of characters that proved difficult when translating into a motion picture. Characters seemed to come and go without care, and those that do appear in the subsequent films, are sometimes portrayed by other actors. Take for example the main character of Yang Kang.

In the first two films, he was played by Li Yi-Min but then replaced by Yu Tai-Ping and further substituted for the fourth film with actor Lung Tien-Hsiang. Another example was Alex's love interest who was initially played by Taiwanese teen idol, Tien Niu, but then relieved by Niu Niu (no relation). Further confusion stemmed when an actor appeared in multiple films but not as the same character. Hong Kong muscleman Lo Mang first appeared as a representative of the Seven Freaks but was later re-cast as Qiu Qianren, leader of the Iron Palm Sect. Lu Feng appeared in all four movies yet ironically played four different characters! The biggest crux of confusion was reserved for the fourth part in which Kwok Chun-Fung took over the role of Gou Ying and Fu Sheng now portrayed Yang Guo.

The Brave Archer (part 1) wrapped in the final week of May and debuted in theaters that summer on the 30th of July. This film would become known in the States as *Kung Fu Warlords* which boasted Fu Sheng as "The Best Kung Fu Actor of the Year!" The film's box office receipts in Hong Kong were roughly the same as *Chinatown Kid* and a sequel was in the pipeline, but before work commenced on that, director Chang was prepping a brand-new action film.

The Life or Death Gamble went into production on August 18 and was later shortened to *Life Gamble (1979)*. Known to some as *Life Combat*, the final product drifted into obscurity after its release and only survived in the hands of hardcore collectors. The BootlegScope version languished in 6th generation VHS hell for many years with the first several minutes cut off. Desperate viewers had to squint and struggle to decipher the murky, washed out images and subtitles of this rare flick.[9] All that thankfully changed in the summer of 2007 when Celestial Pictures released an immaculate, widescreen print.

The screenplay for *Life Gamble* was based on a book by Taiwanese author Zhu Yu. Zhu was born in 1933 and wrote four screenplays and 15 novels in his career and was the ghostwriter on two others. He specialized in popular fiction and noted for his early Republic novels. Zhu used multiple pen names but the one he's best-known for literally meant feather, as this pseudonym gave his writings an impression of lightness such as duckweed floating on water. Though not as famous as his contemporaries, Zhu made many friends in the movie industry and even dabbled in filmmaking himself.

Regrettably, *Life Gamble* (the film) was hardly light as a feather as critics claimed it was overburdened with a convoluted smorgasbord of plot twists and ever shifting alliances. While it didn't offer a ton of action or thrilling choreography, the picture was saturated in vivid colors from the opening sequence to the costumes, sets, and lighting. When production ended, the movie was so far from the original concept the studio decided to reshoot most of it. Choreographer Robert Tai grumbled,

"At the end of the day, I didn't put my name on it. Though it was my idea and my work, I didn't put my name in the credits."[10]

While traditional kung fu was scarce, there was action aplenty to keep most fans enthralled. A medley of weapons was used as the movie resembled more of a Hollywood Western than wuxiapan. One highlight was the quick-draw dueling knife fight between a famous swordsman (Lo Mang) and the silent, cool killer (Fu Sheng). Lo just came off his largest role to date in *Chinatown Kid* and proved a versatile adversary for Alex.

Lo Mang's original name was Hin-lam Lo but given his stage name after director Chang observed the actor to be a bit reckless. Lo is a Hakka from the New Territories and began practicing Chu Gar Praying Mantis as a teenager. His Sifu was Kuen-wa Chu who in turn was a student of Great Grandmaster Lau Soei. Master Lau is acknowledged by many as the leading promoter of Chow Gar Praying Mantis which is an aggressive style with emphasis on close range fighting. Lo's strong will to win was cultivated as a youngster when he trained with a senior student and wouldn't submit even when the pain became overwhelming.

"I spent years practicing hard, from 13-14 years old till now. It's not something you can describe in one sentence, so I challenge any person to draw a conclusion. I've done this many times before and won every time."[11]

Growing up in the '60s, Lo Mang's father worked in the construction sector and had hopes his son might succeed him. Lo worked briefly at his parent's job site after graduating secondary school but quit as he was frequently rebuked by his father. Like Alex, he came from a large family and his elder brother, Lo Bing Gung, was employed as Chang Cheh's driver. Lo Mang wanted to work with the director when the filmmaker started up Changgong but his brother opposed him from pursuing a movie career. Reluctantly, he secured a position in the security department for Changgong's accounting department at the Waterloo Road office.

"When Chang returned from Taiwan, he needed a bunch of people for Shaolin Temple. People who could practice kung fu in unison. But not everyone could do that. He put an ad out in the paper, and out of 8000 people, only 30 were chosen. I was lucky to be included."[12]

Lo Mang went to the interview without letting his brother know and signed a three-year martial artist contract. He developed a lasting friendship with Alex, working on nine films with the fellow New Territories actor, and years later, the two became blood brothers by spilling their own blood into glasses of wine. On his last day alive, Alex is believed to have visited Lo's home for breakfast before the late actor headed to court in San Po Kong.

Life Gamble finalized principal photography five days after Alex's 23rd birthday but audiences had to wait 16 months before it was released. According to Kwok Chun-Fung, its delay was because Chang Cheh had cast him and Lo Mang to be the stars of the film with Fu Sheng appearing as a co-star to help promote the picture. The director then had second thoughts, feeling Alex's star power might steal the limelight from his new talent. He decided the best way to promote Kwok and Lo would be to first release the movie, *The Five Venoms (1978)*, and then he could promote *Life Gamble* as the return of Alex to Chang's new group.

Whether its loved or loathed, this movie can be viewed as a transitional film in which Li Yi-Min's collaboration with Chang was nearing an end, the team of actors known as the Venoms were on the brink, and Alex would soon be exploring new waters. The film's $1.2 million at the Hong Kong box office was the lowest tally for the remainder of Alex's career but those figures were of little consequence. The actor was rather content on his position in life and the idea of being married seemed to suit him well. He had nothing but praise for Jenny and boasted to anyone who lent an ear.

"...in the past I smoked three packs of cigarettes a day. After I met Jenny, she asked if I could smoke less. OK, twenty cigarettes a day. Smoke even less? Ten cigarettes a day. Less? OK, two! Then she asked if I could stop smoking all together. Sure. Now I don't smoke because I want to."[13]

Alex didn't see much downtime after *Life Gamble* completed. He was back the first week of November at Movietown's Studio No. 6 for the filming of *The Brave Archer Part II (1978)*. The sequel set was massive and included a courtyard full of grass covered walkways, a small inn strewn with cobwebs, and mammoth 10,000-watt lamps suspended from the tall structures. While many returned for the continuing escapades of Guo Jing and Huang Rong, the biggest absence was Alex's co-star. Shaw's in-house publications wrote it off as a broken ankle for the actress but Robert Tai recalled the events as slightly less innocent.

"The first episode of Brave Archer was about to be finished and Tien Niu was involved in a relationship with actor Tony Liu Jun-Guk that upset both Miss Fong and Tien's mother. The latter was so angry that she would not let daughter participate in any more films and took her to the United States right after the production was complete."[14]

Chang Cheh and Production Manager Mona Fong recast the part of Huang Rong with actress Esther Niu Niu aka Nau Nau. Niu was a former child actor who made her debut as the younger counterpart to Li Ching in the superb coming of age drama *Susanna (1967)*. Chang didn't seem fazed by the personnel change for *The Brave Archer* sequel and commented,

"From the personality point of view, Tien Niu is more outgoing while Nau Nau is more reserved. Nau looks fairer and prettier in appearance and each has their own interpretation of the role. Nau's a good fit."[15]

Around three in the afternoon on the first day of filming, an enthusiastic Chang walked into the studio sporting a leather hunting outfit. When the production staff saw him, they rushed to his side and produced a director's chair, table, and a portable air conditioner. The boss took a quick glance at the lighting and locations of cameras and nodded before taking his seat. He was a stickler to routine and his briefcase was a microcosm. The script had to be in the left pocket, the fountain pen on the right upper pocket, cigars in the left upper, the lighter in the right upper, etc. Things needed to be in their proper place as Chang demanded order. If he saw any imbalance, he quickly became agitated and had to reorganize again. His preference when filming at Movietown was the middle shift as he felt his best work was after lunch, and after shooting, worked deep into the night planning out the next day's scenes. Chang reflected while observing the rehearsal,

"One night, when Louis Cha and I were chatting in the Peninsula

Hotel coffee shop, we happened to discuss how some of his novels had been made into Cantonese films and a few lengthy TV drama series."[16]

Chang Cheh thought it was time to revisit these works for the silver screen and was given carte blanche from Louis Cha in adapting the novels. Fans of Cha's books gave the first Chang-directed movie a high rating when the film was released. The director's main disappointment was he couldn't tell the complete story in one performance due to the limits posed by the theater's showing times. On the ideal length of a film before editing he noted,

"It's hard to make it just right. Like the first episode of The Brave Archer, I approved 18,000 ft. of shots. But a few thousands were snipped as we need to fit it into the show times of the cinemas. This makes some scenes look hasty or lacking."[17]

The uniqueness of Cha's wuxia novels lay in their tightly knit plots with interlocking episodes. In years prior, many believed his novels weren't suitable for film adaptation. The story of *The Legend of the Condor Heroes* was so elaborate that it didn't appear to be compatible with Chang's bold and decisive style. Sek Kei felt differently and wrote in the Ming Pao that the director grasped the heart of the story and produced a motion picture with a captivating charm.

"It is like an ink splatter painting where it takes someone with brilliant skills and stupendous audacity to create something ingenious out of plainness."[18]

Sek Kei's observations were fitting considering that the filmmaker employed a new way of adapting the novel to the screen. Chang opposed portraying the central characters as hero and beauty and opted to depict the pair as bickering lovers who endured many hardships. That modification made the adventures of this wandering couple, in the rivers and lakes, more believable to the audience.[19]

The Brave Archer Part II had a short lensing schedule, completing in less than 90 days, and its finale set the stage for the third installment.[20] This sequel became a milestone in Alex's career. It was his 25th picture with director Chang, and since joining the cast for *Young People* and *Four Riders*, the cinema "father & son" team seemed inseparable. Alex was a good fit for the ingenuous characters in Chang's movies because he always put on a smile and exhibited a naivety that others lacked. When Alex was with Chang, his juvenile behavior came out and the two winked at one another, talked in codes/signals, and chuckled in the studio.

"I can understand perfectly what my dad wants. If he wants expression #27, I don't do #28. After assigning numbers to them, I stored them in my own brain-computer. This computer never breaks down," Alex said with a grin.[21]

"Oh, it will. Sometimes the wires get stuck together. I wanted #27 and he did #29. So, his brain computer must go under maintenance every few days," Chang chortled in response.[22]

Undeniably, Fu Sheng was Chang's all-time favorite and gave him great latitude. The star was not a fan of make-up so Chang allowed him to go without. Furthermore, Alex preferred not to wear headgear and once again the director permitted it. When Alex needed extra cash, Chang was always ready to dig deep into his pockets. Despite all of this, Fu Sheng entered uncharted territory in the fall of '77, when agreeing to a new project not guided by his mentor.

"Can't help it," Alex sighed. *"I want more work."*[23]

---

[1] See Web and More, "From Dancer to Best Actress."
[2] Originally named Fung Wang-yuen, Wu Ma co-directed over a dozen films with Chang in the 1960s/70s including six that featured Alex. A Shaw icon for 20+ years, he battled cancer in his late life but refused chemotherapy as he believed it would confine him to his deathbed. He died in 2014.
[3] See Web and More, "From Dancer to Best Actress."
[4] "Hui Ying-hung reminisces about Alex." Personal interview. 25 Feb 2014.
[5] Literally translated as "The Vast River and the Heroine."
[6] The title in Chinese translates as "The Legend of the Hawk Shooting Heroes."
[7] See Web and More, Hong Kong Commercial Daily, 1957.
[8] "Johnny Wang talks with Teako." Personal interview. 14 Jan. 2003.
[9] Since Cinemascope was introduced in 1953, it has spawned over five dozen spin-off "scope" formats throughout the globe. "Bootlegscope" is not one of them, but a humorous nod by the author to the black market that kept these films from drifting into oblivion between the 1980s and the Celestial remastered DVDs of the early 2000s. For further information on Cinemascope, refer to Web and More, "A Complete History of CinemaScope with Film Historian David Bordwell."
[10] Life Gamble (1979). Dir. Chang Cheh. 2004. DVD. Region 1 Navarre Corp.
[11] Hong Kong Movie News Oct 1978: 42-43.
[12] Life Gamble (1979). Dir. Chang Cheh. 2004. DVD. Region 1 Navarre Corp.
[13] See Web and More, "Fu Sing & Yan Nei," page 20.

[14] "Q & A with Robert Tai." Personal interview. 12 Nov. 2013.
[15] Southern Screen Jan 1978: 32-33.
[16] Ibid.
[17] Ibid.
[18] Southern Screen Jul 1979: 56-57.
[19] See Chapter 18 for more on the term "rivers and lakes."
[20] Cinema fans had to wait over three years as multiple delays occurred between the second and third film.
[21] Hong Kong Movie News Feb 1978: 33-34.
[22] Ibid.
[23] Ibid.

16

Sun Chung

Director Sun Chung always thought highly of Fu Sheng. The director wanted to cast Alex in one of his earlier pictures but it didn't pan out as Run Run Shaw had no intention of removing him from Chang Cheh's camp.[1] In the autumn of 1977, winds of change were coming to Movietown. Chang shifted the spotlight onto his troupe of Taiwanese performers while Sun was about to start on new martial arts adventures. Prudently, Sun Chung secured Ti Lung in his upcoming production and approached Fu Sheng to star opposite him. Alex agreed and not solely because he was driven to make more money, but as with Chiang Da-Wei, Alex felt a sense of debt to the director.

Several years prior, when Alex was attending the Shaw HK TVB Training Centre, his 1972 screen test wasn't presided over by Chang Cheh but Sun Chung. It was Alex's first audition in front of a camera, and thanks to a bad case of nerves, it didn't turn out well for him. The aspiring talent realized he would not make the short list and begged the director for another chance. Sun reluctantly agreed,

"Fine! You can have one more go."[2]

Alex retook the test and fared much better in this go-around. If Sun had not given Alex that second shot, it's a good bet his acting career would have flatlined. Shaw Brothers Studio, as well as movie fans worldwide, may have never known of the many gifts this up-and-coming performer was capable of bringing to the cinematic table. However, such was not the case as Alex turned on the charm for the second screen test, and now it was time for Alex to pay back the Taiwanese filmmaker.

Sun Chung was born in the Shandong Province in 1941 but grew up in Taiwan and graduated from the directing and screenwriting department of the National Academy of Arts; now known as National Taiwan University of Arts. He began his professional career, after his obligatory stint in the Taiwanese military, at the Central Motion Picture Company as a continuity person and director's assistant. Sun learned from the best, working under director Li Hsing and Pai Ching-jui, two of the four undisputed rulers of Taiwanese cinema in the 1960s & '70s.[3] Sun directed the musical, *Wild Girl (1968)*, but it was the success of his second film, *Tops in Every Trade (1970),* starring Chen Chen that brought him to the attention of the Shaw Brothers.[4] Sun's debut with the studio was the wuxia production, *The Devil's Mirror (1972),* where he injected his signature vertiginous cinematography that hurled the audience into the tale as an unseen participant.

"At that time, I was a new director. I couldn't get good actors. I couldn't even get a studio set, so the production time was extended and it took me a year to shoot. Others thought it was a big production but actually my time was wasted on waiting. I was still tolerant though."[5]

While Chang Cheh was renowned for his blood-spattered cinema, Sun Chung became celebrated for his camerawork. In addition to sweeping use of tracking shots and slo-mo, Sun experimented in removing frames of film to create a choppy or jagged effect. He was also one of the first to exploit a new weapon in the Shaw's arsenal when the studio purchased a Steadicam. This revolutionary stabilizer allowed the filmmaker to enhance mobility and ingenuity of his hand-held camera work without the dreaded camera wobble. Initially, he signed a five-year deal with Shaw and tackled a multitude of genres: true crime, romantic comedies, horror, and sexploitation. He also moonlighted with other companies, such as Summit Film Productions, working under the pseudonym of Tung Ming Shan.

The director returned to the wuxia genre and shot several Shaw classics which underscored the portrayal of conflicts among characters similar to the cowboy genre. He worked almost exclusively with Tong Gai, 11 of 13 films between 1978-82, in which the choreographer brought his own unique touch by introducing inventive weaponry such as those utilized by Fu Sheng's character 'Double Sword Sleeve' Cheuk Yi Fan in *The Avenging Eagle (1978)*.[6] Sun wanted to introduce his vision of Western heroes and their valiant spirit into a Chinese wuxia production with this new production and who better to do that than Ti Lung and Fu Sheng. The filmmaker commented,

"In the beginning, Ti Lung wasn't given any eye-catching roles to prove himself. Now that he has these opportunities, he takes advantage of them and tries to show his best. He treasures his future and takes his job seriously, not wanting to disappoint the audience and the directors."[7]

The filmmaker voiced similar praise for Fu Sheng who tackled a different type of role for this production. Alex's boyish buffoonery was now replaced with atypical still-waters-run-deep persona as he meticulously plotted his revenge.

"Fu Sheng is different from Ti Lung. He is smart and picks things up quick but doesn't seem to care when he gets an NG [no good]. He's always grinning when I counsel him, just like a kid. Sheng grew up in a carefree environment and hasn't really suffered, so he's always happy."[8]

Production on *Cold Blooded Eagle*, as it was initially named, continued through the winter and spring. While Ti Lung and Fu Sheng were battling the diabolic Ku Feng and his brotherhood of assassins, Jenny was also hard at work with overseas meetings and recording in Taiwan. When she was back in Taipei for an extended period, she normally stayed with her elder sister, Judy, who handled her business affairs. Her sister-manager commented,

"We're really ordinary people. We've always kept away from the singer-circuit, the socials, and the partiers. To Jenny, singing is just a job. When she's finished, she goes home and leads a perfectly normal life."[9]

The songstress had made a great deal of money with her career but remained loyal to her family. Their father was the vice-chairman of the Taiwan Radio Station while mom was retired from the police department. Judy's background was in accounting and her money management skills seemed to wear off on her younger sibling.

While Jenny adored Alex's simple outlook on life, there were times when it became an issue. Jenny oversaw their household finances, and when she was out of town, the house chores and bills went unattended. This routinely exasperated her but all Alex needed to do was put on his innocent boy charms and any ill feelings simply melted away. To his credit, Alex also showed he could be extremely thoughtful, and at those times, she was left speechless. When Jenny flew back to Hong Kong for their first wedding anniversary, Alex's work schedule conflicted with her arrival and was unable to pick her up at Kai Tak. A disheartened Jenny proceeded to go home alone, expecting the worst, but instead found flowers, a pearl, and a letter in which Alex wrote,

"Every year on this day, I will present you with a pearl. When we are old and gray, you will wear all of them as a symbol of our love."[10]

Filming on *The Avenging Eagle* concluded on the second of June and was released that September to box office receipts eclipsing $2 million in Hong Kong. The picture also fared well throughout Asia. In Singapore, it added nearly another half million to its total as fans were thrilled with the explosive tale of revenge and redemption. Critics agreed. At the 25th Asian Film Festival, held at the Singapore Conference Hall from July 3-6, 1979, a dozen countries and 450 delegates were represented showcasing 40 feature length films. For their efforts, Ti Lung won the Most Outstanding Actor Award and Alex received the Highest Achievement Award in an action film. Later that year, the movie captured The Best Editing for Drama trophy at the 16th Annual Golden Horse Awards.[11]

Artist and long-time martial arts film fan, Robert "Kung Fu Bob" O'Brien, studied the film's choreography frame-by-frame for one of the fight sequences. In one shot, Fu Sheng throws a long series of fast strikes with his sleeve blades at Ku Feng's face and O'Brien noted,

"...he misses his eye by an inch, and another goes through Feng's beard, just below his chin and super close to his throat! I haven't seen the blades flopping like rubber, so they were either plastic or unsharpened metal. Either way, capable of doing significant harm to someone's face. Damn – Alex was good! These guys really took a lot of risks."[12]

During the spring of 1978, while still working on *The Avenging Eagle*, Alex started on two new productions. The first was on the 7th of April when he rejoined Chang Cheh for *Ten Tigers of Kwantung (1979)*, and on the 25th, he embarked on his second Sun Chung/Ti Lung collaboration, *The Deadly Breaking Sword (1979)*. Tong Gai was again on the set as the action director, a collaboration of over 40 films with Ti Lung starting with *Return of the One-Armed Swordsman*. The actor fondly recalled those early days when Tong was choreographing and how the young actors watched in complete silence from the sidelines. He expressed how the director had his chair, next to which were the assistants, and then the martial arts choreographers.

"The hierarchy was clear and the seniority was respected."[13]

Regrettably, Fu Sheng didn't share in such cherished reminiscing as he and Jenny continued to let business dominate their lives, and despite being married for over a year, had gone without a proper honeymoon. The couple decided that before Alex starts on any new projects, they would take a well-deserved vacation, and caught a flight to the Philippines where they checked into the Mandarin Oriental Manila Hotel. The twosome's hectic schedule seemed to melt away in the record setting heat as they spent several days shopping and sun bathing. Alex was asked by a local writer for his thoughts on the superstar status he enjoyed and Alex's response was rather frank.

"Star? I don't know what a celebrity is or what it takes to be one. I don't care about these things. I only know that I do what I like to do."[14]

Alex pointed out how celebrities drove new sports cars or luxury vehicles but he preferred his old yellow jeep which withstood fender-benders and allowed him to traverse rivers and mountains. On occasion, cinema fans spotted Alex's jeep pulled over by a dai pai dong (open-air food stall) in Tsim Sha Tsui. He'd wear a sleeveless shirt and jeans, while Jenny sported a pair of old shorts. She added to her husband's reply.

"In other people's eyes, movie stars are rich. They wear beautiful clothes, ride fancy cars, meet tycoons. However, these people never see how hard it used to be. Alex's family might be wealthy but I've never seen him take a dollar from them. I felt really good about that."[15]

While on holiday, Alex saw a decorative tobacco pipe in a store display. It was an exquisite piece with superlative craftsmanship and he played with it for some time. While he had no qualms on spending thousands of dollars on a gift for Jenny, even a few hundred on him was too expensive. Alex considered the cost of the pipe and exited the shop empty-handed. When he woke up the next morning, there was a small package on the couple's breakfast table. Alex opened it and a smile of content crossed his face. It was the very pipe from the store which Jenny purchased in secret.

Unfortunately for the honeymooners, all good things must come to an end and it was back to Hong Kong to begin work anew. Despite returning with healthy suntans and feeling optimistic about the future, Alex and Jenny were soon to undergo setbacks that would test their love, careers, and marriage.

---

[1] On 7 Mar. 1978, during the production of Avenging Eagle (1978), Run Run became "Sir Shaw" when he was officially knighted at Buckingham Palace by Queen Elizabeth II.
[2] Hong Kong Movie News Feb 1978: 33-34.
[3] The other two filmmakers were Li Han-hsiang and King Hu.
[4] In a 2004 video interview with Lydia Shum, Sun Chung stated his first film was actually Tops in Every Trade (1970). Some sources list this film as 1969. Unfortunately, the director does not clarify if this film was shot before Wild Girl (1968) and had a delayed release. Refer to #5 below.
[5] See Film Reviews and Interviews, "Suen Zhong and Kam Fei; Episode 9."
[6] Tong Gai, who created Fu Sheng's weapon in this film, also devised other unique weapons for Shaw Brothers Studio including ones used in The Killer Clans (1976) and The Deadly Breaking Sword (1979). See Books, The Making of Martial Arts Films: As Told by Filmmakers and Stars: page 72.
[7] Southern Screen Dec 1978: 42-43.
[8] Ibid.
[9] Dana Lam. "Jenny's big sister." The Straits Times [Singapore] 2 April 1981: 5.
[10] Cinemart Apr 1979: 36-37.
[11] Editor Chiang Hsing-Lung was an iron man of the industry with over 600 editing credits under his belt. He won Golden Horse Awards for Best Editing four times (1962, 1963, 1966, 1979) with a fifth nomination in 1988.
[12] Facebook post
[13] See Books, Ng. Oral History Series (7): Ti Lung, page 130.
[14] Southern Screen Aug 1977: 34-35.
[15] Cinemart Apr 1979: 36-37.

17

Black September 1978

Chang Cheh had few vices. One habit he could not kick was wuxia novels. Chang admitted they weren't well written, but once he started one, he was unable to put it down until finished. His wife Amy vowed to stop buying them, yet whenever she spotted one at the newsstand, she wound up bringing it home. Chang wasn't a fan of TV or other entertainment and Amy didn't want to deprive him of this little luxury. He was passionate for the martial arts, immersing himself into wuxia philosophy, interviewing masters through the years, and even taking lessons earlier in his life. Due to his lasting curiosity with the arts, Chang gathered a star-studded line-up for his latest production highlighting real-life practitioners of the past.

The Renowned Ten Tigers of Five Rams City (working title) recounted the inspiring account of ten martial experts who rescued an anti-Qing revolutionary leader and assisted his escape from Canton. The film was a parade of martial arts systems as each Tiger practiced his own distinctive method. Styles included Wing Chun, Taam Ga Saam Jin Kyun, Praying Mantis, Xia Quan, Hak Fu Mun, Hung Gar Kuen, and others. Chang paid close attention to each actor's specialty, enabling them to bring their best performance into full play. The filmmaker appointed three action choreographers (Leung Ting, Robert Tai, and Lu Feng) to assist in authenticating the action and employed four additional consultants. These renowned kung fu masters were Hung Gar Kuen expert Chiu Wai, Lo Wai Keung of Xia Quan (Lama Style), Wong Cheung of Hak Fu Mun (Black Tiger), and Tam Hon of Taam Ga (Three Extensions).

The historical Tigers were all lay disciples of Shaolin. They did not study at the monastery itself but were instructed by monks and/or other lay disciples before it was razed. The ten fighters lived during the latter part of the Qing Dynasty, though didn't appear at the same time as a group, and are believed to be a few generations after the Five Elders. Chang cast the role for each of the Tigers with Movietown's top martial talent.

Fu Sheng starred as Tam Min. He's a candid and impetuous stylist whose forte was the Three Extensions Fist. Tam Min was also known for his expertise in the Eight Trigram Staff technique. Ti Lung played Li Chen-Chow (Lai Yan-chiu or Li Renchao). He was a composed practitioner of the Hakka Kuen (Southern Praying Mantis). Li Chen-Chow is renowned for his Shaolin Seven Star Fist routine and ran a pawnbroker's shop called Shun Hang.

Kwok Chun-Fung portrayed Beggar So Chen. He was a comical, carefree drunkard who squandered away his fortune. So Chen was a master of Hoong Ka and learned from the Venerable Chan Fook of the southern Shaolin Monastery. Sun Chien was featured as Wong Yin Lin (Wong Yan-Lam). He was a student of Tibetan Monk Sing Lung who was a master of the Lion's Roar style of martial arts. This style eventually evolved into Lama Pai, Hop Gar Kuen, and Baak hok kuen.

Lu Feng played Su Hei Hu (Sou Hak Fu) who resided near the rice wharf and was respected by the boat people. An invincible master, his disciples utilized the Black Tiger Array techniques. Lo Mang was Chan Cheung-Tai, best known by his nickname Tit Chee Chan which meant Iron Finger Chan. Brave but wild, he was an expert at the Shaolin method of Siu Lum Kam Kung Chee and was an Eagle Claw practitioner.

Chiang Sheng portrayed the part of Tzou Tai (Tzou Yu Sheng). Better known as Chau (Chow), his nickname was Iron Head Chau and renowned for his skillful Three-Section Staff, and Cotton Palm techniques. Wai Pak was Wong Kei-Ying. He first studied under his father, Wong Tai, before becoming a student of Luk Ah-Choi. He ran the Po Chi Lam clinic but his greatest claim to fame was being the father to Wong Fei-hung.

Dick Wei was Wong Ching-Hoh. He was also a student of Luk Ah-Choi and became a master of the Nine Dragon Fist style which he created from various styles. It is rumored that he was related to Wong Kei-Ying. Yeung Hung played Leung Kwan. His nickname was Thit Kew Sam which literally meant Iron Bridge Three and his internal strength came from training in the Iron Wire Set. Kwan's most influential and best-known teacher was the Shaolin monk Gwok Yan.

Something worth pointing out is that the film title could be "Fu Sheng and the Nine Tigers of Kwantung" because the role Alex played raises a question. In the movie, he's called Tam Min. According to Sifu Paul Burkinshaw, who's writing a book on the Ten Tigers, Hung Hsi Kuan had a disciple named Tam Min who in turn had a student named Tam Chai-Kwan. Also named Three-Leg Tham, he was famous for his three kicking techniques: sweeping-floor, tiger-tail, and organ-seeking. He was also one of the Ten Tigers. So, Alex was not playing one of the Tigers himself but the master of Tiger Tam Chai-Kwan.

Another contradictory tale is that Tam Min was actually the grandson of Tam Chai-Kwan who refused to teach Tam Min kung fu because of his quick temper.[1] Chang Cheh did mention this occurrence in the movie; however, it still doesn't explain if Chang was intentional in his choice or perhaps the group's mythology has progressively distorted over time. Hopefully with Burkinshaw's efforts, the real history of the Tigers will be preserved for future generations.

Ten Tigers of Kwantung, as it was ultimately released as, commenced shooting on April 7, 1978. Over the years, Chang Cheh developed a reputation of being a man of extremes on set. He'd doze off while his assistants shot fight sequences, while other times, he might be a bit more boisterous.[2] An example of the latter was on the *Ten Tigers* set that spring. While directing a scene with two of the actors, Chang fell into a five-foot-deep pond and Lo Mang jumped in to his rescue. Soaking wet and all eyes paused on him, Chang laughed off the awkward moment.

"I was so busy reprimanding Lu Feng that I didn't see where I was heading. Guess I needed to cool off," he chortled.[3]

Chang expressed his appreciation for Lo's assistance; however, despite his couch-potato physique, the director was in fact a skilled swimmer and possessed exceptional breath control. During the Second Sino-Japanese War, Chang was residing in Sichuan where Japanese bombers targeted the province. The public rushed in panic to the air-raid shelters when the enemy's planes appeared but he had a different plan. According to a reporter, Chang simply dove underwater and surfaced once the bombers left.

During the war years, Chang developed an interest in authority and aspired to be a commander in the army; giving orders and planning strategies. This urge though waned when the conflict ended. Chang opted to channel this impulse now into becoming a filmmaker and directing a crew in the studio. But like Alex, it was not money that drove him. It was par excellence.

Ten Tigers of Kwantung continued production over the summer of 1978 when a freak mishap occurred, on another film set, and shooting came to an abrupt stop. The project was in hiatus for over 15 months before resuming on January 5, 1980. Chang would shoot till the end of February, using a new crop of actors, as many of the original cast moved on to other assignments. He integrated the 1978 footage as flashback sequences while the newer cast recanted the story of these legendary Tigers. Alex's role was relegated to a few scenes, due to the reworking of the tale, though he did have an explosive battle with Lu 'Black Tiger' Feng.

"I have loved acting since I was little. I was the leading actor of the drama club at school. I feel that only when I am acting my life becomes meaningful. Therefore, I work in the film industry and do not treat it as an occupation but as a life pursuit," Lu commented.[4]

The Taiwanese native was born Chu Qi-xue and introduced to the arts at an early age. When Lu Feng was a child he was physically the weakest amongst his siblings, as he weighed around 60 odd pounds, and was sick from time to time. His parents decided to send him to the Lu Kwan Peking Opera School to learn Revolutionary (Jiang Qing) Opera.[5] He studied for over a decade and the training improved his health, in addition to, helping him put on the proper weight. As an actor with the Shaw Brothers Studio, Lu continued his regimen to stay fit and jogged every morning along Clear Water Bay Road. He ran rain or shine and claimed his daily jogs were what kept him with a clean bill of health.

"If I don't jog, I feel like I have missed something. I've never been sick since I started this routine. When I have a few symptoms I only need to sweat it out to recover, so I see jogging as a cure for sickness."[6]

Ten Tigers of Kwantung was the 12th (of 14 films) that Lu Feng and Fu Sheng worked on together. During his downtime, Lu brought his wife of four years and their son to the *Ten Tigers* set. Like Alex and Jenny, they were in a good place in their lives and avoided the limelight. Lu enjoyed the occasional mahjong stake and betting on the horses, though his biggest hobby was the cinema. The couple took in a movie downtown no matter how tired he was after work.

"The reason I like movies isn't for some violent or bloody scene to stimulate my senses. The main reason is that I want to experience and study others' acting skills, which can be helpful to my job."[7]

As noted earlier, Alex was splitting his acting duties between *Ten Tigers* and his second collaboration with Sun Chung which was shooting under the working title of *The Romantic Dagger and The Little Dagger*. Sun's adventure-romance yarn revolved around an exalted courtesan (Shih Szu) who exploited a narcissistic swordsman (Ti Lung) and an unlucky gambler (Fu Sheng) to bring an immoral doctor (Ku Feng) to justice. Ni Kuang's original script allowed the director from getting bogged down with a laundry list of characters and complicated scenarios. Instead, it flowed with a flawless balance of action, suspense, and satire in which Alex delivered his finest comedic performance. As one reviewer stated, it put him right up there with the great physical comedians such as Jerry Lewis, Peter Sellers, and of course, Jackie Chan.

"What he lacks in Jackie's advanced Beijing opera skills, he makes up for in other ways such as twirling his dagger about with impressive skills of his own, sliding under hanging beads, or just by timing a raised eyebrow perfectly while fighting three wannabe thugs."[8]

Production was running smoothly through the spring and summer months until the first Sunday in September. Alex had rested for the last week of August due to a stomach ailment and lost several pounds. He stopped by the studio but his replacement took takes for him, as Alex still looked noticeably pale to his co-workers. On the 3rd of September, Fu Sheng felt he was ready to return and resume filming when the unthinkable happened. He was prepping for a scene when his footing gave way and he lost balance. Alex tumbled backwards and the deafening sound of his skull smashing into a porcelain wine jug caused all personnel to freeze. The prop vase shattered into pieces as Fu Sheng sprawled out onto the stage floor. Several people hurried to the unconscious actor's side while a company aide called emergency services. Alex was rushed off to St. Francis Hospital of Kowloon and his family was informed of the mishap.

At St. Francis, a neurologist examined Fu Sheng's head and requested his transfer to Hong Kong Sanatorium & Hospital in Happy Valley. The diagnosis was that Alex may have suffered a concussion and required further testing. Jenny rode in the ambulance with her husband to prevent his head from jarring and doing any further damage. Alex awoke briefly during the ride, quite confused as to his surroundings, and grumbled that his head was hurting. After arriving at the second hospital, it was determined he suffered an intracranial hemorrhage and a three-inch blood clot had formed. The staff administered medication in hopes the clot might dissolve on its own otherwise surgery was imminent. They fitted Alex with a neck brace as a precaution since a cervical tendon was partially torn and further tearing may possibly lead to paralysis.

The actor suffered from blurry vision for the first few days, but to the family's relief, his eyesight stabilized on its own. Jenny stayed by Alex's bedside throughout his stay at Hong Kong Sanatorium. Colorless and exhausted, she appeared as if she hadn't slept for days. Alex's mishap was regrettably not the only setback for the couple. A short time ago, Jenny lost a great deal of money in her Taipei fashion business, but even more heartbreaking, she recently suffered a crushing miscarriage.[9]

"Alex is a guy who loves kids. When he knew I was pregnant, he was so delighted. He bought three prams at one time and a lot of parenting books. He studied all of them after work and looked like a research student," Jenny disclosed.[10]

The loss was a devastating blow to both Jenny and Alex for this was the second time the singer had miscarried. After the first child was lost, Alex threw away all the baby items and did not wish to bring up the topic. He didn't want Jenny to dwell on something that was out of their hands. Despite Alex's best intentions, Jenny still could not help herself.

"Whenever I see Alex play with my friends' or relatives' kids, I feel really sad for him and sorry for myself."[11]

Their current financial plan was for Jenny to work a couple more years, then retire and become an ordinary housewife. For now, they were squirreling away as much money as possible and Alex's work injury was a setback they weren't prepared for. Jenny admitted she was extremely occupied with work these days and seldom spent time at the house. Alex was often stuck eating instant noodles though never complained, and when his partner had a break, she'd make the best of it.

"...when I am free at the house, I will get up early, prepare a meal for Alex and make him feel like home. Although we seldom have these opportunities, we do treasure those moments."[12]

On Friday the 8th, the hospital staff conferred on the probability of surgery. A final test revealed such would not be necessary as the clot had fortunately dispersed due to the pharmaceuticals. On the 10th, Alex discharged from Hong Kong Sanatorium and the couple returned home after an exhausting and emotional week. His injuries barred him from returning to the set for three months and Alex's parents felt it best if he left the industry for good. His mother commented,

"The film business is too hard for Alex, especially after an accident like this. How can he continue? Both his father and I agree, he can find work with us as we have many family businesses."[13]

The Deadly Breaking Sword continued forward despite the setback of its leading man and concluded production on December 15. When it released in April of the following year, the Hong Kong totals surpassed $2.7 million (#12 overall for 1979) making it the highest grossing movie of Alex's career to date. However, records were made to be broken and a subsequent film would soon shatter all previous personal bests.

---

[1] See Web and More, Hung Gar History.
[2] Chen Kuan-tai said in an interview that Ni Kuang never wrote specifics for a fight sequence, except for which characters would suffer any consequences. The director and martial arts choreographer conversed on the characters' motivations, how the shot should be framed, the location of the cameras, and the result of the scene. The director would then entrust the set to them to film any fight sequences.
[3] Cinemart Oct 1978: 40-41.
[4] Southern Screen May 1981: 48-49.
[5] Also known as Fu Sheng (Fu Xing Ju Xiao), this school has a prestigious list of alumni that includes: Kuo Choi, Chiang Sheng, Lee Yi Min, Angela Mao, James Tien, Chu Ko and Robert Tai. Despite sharing the same roof, Lu Feng was not opera classmates with Kuo Choi or Chiang Sheng. Lu learned Peking opera while Kuo and Chiang studied Taiwanese opera.
[6] Southern Screen May 1981: 48-49.
[7] Ibid.
[8] See Film Reviews and Interviews, The Deadly Breaking Sword (1979).
[9] The couple opened a store called To Ni on Ren'ai Road in Taipei, Taiwan during New Years 1977.
[10] Cinemart Apr 1979: 36-37.

[11] Ibid.
[12] Ibid.
[13] Cinemart Oct 1978: 36-37.

18

Chor Yuen

Alex respected his parents' concerns for his safety and well-being, but then again, was also eager to resume work. He gallantly returned to the studio on December 2, 1978 to the elation of his fans and colleagues, but also fully aware of his wife's reservations. Sun Chung and Chang Cheh had moved on to other projects in his absence, so Alex set his sights on a new movie and a new director. *The Proud Twins (1979)* was the first of four productions in which Fu Sheng paired with Chor Yuen, a certified member of the last generation of Cantonese filmmakers. Chor's output boasted an impressive span of multi-genre productions that include signature works in romantic comedies, period, contemporary, fantasy, and swordplay. In her book, Meredith Lewis described his films as opulent.

"As a director, he found a way to combine extravagant mise en scène, graceful action, striking characters, and compelling stories to make wuxia pian that progressed the expressive capabilities of the genre."[1]

Chor Yuen was born in Guangzhou in 1934 and the son of renowned actor Cheung Wood-yau.[2] His father was initially a stage actor but got his break in cinema when Runje Shaw extended the family's film business to Hong Kong in the early '30s. Chor's fascination with the moving picture was owed much to his father's profession, and he spent most of his free time at the studio during the summer and winter holidays.

When Chor was in Primary Six (age 11), he was selected the leader of his school's drama group. By taking part in school plays he developed a sensibility of the psychological workings of the actor. Some years later, he enrolled at Sun Yat-sen University to study chemistry as they did not offer cinema studies. In his second year, an illness forced him to leave school and seek medical assistance in Hong Kong. It was there that he began to work under Ng Wui as an assistant director and later for Kong Nee Company.[3] Chor stated,

"Kong Nee allowed me freedom despite my youth and inexperience. I was my own boss and could film whatever subject I wanted."[4]

Chor Yuen made his first solo scripted/directed film at the age of 23, and at the time only one other director, Griffin Yueh Feng, could make such a claim. Chor continued to pad his resume, directing and scripting a personal record of 14 films in 1964-65. He eventually left Kong Nee and worked as an independent before joining Cathay in 1969. After making only four pictures in two years with them, he was invited to join the Shaw Organization where he remained until their closure. Chor was credited with the revival of the Cantonese cinema with 1973's biggest hit, *The House of 72 Tenants,* and in the ensuing years, developed a cult following of martial arts films adapted from Gu Long novels.[5] One such book was the source material for *The Proud Twins.*[6]

On the set, Chor Yuen and Fu Sheng's personalities gelled, and when the two were together, they were like wild and uproarious kids. Alex was back to his normal self on stage, despite his long absence from Movietown, and the studio was alive with banter and amusement. The director enjoyed goading his young star, and one afternoon there was a tomboyish female journalist on *The Proud Twins* set who was quite well-liked by Alex, so the director put to him a friendly wager.

"Sheng, I bet you 100 dollars you won't give her a kiss."[7]

Alex never had much pocket change, only scrounging up 30 or so dollars, so he borrowed 500 and upped the challenge. The director didn't want to lose face and cautiously took the bet but said it must be a passionate mouth-to-mouth smooch, not just a weak peck on the cheek. Alex smirked and whispered to the reporter,

"Why not? We split the money. Two hundred and fifty dollars for a little bit of acting."[8]

The journalist refused at first but accepted so long as the other reporters promised they would not snap any photos. It was agreed and the set then came to a standstill as all converged around Alex for his big scene. He deliberated for a moment, gazing over the scrutinizing eyes, but his confidence waned and he threw up his hands.

"Umm, no, no way . . . I don't think this will work. 500 dollars is not worth the mess this will make when my wife finds out about it!"[9]

Everyone erupted into laughter and heckled the star once he balked. Chor Yuen was quick to comment to the crowd that it wasn't easy money since Jenny would become incensed, bet or no bet, if she found out. His banter hardly fazed Alex because it was widely known he was scared of his wife. When Jenny wasn't around he may have talked it up and put on a good show, but in her presence, he withdrew to the background. In truth, Alex admired Jenny for her tact and deferred to her on many decision-making matters. Chor Yuen continued to goad him.

"How much do you think his wife has left him for pocket money? Only 200 dollars! 200 dollars for two weeks for such a famous star?"[10]

Fu Sheng countered with a chortle.

"I actually feel free when I don't have money with me. I don't have to worry about anything. I just enjoy my meal and my wife will pay. If I have food, a car, a home and work, I don't care much for the rest."[11]

Even though Alex lived day-to-day on pocket change, he and Jenny were certainly not destitute. They had recently purchased a three-story Spanish style villa near Hang Hau, for a cool $3.1 million, which was less than two miles from the studio. Jenny oversaw decorating the home and Alex stopped by on his way to/from work. She put a lot of time and effort into the design of the residence and invested over $10,000 which included marble flooring for the sitting room.

"I prefer basic furnishings. The most important thing is comfort. Only a comfortable house feels homey," she said.[12]

Alex gave his wife carte blanche on the entire decor, but nonetheless had one special request. Brothers Edmund Leung-Sing and David Cheung fancied snooker, and Alex requested a billiards table for their new residence. Jenny flatly rejected the idea. Saddened, but wishing to keep the peace, Alex acquiesced to his wife's decision. A few days passed when his housekeeper revealed that Jenny was secretly shopping around for a snooker table as a surprise for him. Alex could not contain his delight after hearing the news.

"My wife likes to keep me in suspense. Often, she would openly reject my request but then does it without my knowing. She's really a gem."[13]

The first week of 1979 brought with it a new film project in which Fu Sheng rejoined Sun Chung for their third and final collaboration. Initially called *Raging Tiger,* Alex was cast as the mischievous son of an authoritarian father played by veteran actor Ku Feng. A mix of action, comedy, and even a brief romance, the film released nearly four years later as *My Rebellious Son (1982).*[14] While Fu Sheng and Ku Feng collaborated on a total of ten productions, it was this project where they shared the most screen time. Alex's elder co-star was the veteran of nearly 100 Shaw productions, 360 movies overall, and worked under *The Avenging Eagle* director on a dozen films. He acknowledged in an interview it was quite intense working for Sun Chung and reflected on their previous outing.

"Rehearsal after rehearsal, we were worn out before the cameras started rolling. After one take, the three of us [himself, Ti Lung, Fu Sheng] we were so exhausted that we had to sit and catch our breath."[15]

Ku Feng was born in 1930 as Chen Si-wen and his family was originally from Shanghai. His father owned a theatre and the youngster fostered an appreciation for the cinema while attending elementary school where he acted in his first production, *Angel Grape*, in which he played a white rabbit. Ku later studied in Beijing where he developed an interest in singing and subsequently landed his first job as a fairground singer. Due to the Second Sino-Japanese War, Ku fled to Hong Kong but the language barrier made it problematic in finding suitable work.

"Life was difficult in Hong Kong, especially if you came from Northern China. The Cantonese called us Lao Xiong; the northerners."[16]

After doing assorted manual labor jobs, an old classmate who was now a Beijing producer introduced him to the film industry. Ku landed some bit parts as an extra but there were only a handful of Mandarin speaking movies at the time. He eventually joined a theater company and toured various countries throughout Southeast Asia before returning to the colony in 1960. The novice actor began securing more movie roles as Mandarin films were gaining popularity, and in 1968, signed his first contract with Shaw Brothers Studio.

Ku Feng was never a martial artist like other performers at Shaw, but he learned from the best. His instructors included Lau Kar-Leung, Tong Gai, and Simon Yuen Siu-Tin who taught him while on the set. He said there was no room for error in Lau's films as they featured authentic kung fu.[17] Moreover, Sun Chung also had high standards and expected perfection in every move. Regardless of his limited martial skills, Ku Feng was able to adapt and rose to the top of the studio's most sought-after stars. When *My Rebellious Son* went into hiatus in the fall of '79, the actor was averaging 10-12 films per year.

Alex's schedule was not as hectic as his co-star but he continued as the leading actor on several projects. *My Rebellious Son* was one of five different productions he took on in 1979. He returned to work with his cinema dad on the third installment of *The Brave Archer* in March and became involved in a trio of projects with Chor Yuen; two in May and a third in June. Prior to starting on his multiple duties, Alex flew off to Indonesia during the Chinese New Year for one of Jenny's concert. Once her engagement was complete, they remained in the multi-island nation for three weeks of sightseeing. Jenny reflected,

"Alex loved Bali the most. Sea, beach, waves. It was truly breathtaking. When we came back to Hong Kong I asked him how much we spent on our vacation. He thought for a while and then said he had forgotten as being together was all that mattered."[18]

On the 20th of March, Alex returned to Movietown. Nearly 14 months passed since production ended on the second *Brave Archer* film and everyone was anxious to begin working on the third chapter. In this latest installment, Ti Lung was featured as Duan Zhixing, the Southern Emperor, and one of Five Supreme Martial Artists in the Jianghu. The megastar had appeared in the opening credits of the first film but his character never surfaced until now. Duan was the 18th ruler of the Kingdom of Dali but left the secular world to live a spiritual life. Ching Li was cast as Auntie Ying, aka Lady Liu Yinggu, and was the former emperor's scorned courtesan. She had an unbecoming relationship and gave birth to a lovechild whom Duan later refused to save. His jealousy and her rage created the backstory that filled a good portion of this film.[19]

Despite his increasing workload and slight weight gain, Fu Sheng was still the light and frivolous guy on stage. Alex had developed a passion for ice cream, and in the middle of the night, would sneak into his kitchen and wolf down spoonful after spoonful until satisfied. When Alex was involved in few NG's on *The Brave Archer Part III (1981)* set, a cameraman decided to badger him a bit. He quipped,

"Sheng Goh, why don't you move to this side a bit? That'd make it a nicer shot. When we're finished, I'll treat you to a nice ice cream cone."[20]

Ever the professional, Fu Sheng waited until Chang Cheh hollered cut with a thumb up. Alex then ran off set and chased down the cameraman with his sabre. It was all in good fun of course and Alex loved to dish it out as well. He especially enjoyed teasing Ching Li and there were times when she was so provoked that she'd snatch up a broom, and he a dustpan, and they'd have an improvised off-screen battle in the make-up room.

Unfortunately, filming on *The Brave Archer Part III* came to an abrupt halt in September and wasn't finalized until May 14, 1981. It released that November and its box office ranking was #47 for the year. Despite its poor placement, the near $1.9 million gross was the highest of all the *Archer* films. Many Shaw fans consider *Blast of the Iron Palm* (an alternate title) as part of the Venoms filmography for it featured five of the six actors in significant roles. Taking this into consideration, this motion picture would be the highest grossing Venoms movie as it surpassed *The Five Venoms* by $75,000 in HK receipts.

The Brave Archer Part III brought an end to *The Legend of the Condor Heroes* novel, though a fourth film would be shot in 1981 which tackled the second book of *The Condor Trilogy*. Shaw aficionado Linn Haynes commented that these three installments were meant to be seen as one film, and if viewed with that mindset, instead of three separate movies, the trilogy would be more gratifying.

"It's like the first movie is a prologue to the main action that happens in the following films. Unlike Chor Yuen's films that cram a large story into an hour and a half, it's laid out in the form you'd normally see on TV; not as a film. Shame things didn't work out with the series as he wanted."[21]

What Haynes refers to in his closing comment is the statement made by director Chang who believed his reworkings did not do Louis Cha's work justice. The better ones, Chang admitted, included *The Brave Archer Part III* but he only recreated select episodes and felt he failed to capture the source material's grandiosity. The filmmaker remarked in 2001,

"Louis Cha is composed and profound; his novels flow with the mightiness and grandeur of a great river. Myself, however, more rebellious and ferocious; like rapids and falls."[22]

On the 15th of May, Alex's work on *The Proud Twins* ended as the project moved into post-production. Two months later, the film was in theaters and raked in over four million in receipts. This was Alex's biggest box office to date but he had little time to relax. Cameras rolled on *Mark of the Eagle* on May 16 and ultimately terminated on July 14, two years later, in what became Alex's best-known incomplete film. While the studio planned various projects, most never saw a single frame shot. *Mark of the Eagle* aka *Sign of the Eagle* was supposedly not the case.[23]

Promotional articles published in the trades touted this as an early Republic Era (A.D. 1912-1949) crime drama. The project featured Fu Sheng and Ti Lung with co-stars Ku Kuan-Chung, Chan Sen, Chow Kin-Ping, and Wan Ling-Kwong. The leading actress (never cast) was to be Ti Lung's love interest, who becomes so downhearted by the story's end, she runs off to a Buddhist nunnery to escape the severity of her lover's world.

In the film, Ti Lung starred as the character To Ying who was the honorable head of a crime investigation team. Alex played his cheerful sidekick, Ma Kin, who looked to his superior as a worthy role model. The Batman & Robin duo find themselves embroiled in an underworld caper in which a cryptic criminal is assassinating corrupted officials. At each murder scene, he leaves the mark of the goshawk (bird of prey) as his calling card. When the goshawk hitman slays the superintendent, it's up to To Ying and Ma Kin to hunt down the assassin.

While the plot didn't sound too complicated, the film was meant to take its viewers through a Dantesque journey of the underworld as the twosome sought out their nemesis. The term underworld here does not refer to the Greek concept of the afterlife or that of organized crime. Here it signified the ancient Chinese notion that almost all people who made a living outside their hometown (entertainers, salesmen, etc.) were said to be traveling across the rivers and lakes. As society changed, the meaning has narrowed to refer to anyone who leads an unstable, risky life and may or may not be involved in illegal or immoral activities. Bandits and murderers are of course "in the rivers and lakes" but since the police must deal with them, they too have become part of this underworld society.

There are several similarities between *Mark of the Eagle* and *The Convict Killer (1980)*. They are both adapted works of author Zhu Yu and directed by Chor Yuen. They both have Ti Lung as the lead and deal with similar themes. The thinking is that when *Mark of the Eagle* was shelved it ultimately became *The Convict Killer;* however, this is inaccurate. Chor kicked off *The Avenger* (*The Convict Killer's* working title) the year before and it arrived in theaters in June 1980. *Mark of the Eagle* did not shut down production until a year after *The Convict Killer's* release. Chor recalled how he was making films so chaotically at the time, that he was juggling eight separate projects. One such assignment was the second Fu Sheng/Ti Lung collaboration written by Gu Long and titled *Return of the Sentimental Swordsman (1981)*.

Gu Long is not a name as widely known as Louis Cha or Liang Yusheng. Gu preferred to take to the shadows and leave the spotlight for his more famous colleagues.[24] The reclusive scribe penned 66 novels between 1960 and 1984 in which 31 adapted to film (49 if counting the remakes) and 18 into television dramas (40 in total). He was born Xiong Yaohua, a native of Nanchang of the Jiangxi Province in Southeast China, and his date of birth (1936-38) varies depending on the source. As a young man, he enjoyed reading wuxia fiction but also appreciated Western literary works and was influenced by authors Ernest Hemmingway, Jack London, Friedrich Nietzsche, John Steinbeck, and Japanese historical novelist, Eiji Yoshikawa. In 1952, he moved to Taiwan and graduated from the Foreign Language Department of the University of Danjiang.

Xiong Yaohua grew up in a broken household and bore the solitude of a wanderer in his heart. He had three sons by three different lovers over the years and admitted, that without women, he could not live. His close friends said Xiong Yaohua saw himself as the narcissistic knight-errant who lay inebriated in a mountain village with fine wine and even finer women. The aspiring writer's first work was published in 1960, under the pen name of Gu Long, and he churned out several more novels before retreating to the suburb of Ruifang. He initially attempted to mimic the styles of Louis Cha and others, but his exposure to Japanese literature and Western works, such as the *Godfather* novels and the *007* series, enabled him to establish a distinctive approach. Gu Long's sizable output from the late 1960s through the 1970s secured him a place in the annals of modern wuxia fiction.

Gu Long's passion for writing equally matched his love of alcohol. Whenever he received payment for a manuscript, he purchased a pile of books and several bottles of spirits before resuming the life of a country hermit. When Gu drank, he emptied his cup with a swift backward tilt of his head. It was a pastime he cherished but one that inevitably brought him ruin. At his 1985 funeral, mourners brought 48 bottles (one for each year of his life) of his beloved XO Cognac. While Louis Cha and Liang Yusheng retired from the world of wuxia fiction and left readers with wisdom and rapture, Gu Long's writing ceased with his untimely death and left his fans with pessimism and anguish.

The *Flying Dagger Series* aka *Xiaoli Feidao* was published between 1968 and 1981 and is the source material for *The Sentimental Swordsman (1977)* and its 1981 sequel. Both films were based on *Sentimental Swordsman, Ruthless Sword*, the first novel of five in the series that detailed the adventures of Li Xunhuan (Ti Lung) and his friend A'fei (Derek Yee Tung-Sing). It's worth noting the third film in this trilogy, *Perils of the Sentimental Swordsman (1982)*, was sourced from the *Chu Liuxiang* series which included the Shaw Brother adaptations *Clans of Intrigue (1977)* and *Legend of the Bat (1978)*.

Poshek Fu and David Desser noted in their 2000 publication that Chor Yuen created a virtual sub-genre of films while employed at Shaw, and his movies adapted from the novels of Gu Long were,

"...leaden with Gothic mysticism haunting both its loner heroes and its villains...its heroes moving like zombies in the cloistered landscape."[25]

The character of Li Xunhuan was born into a respectable family of scholars who served as imperial court officials. He acquired prominence throughout the Wulin, a community of martial artists, due to his combative expertise. His speed and precision in using his dagger, Xiaoli Feidao, was highly acclaimed and ranked him third in the renowned book of weapons; Binqipu. In the sequel, the legendary swordsman had abandoned his prior way of life and settled into an alcoholic haze of seclusion, which is possibly how the author viewed his own existence. His retirement wasn't permanent though, as he is hurled back into the world he hoped to forsake. It's there that he becomes entangled with the eccentric left-handed warrior Jing Wuming (Fu Sheng) and Money Clan Shangguan Jinhong (Ku Feng) in a series of contests to determine the leadership of the martial world.

Ti Lung believed that a wuxia film must uphold the wuxia spirit. That one must honor one's Sifu and never slay the innocent. He was always willing to take on a role that moviegoers would find entertaining but he rejected any parts which were against the moral conscience. Ti said he was nurtured by martial arts films, growing up on the Wong Fei-hung series, and was motivated by compelling screenplays so long as they were not harmful to China's dignity.

Return of the Sentimental Swordsman started production one week after *Mark of the Eagle* but came to a standstill that September. This was the fourth film to stall due to an incident occurring on the set of *Heroes Shed No Tears*.[26] This latest project was the third Chor Yuen/Fu Sheng collaboration, which initiated June 26. Besides directing, Chor also took screenwriting credit for an adapted work from the Gu Long novel titled *Ying Xiong Wu Lei* aka *A Hero without Tears*.

Gu Long's writing style was harmonious for cinema adaptation, and in the 1980s, the author even established his own movie company named Bao Sian. Instead of sticking with the traditional style of the genre that invoked Chinese history, culture, and philosophy, his works emphasized action and character interplay with terse and witty dialogue. Gu's prose was succinct and thus more like a screenwriter where less is more. In the novel, Little Gao aka Gao Chien Fei, Fu Sheng's character in the movie, made his introduction on page 13.

"*Dusk.*

Inside the little restaurant, the fragrances of lard and stir-fry, the sweat of coolies and rickshaw drivers, the odor of hard liquor, hot peppers, leeks and garlic, all mixed together to create a strange, hard-to-describe smell.

Little Gao liked this smell.

He liked the smell of clouds floating past a mountain peak, and the delicate fragrance a cold wind passing through trees and leaves. And yet, he also liked this smell.

He liked the smell of noble and elegant scholars, but he also liked these sweaty men, who sat eating flatbread-wrapped leeks, garlic heads and fatty meat, and drank hard liquor.

He liked people.

This was because he had been alone for too long, and rarely saw people, only the green mountains, white clouds, flowing water and ancient pines. Three months ago, he had finally returned to the world of men. And in three months' time he had already killed four people.

Four local overlords with illustrious reputations, people who deserved to die, and yet couldn't be killed.

He liked people, and yet he killed people.

He didn't like killing people, and yet he killed them."[27]

---

[1] See Books, Ask for the Moon, page 96.
[2] According to the director, his professional name was derived from two random words he spotted while flipping through a dictionary.
[3] Ng Wui had an illustrious career in the 1950s/60s in which he acted in over 100 films and directed over 200.
[4] See Books, Ng. Oral History Series (3): Director Chor Yuen, page 21.
[5] The decline of Cantonese Cinema was attributed to a variety of factors including the 1967 Riots and Shaw/Cathay's monopoly of local and foreign distribution. For further reading, see Books, Yu Mo-wan: Swords, Chivalry and Palm Power.
[6] The 127-chapter "Legendary Siblings" was penned in 1967 and a milestone in Gu Long's career that marked the dawn of a more mature style of writing. It has spawned three movie and six television adaptations.
[7] Southern Screen Jun 1979: 36-37.
[8] Ibid.
[9] Ibid.
[10] Ibid.
[11] Ibid.
[12] Ibid.
[13] Ibid.
[14] See Chapter 21
[15] Life Gamble (1979). Dir. Chang Cheh. 2004. DVD. Region 1 Navarre Corp.
[16] Ibid.
[17] Tong Gai was one of Simon Yuen's three disciples. See Books, The Making of Martial Arts Films: As Told by Filmmakers and Stars, page 71.
[18] Cinemart Apr 1979: 36-37.
[19] See Web and More, Brendan Davis: Brave Archer 3.
[20] Southern Screen Aug 1979: 28-29.
[21] "Shaw Brothers Films: The Brave Archer Movies." Kung Fu Fandom. 11 Jan. 2005.
[22] See Books, Chang Cheh: A Memoir, page 109.
[23] In an August 2002 post on Kung Fu Fandom, the late Linn Haynes wrote: "Some footage was filmed for it and exists in the hands of some BIG collectors."
[24] At that time, the wuxia fiction scene in Taiwan was monopolized by Wolong Sheng, Zhuge Qingyun, and Sima Ling who were known as the "Three Swordsmen" aka "Three Musketeers."

[25] See Books, The Cinema of Hong Kong: History, Arts, Identity, page 99.
[26] Five films paused production when Alex injured his leg in Sept., '79. In production order, they were: My Rebellious Son (1982), The Brave Archer Part III (1981), Mark of the Eagle (n/r), Return of the Sentimental Swordsman (1981), Heroes Shed No Tears (1980).
[27] See Books, Yingxiong Wu Lei a.k.a. A Hero without Tears.

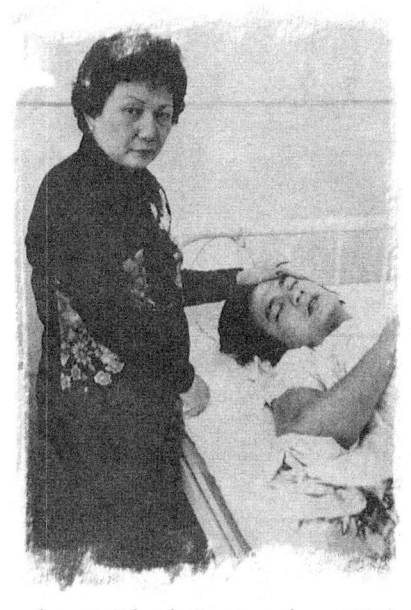

Ti Lung & Alex, 1979

above: Black September 1978
below: Shaw Training Class of '72

Jenny, Alex, Angelea
Cheung; Fall '75

Alex Spring '76

Marco Polo set with Richard Harrison and Carter Wong

Alexander Fu Sheng: Biography of the Chinatown Kid

right: The "Brave Archer"
at Movietown, 1977

bottom: The Lau take three Cheungs
as new students; October 1980

left: Jenny & Alex
on vacation, 1979

middle:
Boxer Rebellion
with Chi Kuan-chun

bottom: Lau Kar-Leung
with Mrs. Cheung, 1980

Alexander Fu Sheng: Biography of the Chinatown Kid

Cheung Siblings #8-#11 in the U.K., late 70's

Alex in his prime

David and Alex, 1979

19

Black September: The Sequel

September 19, 1979 began like any other ordinary Wednesday. Alex took the short drive to the studio for another day's shooting on *Heroes Shed No Tears*. He and co-star Derek Yee Tung-Sing were preparing for a scene and suspended several feet up in the air. They clowned with one another on who was to be the unlucky man to fall. Derek was hanging over a bed of rocks and joked Alex must be the one for he was dangling over a body of water. If Alex slipped, the water would certainly help break his fall. Whether it was coincidence or premonition, the wire holding Alex snapped and the actor plunged towards the studio floor. Alex was hydrophobic and shifted his body to avoid the pond.[1] He strained to lean backwards which caused his right leg to take the full brunt. Like a replay from last September, emergency services rushed to the scene. The injured star was transported to Hong Kong Baptist Hospital and underwent several hours of surgery in which a series of screws were inserted into his leg.

Alex underwent further surgery on the morning of September 26 to remove multiple bone fragments. Jenny kept the bone chips in a small jar by Alex's bedside to remind him he wasn't Superman despite the nickname many came to know him by. According to Lau Kar-Leung, Alex failed to heed his physician's recommendation to stay off the leg, and two days after the first surgery, he hopped out of bed to the bathroom. Director Chor took Alex's mishap to heart and insisted Jenny blame him for the accident but she felt it unnecessary. Jenny wasn't as forgiving though with the studio, venting her rage, and condemning them for their carelessness and lack of proper safety equipment.

"Last year he suffered a serious head injury and needed several months to recover. Now it's happened again and the production of several movies have paused making all suffer. Why can't they just get some safety equipment which could have prevented such a severe injury?"[2]

Jenny spent day and night at the hospital making sure Alex's needs were met. He was in a good deal of discomfort and she bathed him daily which exacerbated her already inflamed sciatic nerve. Their emotional state became heightened as both patient and nurse endured some tense weeks together before Alex's discharge in October. Jenny was forced to return to work as her promotor refused to postpone prior engagements, so she had to leave Alex behind in the hands of caregivers. After concerts in Canada and New York, she flew to Los Angeles and performed to a packed house at the Shrine Auditorium. On the evening of her final engagement, the audience requested the man standing behind the curtain come out to greet the crowd. Who was the mystery man? It was Fu Sheng who flew to L.A. to witness his wife's closing performance. He joined her on stage with the aid of a walking stick to the applause of 3000 fans.

Alex underwent his third operation a few days after Christmas to remove the screws still inserted in his leg. The procedure went well but it would be some time before he could return to Movietown. In the meantime, Alex found ways to keep himself busy at home by building models and practicing his singing. Jenny teased him if he entertained plans to take over her career but Alex joked that he only sang for her. When asked about his feelings on returning to work and how Shaw was managing without him, he was a bit more despondent.

"Popularity is useless. Some directors in the Shaw Studios are really practical. Once they saw my leg was hurt, they replaced me with other actors immediately. There are no friends in the studios."[3]

The couple went on the road in the spring of '80 when Jenny began several tour dates. On April 2, they arrived in the Philippines for multi-city concerts. Jenny wowed her fans at Baguio Convention Center with a lineup of hits that included "Intervals of Sun and Clouds with Occasional Showers," "Solemn Vows," and "You Light Up My Life." However, nothing compared to when Alex, with his injured right leg roughly 85% recovered, approached the stage for a duet.[4] The music started anew and the duo sang "You Don't Have to be a Star" for the finale which electrified the crowd. They remained in the Philippines for another week where additional concerts were held in Manila, Cebu City, and then farther south to Zamboanga and Davao City.

After a brief return to Hong Kong for a few local performances, they set off to Europe for *The Monte Carlo Show*. The short-lived variety series, hosted by the son of actor John Wayne, had a wide array of international talent that included dance routines, comedy sketches, and celebrity interviews. Alex and Jenny's flight to Switzerland took close to 17 hours, not to mention a half-day layover, and a second flight to Nice tacked on another hour. Jenny was concerned the extensive traveling might hamper Alex's recovery but he persevered.

At the Nice Côte d'Azur International Airport, they felt like rural villagers from the New Territories who were entering a big city. None of the locals spoke much English, let alone Cantonese, but luckily the couple was soon greeted by the show's public relations manager who held a huge sign with their names in English.

The trio boarded a train to Monaco where Jenny and the PR director engaged in shop talk while Alex kept his eyes glued to the window as the train hugged the coastline of the Ligurian Sea. There were numerous beaches on the way where vacationers played and swam in the water, and to their surprise, included many topless sunbathers. Jenny joked that Alex was in such a good mood, as he judged the passing European beauties, he almost forgot his leg was broken and that he was sitting next to her.

When they arrived, Alex and Jenny still had a few days before the show's live performance, so they amused themselves by watching the other entertainers practice. Liberace was in attendance and Jenny was scheduled to perform in the same session. The world-renowned pianist's rehearsal went without flaw, and after he finished, she confessed he was a hard act to follow.

"I couldn't describe the excitement in words and told myself... Jenny Tseng, stay calm. Have some self-restraint. Maintain your standard."[5]

She completed her set and received a reassuring applause from Liberace and host Patrick Wayne, who then posed with her for a photo-op. Their approval gave Jenny a much-needed confidence boost and afterwards, she and Alex rented a car to take in some of the sights of the Italian countryside. Jenny's butterflies would come back with a vengeance on opening night and Alex couldn't contain himself in poking fun at her anxiety. Jenny was extremely irritated but all that changed when it was time for her to perform. Alex gave her the courage she required by taking his wife's hand and escorting her onto the stage. Jenny was thankful for the warm gesture and later laughed that the moment was even more embarrassing than when they got married.

In June, Jenny and Alex traveled back to the States where she entertained audiences at the Las Vegas Hilton and worked on an album for an American record label. That summer, Fu Sheng found himself back in the studio as well, not to shoot a movie, but to negotiate his new contract as the old one was set to expire on October 15. He understood his worth to the company and Alex told Run Run Shaw that he wished to expand his horizons by working behind the camera. As an actor, he commanded a high salary but as a director he was still a novice and much more cautious in his demands.

"The problem is sharing the profit. I must have a share of the bonus. Every director does. I want to be like Wong Jing, not caring about the director's wage, but getting a larger share of the bonus."[6]

Fu Sheng still had a few films attached to his old contract and Run Run Shaw expected those finished before agreeing to any new terms. Alex knew he could wait it out, and once his contract expired, would become a free agent working for whomever he wanted. The studio head wasn't going to take any chances though and invited his multifaceted star out for lunch in mid-July to discuss options, but as the summer drew to a close, there still wasn't a deal on the table. While this was discouraging news, it didn't hamper the actor's spirits as the Cheungs and Alex's kung fu family grew even closer that August with a celebration.

On the 30th, Lau Kar-Leung and younger brother Lau Kar-wing took on three of Alex's siblings (Eva Yuen-Wah, Simon, and David Cheung) as their new apprentices. Alex had been training with Sifu Lau for several years, and at the time, was only one of five formal apprentices of this legendary martial artist.[7] Alex acted as the coordinator for the event despite still having some challenges in walking with his injured leg. The Lau brothers held two ceremonies, one casual and one formal, in which the latter was at the residence of Alex's Sifu where dedications were offered to Lau Jaam and Wong Fei-hung. Lau Kar-Leung sported a tailor-made shirt with his name embroidered in red cursive script. There was also an inscription that read, *"Couple hardness and softness to decide the force; the principles of deciding the act in the universe,"* to which the kung fu expert disclosed,

"These two lines are the essence of Hung Gar Kuen, which I introduced in my film, Challenge of the Masters."[8]

The cheerful host greeted his guests and accepted their praises. Among the callers were several actors that included Lau Kar-fai, Robert Mak, and Wong Yu. Kar-fai became a senior on this day and returned to Hong Kong just for the event, as he was abroad dealing with a family crisis. His follow-up film in the Chamber Trilogy, *Return to the 36th Chamber (1980)*, had just been released and he wore a wig in which everyone joked how he looked like a cartoon character.[9] Alex was also enjoying a hearty laugh. He took great pleasure in having his elder sister serve him tea as he was officially now her senior. After the ritual, Angela Liu Cheung handed out red packets to everyone before they congregated around the mahjong tables to try their luck with the game of tiles.

In September, Alex's younger brother returned from his studies in the U.K., so the actor decided it was time for a family holiday. They were joined by David Cheung, Lau Kar-Leung, and several others as the group ventured south to Thailand for a week of fun and sun. Alex stated to the group that he would no longer shoot movies during the month of September, and if a contract was presented, he'd make his official return on October 8. Alex chose to travel to Thailand so he could worship Phra Phrom who's regarded as an idol of good fortune and protection. Regrettably, the four-faced deity outlook wasn't optimistic.

"I got three lotteries and all of them were bad," Alex moaned. *"One of them concerning myself is so-so. Another one concerning my career is medium-luck. Both say there will be troubles."*[10]

Fu Sheng and the film mogul finally came to a resolution the following month with a new agreement. The terms were three years without loans in which he was to earn $700,000 per film. Alex committed to shoot two films per year at this rate; however, for films already in progress, he would be paid his previous salary. This new contract was tops among actors at Shaw Brothers Studio but Alex was reluctant to reveal the details. He kept silent as he had many good friends in Movietown and didn't wish to drive a wedge between him and his co-workers.

The no-loans clause was significant as other companies continued to vie for Fu Sheng. One Taiwanese company proposed a three-film deal at one million dollars per. He admitted the temptation was great and thought of taking the money to purchase a new home but remained loyal to Shaw nonetheless. A few years' prior, director Yuen Woo-ping invited Alex to take part in his new company but was turned down. Some have stated that Run Run Shaw forbade Fu Sheng from being a party to an outside project, but Yuen expressed it differently.

"The price he named was too high. It is risky as the production cost is also high, so I had to give up. Since it didn't work out this time, I don't want to reveal it to cause any misunderstanding."[11]

Sources said the price Alex quoted was $1.5 million which would be a huge burden to the fledgling independent. Strangely though, when questioned via email in May 2014, Yuen stated they never reached out to Alex as they knew he was a Shaw contract player. He also commented that they didn't attempt to replicate a Fu Sheng character for his film, *Snake in the Eagle's Shadow,* but create a novel personality for Jackie Chan. Yuen did admit he contacted another major Shaw star, Ku Feng, to play Beggar So, but he was too busy and the filmmaker opted to have his own father, Simon Yuen Siu-Tin, immortalize the role of the drunk beggar.

Alex was ready to get back to business now that the ink was dry on his new pact. One project on the immediate horizon was the modern comedy *Disco Bumpkins (1980)* directed by Ricky Chan Ga-Suen. Alex agreed to star but had a contractual obligation to first work on *Treasure Hunters (1981)*. This picture was to be directed by his senior, Lau Kar-wing, and while the action choreographer turned director previously worked on several films with Alex, this was the first movie in which he was to direct the star. Like his elder brother, Kar-wing was a twenty-year film veteran and started visiting his father's sets when was around 11 years of age. Kar-wing reflected on those early days.

"I would follow him with a vegetable basket with water and food and a folding stool. When they needed people for the lion dance scene, I would be positioned at the lion's tail or playing drums on the side."[12]

Besides being Alex's return project and Kar-wing's directorial premiere at Shaw, this film held an even greater significance as it was the film debut of David Cheung. Alex had earlier considered his younger brother to act opposite of him in *The Proud Twins*, but the college junior still had another year of studies and the star did not wish to interfere. Now, David had graduated from school and was ready to follow in his brother's footsteps. When a journalist questioned Alex, he was both optimistic and apprehensive about his sibling joining the film industry.

"He's my brother. Of course, I must take care of him in every aspect. Seeing myself in him, I surely hope he will be as successful if not more."[13]

---

[1] By his own admission, Alex was scared of water as he almost drowned once. The actor overcame his fear at age 25 when he finally learned how to swim in the summer 1980.
[2] Cinemart Oct 1978: 36-37.
[3] Cinemart Dec 1979: 44-45.
[4] Erroneously reported on the web and elsewhere that he broke "both legs."
[5] Cinemart July 1980: 30-31.
[6] See Web and More, "Fu Sing & Yan Nei," page 24.
[7] In the fall of 1980, LKL had five formal apprentices. Fu Sheng, Wong Yu, Hui Ying-hung, a singer named Ling Fung, and a Filipino child called Jo-jo.
[8] Southern Screen Nov 1980: 12-13.
[9] Though Lau Kar-fai has acquired worldwide fame playing a Shaolin monk, he was originally a Catholic altar boy while attending the Salesian boarding school as a teen. When Pope Paul VI visited HK in 1970, the pontiff hosted an open-air mass at Government Stadium in So Kon Po (now Hong Kong Stadium) in which Gordon was chosen to take part in as an altar server.
[10] See Web and More, "Fu Sing & Yan Nei," page 24.
[11] Southern Screen Dec 1980: 6-7.
[12] See Books, Ng. Oral History Series (7): Lau Kar-wing, page 117.
[13] Southern Screen Dec 1980: 6-7.

20

The Return of Alex

The first day of filming for *Treasure Hunters* was Monday, November 24, 1980 and both Lau Kar-wing and David Cheung arrived at the studio earlier than most. The initial day was always hectic but even more so for the director and newbie actor. Angela Liu Cheung drove out to the set with daughter Eva Yuen-Wah and brought along boxes of cakes for the workers. She gave red packets to Alex and David for luck and told reporters that the Cheung family was proud of David's new career path.

Treasure Hunters kick-off ceremony began mid-afternoon and the whole crew gathered to worship. Even the uproarious Alex became serious and silently prayed with joss sticks in hand. A roasted pig and fresh fruits laid out on a table near the studio entrance and all were excited to start…except for one. David often visited Movietown to learn about the filming process, but on this particular day, broke out into a flop sweat when his first scene was being prepped. Kar-wing settled his actor down by going over lines, and once the novice got a few takes in, the day's workload proceeded without a hitch. His star brother wrapped his arms around David afterwards to congratulate him. Alex praised the freshman considering he hadn't any prior experience, whereas Alex cut his teeth as an extra in several roles before making the leap to lead performer.

Production continued through the holidays and the following spring with a wrap party in the first week of June. *Treasure Hunters'* brief seven day run in theaters diminished its box office gross; however, the film has gained in popularity over the years, thanks to its many supporters. Shaw enthusiast Paul Nice commented,

"Fu Sheng's proper comeback film after recuperating from his Black September injuries is one for the ages. Fu Sheng and David Cheung Chin-Pang have a natural comedic chemistry and timing in which they bring out the best in each other. This is especially evident in the scene in which

they rob an old man's house. That scene alone is nothing short of kung fu comedy brilliance. Jackie Chan be damned."[1]

When *Treasure Hunters* was in mid-production, Alex began a pair of additional assignments two weeks prior to the Chinese New Year. On January 26, 1981 he joined Chang Cheh for the final installment of *The Brave Archer,* which became the 28th occasion the cinema "father & son" team shared a studio set. Regrettably, it was also their last. Two days before the start of that movie, Alex paired up with his Sifu for a three-film collaboration commencing with *Legendary Weapons of China (1982).*

Lau Kar-Leung is a name linked to martial arts throughout Asia and is one that's well reputed. Despite not reaching global stature along the likes of Akira Kurosawa or Yuen Woo-ping, his proficiency in martial arts is unquestionable. One might surmise that, given Lau's illustrious background, the making of *Legendary Weapons of China* would be an effortless task. The project's assistant director, Lee Tai-Hang, begged to differ explaining that his boss demanded, not only an exhibition of authentic kung fu, but a meticulous correlation between the martial choreography and the narrative. Lee commented,

"Director Lau was rather strict in order to catch the perfect shot. The film employed more special effects than any of Lau's previous films which added another layer of difficulty."[2]

One example he alluded to was the roof crawlspace sequence which pitted actor Hsiao Ho against Hui Ying-hung. Taking place in Studio 3, the scene was scheduled to be a three-day shoot but ultimately took a total of ten days as Lau Kar-Leung and staff strived for the perfect rendering. Though the scene was an exhausting undertaking, it nevertheless showed the director's dedication and fervent desire to be a visionary. Fu Sheng praised his master,

"My teacher is rather inventive. For example, he will try different positions for a shot. While no one knows if the desired effect will look good, not everyone has the courage for being an innovator like Sifu."[3]

The story of *Legendary Weapons of China* is a fanciful one towards the end of the Qing Dynasty where the use of Mao Shan sorcery was utilized to combat non-nationals. The enigma of these magi was unknown to outsiders and it's alleged they manipulated black magic to protect them from swords, knives, and even gunfire. Lau Kar-Leung scoffed at the notion and believed these so-called invincible ruses needed to be grounded with authentic kung fu otherwise they were merely parlor tricks; smoke and mirrors to manipulate the masses.

Actress Hui Ying-hung agreed that vigorous training was the key for any style in reaching its summit and cherished working on this project.[4] While she was familiar with some of the weapons on set, others were quite alien to her. Hui practiced them between takes and endured multiple cuts and bruises. She loved how the film did not cater to the superstitious but created a valuable history lesson to the viewing audience with its depiction of Eighteen Arms of Wushu. Hui Ying-hung explained,

"Each one has a different meaning and must be used in a particular way, representative of either the Northern or Southern styles of Chinese martial arts. This movie shows the difference between martial arts for performance and for combat. This is what makes the film a great representation of both Chinese and Hong Kong Cinema."[5]

As for Fu Sheng, he got off easy. Due to his contractual disputes and injury, his participation was downgraded to a minor but comical effort. Alex's character made a mockery of the so-called invincible shaman by staging a series of ruses and mock battles. He relished in the role of the bogus martial arts master, exposing how absurd the conjurers were, which allowed him to delve deeper into his comedic faculties. Critics have grumbled that his inclusion was unnecessary and it compromised the overall serious tone or message. Alex though didn't see it that way. While its completion took nearly a full year, the wait was well worth it for Lau Kar-Leung and company. Box office totals were a hair under ten million dollars making it the highest return in Alex's career.

Whereas *Legendary Weapons of China* shot throughout the majority of 1981, Alex's concluding assignment with Chang Cheh took a mere six weeks to complete. Based on the second book of *The Condor Trilogy*, *The Return of the Condors* aka *Divine Eagle, Gallant Knight* was first serialized between May 1959 and July 1961 in Ming Pao. The book's setting was two decades after *The Legend of the Condor Heroes* in which the Mongolian hordes are invading China and Guo Jing and Huang Rong are trying to save the city of Xiangyang.[6] While Guo and Huang are featured prominently in the novel, the principal hero is the orphaned son of Mu Nianci, not to mention the offspring of sworn enemy, Yang Kang.

The Brave Archer and His Mate (1982) saw several fresh faces as well as old ones in new roles. Gigi Wong Suk-yee was the third actress to play the starring lead of Huang Rong while Kwok Chun-Fung (Uncle Naughty in parts 1-3) took over the role of Guo Jing that Fu Sheng had previously played. Alex was cast as Yang Guo, son of Mu Nianci, which is rather curious considering Hui Ying-hung portrayed the character Mu Nianci in *The Brave Archer (part 1)* and was Alex's step-sister in that film!

The shifting of characters has always made viewing the *Brave Archer* films an arduous task but the change involving Alex and Kwok left viewers bewildered. To the casual observer, it appeared they simply swapped characters but this was not the case. Alex's character (Yang Guo) was a new addition to the tale, and according to Chu Ko who was the assistant action director and cast member, Chang Cheh felt the switch was a necessary modification for this new storyline.

"The first three films featured a young Guo Jing and so Fu Sheng fit the role perfectly, but in the fourth film the story was set some 20 years later," Chu Ko pointed out. *"No longer is Guo Jing the smarmy youngster but a more mature middle-aged man. Director Chang felt that Kwok Chun-Fung, who was nearly a decade older than Alex, would be better suited in that role. Not to mention, the character of Yang Guo was much more mischievous and youthful and who better to play that role than Alex?"*[7]

Kwok and Fu Sheng worked together on over a dozen projects but it was a tragic twist of fate that their final film featured them as father and son. In real life, Kwok's only son was born when his acting career was just starting out. Chan Yip-Shing did not inherit his father's interest in cinema or martial arts, so Kwok told him that he needn't pursue a similar career path. Chan instead aspired to work in law enforcement and joined the Royal Hong Kong Police Force where he served with various units, including the Hong Kong Airport Security Force and the Police Tactical Unit; popularly referred to as the Blue Berets.

Officer Chan's last unit was in the motorcycle division of Kowloon West Traffic. In the early morning of March 18, 2004, he was driving on Gascoigne Road Flyover in Yau Ma Tei when his motorcycle was rammed head on by a drunk driver who crossed over the median. The collision sent Chan and his bike hurtling off the flyover to the street twenty feet below. Emergency services rushed him to Queen Elizabeth Hospital where he was certified dead. A distraught Kwok, then employed for TVB as a choreographer, attempted to hold back his tears,

"*I have raised my son for 28 years and now . . . he's gone.*"[8]

The Brave Archer and His Mate would not release until February 1982. It fared better than the first two *Brave Archer* movies but heavy competition from Golden Harvest and others forced this installment into 76th place overall. It did nevertheless edge Hua Shan's *Little Dragon Maiden (1983),* another adaptation of *The Return of the Condors*, which featured Chen Kuan-tai (Guo Jing), Leslie Cheung (Yang Guo), and Yung Jing-Jing; future wife to Lau Kar-Leung.[9]

As he did in 1977-78, Chang Cheh shifted directions after *Brave Archer and His Mate* was complete. His original Venoms team had run its course and the director was grooming a new set of actors. Run Run Shaw eventually dissolved Chang's contract with the studio allowing the director one final hoorah. The filmmaker established the Chang Ho film company in the mid-80s, where he made several movies on the mainland before hanging up his megaphone for good.

As for Alex, he was steadfast in getting his career back on track after his long recuperation but fate continued to wreak havoc in his personal life. In late 1980, Jenny survived a health scare in which she became hospitalized after an overdose of prescription pills. Speculation was fueled by reports that she and Alex were fighting and swallowed the capsules to anger him. Jenny dismissed the rumor stating she was overworked and only took Alex's prescribed medication to help her sleep.

Alex was enduring his own disorders as well. He put on some additional weight during his latest recovery and suffered from stomach ailments. To make matters worse, their Filipino domestic helper deep fried nearly everything, and turned appetizing meals into bland tasting soups. Alex paid close attention to Jenny whenever she was in the kitchen to pick up possible cooking tricks. He savored his wife's succulent steaks, but if someone heard him praise her seafood dishes, they might presume he was a cat. When Jenny was out of town on business, and he wasn't in the mood for deep fried soup, Alex went to great lengths to feed himself. One evening he had an insatiable craving for an omelet so he ventured out into the night, knocking on closed shop doors, until he found someone willing to sell him a dozen eggs.

Since *Brave Archer and His Mate* was such a quick shoot, Alex's schedule opened up, and on the 10th of April, started on his second film directed by Lau Kar-Leung. *The 8 Diagram Pole Fighter (1984)* began with a working title of *The Heroic Family* and featured the impressive cast of Hui Ying-hung, Lily Li, Phillip Ko Fei, Li King-Chu, and Lau Kar-fai. The film has ultimately been touted as one of Fu Sheng's best-known movies despite its posthumous release in 1984. Lau Kar-fai stated it's his favorite picture due to the emphasis placed on the characters' emotions and how he interpreted his own internal struggle as Yang 5th brother.

"I remember the scene when my character was rejected from the temple and he shaved his head to prove his sincerity. Yande was devastated by his family's violent demise, yet he needed to suppress the trauma and keep it to himself. That particularly powerful scene illustrates the essence of the whole film."[10]

While relatively unknown to the Western world, the *Yang Jia Jiang* is a millennium old tale steeped in history. As mentioned in the chapter on *The 14 Amazons*, this collection of stories was also known as *Generals of the Yang Family*, which detailed the exploits of this military family over four generations during the Song Dynasty. The Northern Song (A.D. 960-1127) was ruled by a debauched court which teetered on the edge of destruction due to repeated invasions from the north. The Yangs were the one family who owned the courage to keep the dynasty from obliteration and risked everything to defend their beloved nation. It is their legacy that is chronicled in the *Yang Jia Jiang*.

Towards the end of the 10th century, Emperor Taizong of Song called for an epic campaign to retake lands from the Khitan Empire aka the Liao Dynasty (A.D. 907-1125). To do this, Taizong divided his armed forces into three divisions. The East Army was led by Cao Bin, the Central Army by Tian Zhongjin, and the West Army by Pan Mei and Yang Ye. This latter general was the Yang's foremost warrior and nicknamed the Peerless Yang, as his prowess at war brought favoritism from the emperor but envy from the other generals.

The Yongxi Campaign, as it was known, saw initial victories in four prefectures before miscommunication drove a wedge between their forces and the eastern division was overrun. Generals Pan and Yang were to escort civilians back to the Song territory when one of the four prefectures fell to the advancing enemy. Pan suggested an audacious strategy to salvage the operation which required Yang's troops to take the battle to the Khitan. Yang Ye feared the plan to be suicidal, but with his reputation on the line, the general proposed that the Song commanders fortify the end of Chenjiagu Valley with archers in case his forces needed to withdraw.

Yang's army advanced forward, clashing with the Khitan in a bloodstained struggle, until he ordered his feigned retreat to Chenjiagu's rear. Unknown to Yang Ye, there weren't any Song archers waiting for his men. The deceptive Pan had abandoned him and Yang's forces were now cornered and outnumbered. Each of the general's sons succumbed to the enemy as they fought a valiant but unwinnable campaign. When the skirmish concluded, Yang Ye discovered his family annihilated. Though the general was captured alive, he showed his loyalty to the end while a prisoner of the Khitan, dying of a hunger strike.

Extracting actual history or fact from the tales of *Yang Jia Jiang*, or other works based on folktales, is like any other mystery. In the film, Yang Ye refused defeat by smashing his forehead against the burial stele of Li Ling.[11] Of Yang Ye's famous sons, three in the book survived. The 4th son (Yanhui) was captured and eventually married a Khitan princess, the 5th (Yande) took the path of a monk, and the 6th (Yanzhao) became a renowned general himself. He continued to battle the Khitan for the next 25 years until his death in 1014.

In the film, only two survived. Fu Sheng played the Yang 6th brother who endured the unspeakable horrors of combat. While war is often romanticized as honorable and glorious, the experience of losing his kin in battle has put a profound toll on his mental faculties. Despite safely returning to his family's home, Alex's character inexplicably vanished without resolution, as the movie's focus shifted onto Yang 5th brother.

One of the first sequences that Lau Kar-Leung wanted to shoot that second week of April 1981 was the pivotal opening battle. It was a theatrically staged kung fu masterstroke by the director in which his brave warriors perished *"standing erect in postures of statuesque greatness."*[12] Lau Kar-fai recalled the sequence as poignant and resourceful.

"In the Jinsha Beach scene, Master Lau adopted the abstract presentation of Cantonese Opera over the traditional bloody massacre. It leaves room for the audience's imagination while successfully retaining the essence of the scene."[13]

Six weeks after the start of *The 8 Diagram Pole Fighter*, Fu Sheng further juggled his calendar and rejoined David Cheung on their next project with Lau Kar-wing, a comedy titled *The Fake Ghost Catchers (1982)*. Though David had only recently become an official student of Kar-wing, he started studying martial arts under the director some years prior. When David wasn't on the set, he practiced his kung fu to maintain his physique and sharpen his skills. David also possessed a genuine interest in films from an early age, and as a senior at the University of Calgary, took a one-year course on cinema studies to equip himself with the necessary techniques of filmmaking.

"Psychology was only my major in school but my real, more profound interest lies in film. I thought with the credentials of Fu Sheng in the circle, I could also make this my profession."[14]

It was well known in Movietown that Alex enjoyed playing practical jokes and his younger sibling certainly followed in his footsteps. Some say that David's shenanigans outmatched his brother, but when it came to martial arts, he exhibited a more serious tone. David believed that using kung fu to teach someone a lesson was arrogant and that fighting never resolved a problem. As for working alongside his superstar brother once again, he was unable to contain his exuberance.

"As a kid, I saw Fu Sheng on the screen and admired this heroic image of his. I was already dreaming then about appearing on the screen one day and how impressive that would be!"[15]

---

[1] Facebook post.
[2] Southern Screen Jun 1981: 36-37.
[3] Southern Screen May 1981: 46-47.
[4] Hui initially learned weaponry skills from Bow-sim Mark; mother of Donnie Yen.
[5] See Film Reviews and Interviews, "Paris Cinema IFF Interview: Kara Wai Ying Hung on

Kung-Fu and Comebacks."
[6] For further reading on the Siege of Xiangyan, go to: http://deremilitari.org/2014/05/the-mongol-siege-of-xiangyang-and-fan-cheng-and-the-song-military
[7] "Chu Ko and his memories of Movietown." Personal interview. 9 Nov. 2013.
[8] See Web and More, "Police Officer's Father: Drunk Driver Should Be Sentenced to Prison."
[9] Movie has been misleadingly labeled by some bootleg outfits as "Brave Archer, Part 5."
[10] The 8 Diagram Pole Fighter (1984). Dir. Lau Kar-Leung. 2004. DVD (insert), Region 3 IVL.
[11] Li Ling was a famous Han Dynasty general who, similar to Yang Ye, fought an overwhelming force in 99BC. When he did not receive any reinforcements, Li Ling defected to the enemy's side which resulted in the execution of his entire family.
[12] See Books, Hong Kong Cinema: The Extra Dimensions, page 107.
[13] The 8 Diagram Pole Fighter (1984). Dir. Lau Kar-Leung. 2004. DVD (insert), Region 3 IVL.
[14] Southern Screen Mar 1982: 60-61.
[15] Ibid.

21

Trouble in Paradise

The year 1981 showed promise for Fu Sheng and Jenny Tseng. Alex began work on five separate projects, since returning to the studio in October, while Jenny took the Best Female Singer Award at the 16th Golden Bell Awards. The twosome also announced they were again expecting a child later in the year. A few months prior to the happy couple's conception, Alex made a prophetic statement at Chang Cheh's birthday party. He proclaimed that when he had a son, the director was to be the godfather, and when Chang passed, Alex and his son would be responsible for handling the filmmaker's funeral.[1] Alex joked upon first hearing news of the impending child that he was going to purchase a saddle for his 100lb dog and let his son ride him like a horse.

"Ride the four-legged one first. When he gets older, he can ride on his dad," Alex beamed.[2]

Alas, the happy moments were short-lived as Jenny miscarried later that year and the couple was forced to endure the harsh disappointment of another child lost. Alex became a bit despondent and began questioning why this cycle continued. He realized they both partook in demanding occupations and wondered if that was the underlying factor.

"Yes, her job is stressful but so is mine. Especially if we just had a fight and then I go shoot a combat scene. If I can't focus, it's easy to get injured. She only needs to be on the stage for an hour or two, but sometimes I've several scenes to film, which may take all day/night."[3]

The growing weight of a full workload after his injury and a continued empty nest started to create small fractures in the otherwise fairy tale marriage. Alex grumbled that when he came home from the studio, he just wanted a half hour to decompress from the day's tasks. Some days though that was asking for too much as Alex complained Jenny wouldn't give him the space to unwind.

"She always has something to bother me. Sometimes it's just something small and keeps hanging on it. To avoid an argument, I usually remain silent and take the blame. My friends always say that I spoil her, but if I wasn't so tolerant, would our relationship have lasted till now?"[4]

In early June 1981, Alex went to Mona Fong to request a loan but was declined. In his new contract, there was a clause for advanced payment, which he had already received during his recovery. When Fong refused to lend him any additional funds, he assumed she didn't wish to honor the agreement and boycotted his entire filming schedule. Alex contacted his physician, complaining his leg was in pain, and said that he needed to take time off. He submitted his doctor's note to the studio for a two-week leave of absence, noting he'd fight Shaw to the end, and then flew off to Taiwan.

The second day after Alex left for Taiwan, Lau Kar-wing committed to direct *Shaolin Prince (1983)* in which Alex was slated to co-star. Fong wasn't pleased with the actor's abrupt departure and expressed her irritation by requesting a lead change. Alex was mortified when he heard the news but that humiliation soon changed to rage. On the 11th of June, the day he was supposed to return to work, the star bypassed the stage and marched right into Fong's office. Alex demanded his contract to be nullified. He was no longer concerned about money and declared,

"I can't work in the Shaw Studios any more. I hurt myself while I was filming and now the old injury has come back. The company though does not respect me and has recast the role."[5]

Mona Fong refused to dissolve the contract stating she didn't have the authority to terminate their pact without consulting the shareholders. Alex reminded her of the $60,000 in medical expenses he incurred, for his treatment in the United Kingdom, which the studio had failed to compensate him for. He also pointed out that the British specialist informed him to rethink his career for the sake of his leg, or not take part in future action movies, otherwise the conditions may worsen. Fong was smug in her reply,

"Well, if your leg is still injured and you cannot make any movies, why then did you renew the contract?"[6]

Push had come to shove and the two erupted. Several journalists were present that day and Lau Kar-Leung stepped in to drag the hot-headed Alex away. Flash bulbs popped and reporters were quick to scribble in their notepads as the producer did her best on damage control. Fong's biggest fear was they might report Shaw not wanting to honor Alex's contract. She rationalized on how her staff sent chicken broth to the star while he was injured, to show how much management cared about his well-being. Whereas Alex saw members of the press as his adversary earlier in his career, he now developed a close relationship with several. On occasion, he would invite a group to his home and play mahjong till dawn. Alex discovered their usefulness knowing they could be an asset in times such as these.

Fu Sheng became so incensed after his blow up with Fong that he was determined to unionize the actors. When questioned about the feud, Sifu Lau deferred to Chang Cheh stating Chang helped negotiate Alex's new contract and should be the one to deal with this matter. Chang though was shrewd and always one to avoid controversy. He said he knew nothing of the quarrel other than what was in the papers and wouldn't be a good advocate. Finally, it was Run Run Shaw who stepped in as arbitrator of the disputing parties and arranged a dinner between Alex and Fong. She ultimately apologized, and while Alex was a bit reluctant, he agreed to get back to work. He saved face when reporters questioned if he was still upset about his request for an advance.

"*Money is not as important as one's dignity.*"[7]

Alex continued to pursue his dream of directing, and when he was recovering from his injuries, brainstormed an idea for his first directorial project titled *Na Cha versus Red Boy*. A fresh set of techniques was to be used for his inaugural project with minimal special effects and emphasis on real kung fu techniques. He planned to reprise his role from 1974, and David Cheung was to be cast as Red Boy. Lau Kar-Leung and Lau Kar-wing agreed to join the project with his teacher playing the role of the Monkey King. Alex was determined not to follow in the footsteps of Chang Cheh who employed crude special effects for *Na Cha the Great*. The aspiring director boasted that once shooting started, he would focus solely on the task of directing and all his other acting assignments would be put on the back burner.

"Every kind of special effect is basically used in Star Wars so it's not easy to surpass its achievement. However, nothing is impossible and if money is not an issue, anything can be produced. It just depends on whether Shaw is willing to spend the money!"[8]

Of course, up to that point, Alex's dream of directing was just that; however, that was about to change. Some weeks prior, the production department suggested to Lau Kar-Leung that he take on a co-directing role. The studio felt he was making far less films than Chor Yuen or Chang Cheh, a loss for the company and for himself. Lau agreed and mulled over who was most worthy to direct a film. After a short deliberation, he returned to the main office with only one name in mind...Fu Sheng.

Run Run Shaw was optimistic about having his prized performer move behind the camera but also had reservations. First, there was the question of how to split the bonus under this co-directing arrangement, an additional expense for the company, as both Lau and Fu Sheng expected to share in the bounty. The second issue was Alex's unfinished projects and his earlier comments, about back burning those films, did not bode well with the mogul. Shaw concluded that Alex's new career path needed further discussion, so the actor returned to the set to finish his backload of movies. On July 14, the partially completed *Mark of the Eagle* ceased production taking one film off his plate. On December 18, *Legendary Weapons of China* finally finished, thus allowing Alex to take on a new comedy titled *Cat vs Rat (1982)*.

Sourced from the late 19th century novel, *The Seven Heroes and Five Gallants*, this Shi Yukun tale has had multiple film and television adaptations. It was a surprise choice to many as all the movies Lau Kar-Leung previously made were hardcore kung fu films committed to symbolizing the virtues and morals of the martial arts. The director said he intended to shoot *Cat vs Rat* as a lighthearted and brisk paced martial comedy in which he would not adapt the script verbatim as portrayed in the novel. Lau instead planned to use a different angle to portray the background and kinship of these two legendary figures; Jien Chiu (Cat) and Bai Yu Tong (Rat).

Adam Cheng Siu-Chow played the film's protagonist and his character was a noble knight-errant skilled in the martial arts. Jien Chiu was upright, generous, and although he desired to excel, he did not compromise his demeanor. The Cat learned martial arts from Master Si Da Fu (Lau Kar-wing) and lived across from Bai Yu Tong (Fu Sheng). Bai was the opposite of his senior. He was arrogant, desired to win at any cost, and refused to admit failure. The Rat was proficient in martial arts as well but inferior to the Cat because of his mischievous nature.

Cat vs Rat was a first for Adam in two regards. It was the only movie he co-starred with Alex and his first film after becoming a disciple of Sifu Lau. At the time of production, Adam was involved in a relationship with actress Lydia Shum Tin-Ha, who portrayed Alex's mother in the movie.[9] The picture was marketed to feature Adam who had a reputation for playing lead roles in TVB wuxia dramas. With the spotlight on the Cat, Alex found himself in an awkward situation. Debates on who got more lines, received the most close-ups, and other gripes eventually boiled over. Even when the film released, the poster became an issue on who's image should be larger. The growing grievances ultimately put a strain on Alex's relations with Lau Kar-Leung.

Cast member Hsiao Ho recalled the project in an interview with Toby Russell. Ho reiterated what other performers have said in that Lau was a perfectionist; however, despite being a demanding director, never got upset with his cast or crew. Ho understood they were all working together to get the best take and if it took ten or even twenty takes, so be it.

"I went absolutely mad making this film. My brain just went. We had seven techniques and then six, five, four . . . I couldn't remember any moves. I was aching all over. Ran out of breath. Muscles broken. Took me a while before I could recover and regain my strength."[10]

Cat vs Rat finished up production on September 6 to become Alex's third highest grossing movie with nearly $4.5 million in receipts. A month prior, Sun Chung's *My Rebellious Son,* also wrapped. With a sum of 1315 days from start to finish, this was Alex's second longest film in production, including hiatuses, only surpassed by *Heaven and Hell* which stretched over five years for a staggering 1766 days!

In the new footage shot for *My Rebellious Son,* a significant change with the leading actress took place. Jenny Tseng was to co-star initially but replaced by Cecilia Wong Hang-Sau when filming resumed in mid-

1982. Wong appeared in films such as *Shaolin Mantis (1978)* with Chiang Da-Wei and *Spiritual Boxer, Part II (1979)* with Wong Yu but was nearing the end of her career when cast in *My Rebellious Son*.[11] She performed in roughly thirty productions though is best known as the wife of Nat Chan Pak-Cheung, who worked with Alex on his final two film projects.

With Fu Sheng's backlog of films behind him, with the exception of *The 8 Diagram Pole Fighter*, the final four months of 1982 were looking up. The star began two new productions with director Wong Jing but was also moving forward with his first directorial duties. With *Na Cha versus Red Boy* in limbo, a new project titled *The Beggar So* was in pre-planning and slated for a September start. This quasi bio-pic of Ten Tigers' Beggar So was to depict his early dealings with the foreign influence in his homeland, and his transformation into a drunken master of the martial arts. The script was still not complete but Alex confirmed it would feature himself, David Cheung, Wang Lung-Wei, and Hui Ying-hung. He was quite energized and commented,

"I have seen it many times before and have learnt much. Now is the time for me to do it. If I learn from the strengths of each director and integrate them together, naturally I can create my own style."[12]

Alex had done just that over the years with his acting. He embraced youthful innocence on the cusp of manhood in Chang's xiaozi hero and perfected that method of performance. Like his on-screen personality, Alex readily admitted he was still a tad immature and didn't always exhibit the best judgement. On occasion, when he was in a foul mood, it was somewhat difficult for him to communicate with others. Alex realized the need to work on this if he was going to be a successful director, but acknowledged this was the lesser of two struggles.

"Whenever someone tells me what difficulties they have, I offer my help without a second thought. There were times I was used but others when they were thankful for what I did. Still, I think I am too careless when it comes to socializing."[13]

Fu Sheng's directional launch hit a roadblock when *The Beggar So* was delayed and his dream stalled once again. Shaw Brothers Studio eventually produced the film, a few years later, as *The Young Vagabond (1985)*. The motion picture featured some of Alex's good friends, Wong

Yu, Wang Lung-Wei, and Lau Kar-fai in the lead role of Beggar So.

Needless to say, while directing continued to be Alex's predominant professional pursuit, he did not let the setback discourage him from pursuing equally ambitious plans in his personal life. He expressed his continued hope in starting a family and the yearning showed in his eyes whenever the topic was broached. The couple was still fairly young but Alex was aware the clock was ticking and having a child was never a sure thing. His voice though swelled with confidence that time was on his side and reiterated,

"If I have children, I don't hope for anything else."[14]

---

[1] Chang Cheh was buried on the same day that Alex died; 19 years later (7 July 2002).
[2] See Web and More, "Fu Sing & Yan Nei," page 27.
[3] Ibid., 21.
[4] Ibid.
[5] Cinemart Aug 1981: 32-33.
[6] Ibid.
[7] Ibid.
[8] Southern Screen May 1981: 46-47.
[9] Shum Tin-Ha was a notable MC on TVB's popular variety show, "Enjoy Yourself Tonight," which gave Jenny one of her earliest televised performances in Hong Kong.
[10] Shaolin Iron Claws (1978). Dir. Ko Pao. 2003. DVD. Region 1 VideoAsia.
[11] Two of Cecilia Wong's last roles were directed by Chang Cheh, Slaughter in Xian (1990) and Hidden Hero (1990), when he was shooting his final slew of films on the mainland.
[12] Southern Screen Oct 1982: 18-19.
[13] Ibid.
[14] Ibid.

22

Fatal Crash

Hong Kong Playboys (1983) was the first of two Wong Jing/Fu Sheng efforts. Alex was enthusiastic to begin work with a new director, although when cameras rolled August 28, 1982, it wasn't Alex who basked in the spotlight but rather his co-star, Chung Cho-Hung (Cherie Chung). Dubbed the "Marilyn Monroe of Hong Kong," Chung's future resume included collaborations with megastars Chow Yun Fat, Sammo Hung, Leslie Cheung, and Andy Lau. While considered as among Hong Kong's most glamorous actresses, her early life was far from stylish.[1]

Chung's parents ran a small female clothing shop, and starting at age 11, she juggled both school and working at the family business. It was her mother's idea for Chung to enter the 1979 Miss Hong Kong Competition but high heels were unfamiliar to the impoverished teen and she made some rookie blunders. Despite placing fourth overall, she was noticed by Damian Lau Chung-Yan who recommended her to participate in a new movie, *The Enigmatic Case (1980),* directed by Johnnie To Kei-Fung. This led to other productions such as *Postman Strikes Back (1982), Twinkle Twinkle Little Star (1983),* and *Winners and Sinners (1983).*

Chung's magnetism attracted other movie producers and her career flourished. Due to her popularity and the media's insatiable pursuit for gossip, rumors spiraled that she engaged in relationships with many in the industry, including George Lam Chi-Cheung and Jackie Chan. Fu Sheng also found himself an unwillingly participant in the paparazzi's "Cherie Show," putting the star in an awkward position. While Jenny and Alex had avoided the social scene and rebuffed the tabloids, the fatigue of living under the media microscope was gradually simmering to a boil.

Six weeks into the *Hong Kong Playboys* shoot, Alex's aspiration of directing finally became a reality. On the 9th of October, the comedy *Wits of the Brats (1984)* was set to commence with Fu Sheng in the director's chair, but like the day of his wedding, he was nowhere to be found. Alex was disappointed with the story, so he and co-director Lau Kar-wing left the studio to find writer Wong Jing for last minute rewrites. The trio returned much later in the day although Alex wasn't himself. Normally everyone's clown, everyone's hero, a more serious Alex barely spoke to reporters as he, David Cheung, and Lau Kar-wing lit incense sticks and prayed. Wong Jing tried to downplay the serious tone saying all was well but Alex's demeanor didn't convey the writer's sentiments. Previously, Alex boasted he could direct a movie with his eyes closed yet now, he was quick to change his bravado.

"This one is different. I must direct and act at the same time. It's much harder than one can imagine. There are so many things to be done. I don't even like this script."[2]

While Alex himself had a small part, brother David took the lead as the brat of a wealthy Kwangtung household who incites trouble due to his kung fu antics. He's shipped off to the north, where his mother hopes he will settle down, but his only ambition is to vie with three northern masters. One of the contenders is played by Fu Sheng, a conman who not only cheats David's character out of his belongings but gets him into an even tighter spot. Screenwriter and (eventual) co-director Wong is also in on the action, as Mr. Blinker, in this chuckle-fu production which became suspended due to the events of July 7 the following year.

The winter holiday season came and went with little fanfare. Alex was hampered by some minor injuries of late and admitted he was, at best, 80% recovered. The star didn't see himself ever returning to a clean bill of health and limited his extent of fight choreography although it didn't seem to slow his drive. He expressed in an early 1983 interview that Asian actors were underrepresented in the U.S. and Europe, and he saw much potential abroad. Hollywood had taken notice of the "Fu Sheng craze," as it was coined in a July '76 Variety article, and according to a good friend, a representative from Warner Brothers had reached out to him. His career was on the uptick and Alex didn't want to lose sight of that by withdrawing to a bar, drinking and playing cards, in his middle years. *Hong Kong Playboys* completed in May 1983, so Alex was exploring future directing assignments that included a new project with a popular Japanese singer.

There was a tradeoff though for this promising future — a costly one.

"The trigger was a toy. I gave this wooden toy to someone. Jenny noticed it gone and blamed me," he sighed.[3]

Alexander Fu Sheng and Jenny Tseng. The darlings of Hong Kong show biz. In the late spring of '83, their careers were sky rocketing, they owned multiple properties and businesses, and efforts in starting a family made it seem like nothing could derail this union. Regrettably, being in the perpetual public eye put an unmeasurable amount of stress on the couple and the facade of normalcy was finally exposed. Alex confessed he and Jenny had numerous squabbles and did their best to keep it from the prying eyes of the masses. While many assumed the celebrated couple were immune to the everyday problems of the commoner, they were in fact just as human as the next person and susceptible to the doldrums of married life. What seemed to Alex as just another fight proved to be not so routine,

"After the fight, I watched TV alone thinking everything would return to normal. Whenever Jenny argued with me in the past, she mentioned divorce, so I was so used to it. However, when I went back to the bedroom, she had packed a suitcase for me. She was serious this time."[4]

Alex refused to tuck tail and run. He picked up his bag and made an ominous statement as he exited their Clear Water Bay home,

"Once I walk through this door, don't think I'll ever come back."[5]

The actor moved in with elder brother Edmund Leung-Sing in Mei Foo Sun Cheun, while Jenny opted to leave the colony and traveled alone to the States.[6] She hoped the distance would be a distracter but the news of the power couple's separation rapidly became public. Good friends, Steven Liu Chia-Chang and wife Chen Chen, attempted to get the pair to reconcile but Alex refused to meet.[7] He instead decided to air his personal grievances with a reporter which became known as "The 28 Reasons." In prior interviews, Alex spoke kindly of his wife to the press, even coming to her defense, stating he admired how she took care of their finances and that his small allowance was never an issue. This time though Alex made it clear he was quite bitter about that arrangement.

"For a grown man, a few dollars a day isn't enough. I like to play snooker with Yee Tung-Sing but I always have to let others pay the bill. That doesn't suit me so I begged Jenny for $5000 pocket money. Although

it's in my pocket now, I still don't have the freedom to use it."[8]

Jenny admitted that, at the beginning of their separation, she longed for Alex to come home. As the days turned to weeks, her emotions cooled and was quick to defend herself after Alex's expose went public. Jenny remarked that a husband should always be the responsible party for the domestic expenses, no matter how much the wife made, but felt it best if she oversaw their budget. Even though she managed the household finances, she made it clear she wasn't frivolous on her own needs.

Matters of finances were just one of Alex's many grievances in how Jenny influenced him. He recanted how he kept a pager so she could locate him at any given time. The actor routinely handed it over to the make-up artist while on set, but as luck would have it, it was turned off by accident one day and Jenny was unable to reach him. When Alex went home that evening and tried to explain the situation, he fought a losing battle.

"She knows where I go. I'm on the set or at a friend's. If I don't have to work at night, I'm home by eleven. I've never been to any clubs. Once, I forgot to tell her I was going out, and got scolded. Next day, she was out till 3 in the morning and wouldn't let me ask her where she'd been."[9]

While the 28 Reasons possibly pained Alex, rumors of his infidelity truly wounded Jenny. A few years' prior, tales of relationships with singer Sally Yeh and a designer named Niu Yen Yeng were splattered across the tabloids. When *Hong Kong Playboys* started production, Jenny had to tolerate reports of Alex and co-star Cherie Chung, as well as, other beauty pageant contestants. Alex admitted he befriended Cally Kwong, but only after the couple separated, and strongly objected to claims he and Winnie Chin Wai-Yee were involved in anything other a platonic relationship. It became so bad for Chin Wai-Yee that her parents were ready to ship her off to the States after scandals of an abortion circulated.[10] The actress insisted upon staying quiet, but that only fueled speculation, and eventually broke her silence.

"Sheng Fu and I aren't close at all. When we're filming, we would all eat together but limit ourselves to topics between friends. To be quite frank, he never talked about his marital issues or wanting to date me."[11]

Fu Sheng's family had noticed Alex wasn't happy for a long time and one childhood pal commented that Alex had "left them" during the time he was with Jenny. He was there physically but not the same. When the couple separated, Alex came back to his friends and family and reverted to his normal self. According to a close colleague, the film star's finances were now independent and he could finally do whatever he desired. Alex was looking to invest his latest $500,000 paycheck and one option was a snooker club with his older brother and two associates.

The model couple, as they were known in the industry, met for the final time on Friday, July 1. Alas, it was at a law firm to discuss the divorce proceedings. Alex lamented,

"Among these years I've endured much, although we've had happy moments. When she treats someone well, how good it is, is unimaginable. But sometimes when she goes too far, no man can put up with it."[12]

The husband and wife were co-owners of an international company and held various assets and properties that needed to be divided. The singer employed five lawyers and revealed that both sides agreed on the terms of divorce. If their case was accepted by the court, they could divorce without further ado and not wait for two years of separation. Jenny commented,

"In the seven years of marriage, there's a lot to calculate. We can distribute our assets equally or he can take what he's earned. If Alex truly needs it, I instructed my lawyer to give him my last cent."[13]

Wednesday, July 6. Jenny and her younger sister flew to Japan with plans to stay there for several days. Meanwhile, Alex was invited by a family friend for 18 holes at the newly opened Clear Water Bay Golf & Country Club. The actor recently took up the game and showed great potential, plus the soothing environment of the fairway alleviated the stress of his hectic workload. Unfortunately for Alex, he had to decline as he was required to appear at San Po Kong Court that morning. Alex had been charged with reckless driving on May 29, after two officers observed him at high speeds at the junction of Hiram's Highway and Clear Water Bay Road. He pleaded not guilty, accepting the lesser charge of careless driving, and was fined $1000 and disqualified from holding a license for one month.

Later that evening, Alex and his older brother Horatio Chun-Sing went to the members-only club for a meal and tennis. Around 10pm, David Cheung and Shaw actor Wong Yu joined them. Alex needed to be at the

Tsuen Wan Bowling Centre by 11:30pm for an outdoor shoot but wasn't in any rush.[14] The bowling alley was a 45-minute drive, and he's typically not required on the set right away. Once the restaurant closed, the foursome left the club in two separate cars and headed out into the night.

Clear Water Bay is a rugged peninsula in the southeastern part of the New Territories and the polar opposite to the congested streets of downtown Kowloon. The rural expanse is fringed by a country park on its eastern shore and peppered with an abundance of beaches, rocky inlets, and higgledy-piggledy villages. A narrow two-lane road cuts through the southern tip of the area with cliffs on the west side and the bay to the east. This is Tai Au Mun Road.[15] Initiating at the club, it can be a treacherous lane with limited visibility as it dips and winds through the lush green vegetation and breathtaking views of the inlet.

David and Wong Yu were first to start off, in Wong's Honda Civic, while Alex and Horatio followed in the star's Porsche 911. As Alex's license was suspended, he took to the passenger side and let his brother drive. Horatio had driven the two-seater a few times prior but Alex had recently retrofitted the engine and added racing tires. The Porsche's windows were rolled down, as they hadn't turned on the air-conditioner, and enjoying the bay breeze. The hum of the rubber on the road drowned out the night noises of the rural vastness.

The brothers drove for several minutes and were well behind the Civic. The drops and turns impeded their line of sight as they made their way towards the Tai Au Mun Bus Terminal at the Clear Water Bay Second Beach. The street lights were off, as they were usually turned on just for weekends or holidays, but the road was dry and no other traffic was entering the Porsche's path. The lane curved to the right and then to left as the first sign of light was from the approaching bus terminus. The sports car, which has a top speed of 160mph, swerved through the bends in the road but the vehicle overcompensated and the driver was unable to maintain control. The Porsche plowed into a concrete post, flipped, and slammed against the hillside. Fiberglass and paint collided with concrete and rock. The horrendous impact was thunderous and decisive.

The Honda slowed upon hearing the screeching sounds of the Porsche careening into the hillside. David and Wong turned back as several witnesses converged on the wreckage. The Flachbau front end was collapsed like an accordion and the 911's tires all face skyward. The windscreen and windows had exploded as parts of the vehicle were plastered onto the rocky slope. A shaken Alex, who was not wearing his seatbelt, crawled out of the wreck and his first concern was if his face suffered any cuts or bruises.[16] A trickle of blood dripped from the corner of his eye. His head went into a spin as the reality of what just occurred came crashing down. A stunned Wong Yu recalled,

"I could see the high beams of his car in the rear-view mirror. In the middle of the drive, they switched to dipped beams. Later, I noticed there were no beams. The Porsche wasn't following anymore. I turned around and when I arrived at the scene, Fu Sheng's face was turning white."[17]

Emergency vehicles soon arrived at the crash site. A crowd had now gathered as Alex and Horatio were rushed off to the Accident and Emergency unit of Kwun Tong United Christian Hospital. Alex's heartbeat allegedly ceased during the eight-mile trip as the paramedics did their best to stabilize him. The ambulance reached the hospital where the ER staff administered a cardiotonic injection and initiated an extensive blood transfusion. Alex was suffering from severe internal hemorrhaging, and despite the massive amounts of blood, the medical team's attempts to contain the bleeding continued to prove unsuccessful.

Thursday, July 7. The Cheungs arrived at the hospital shortly after midnight. Mona Fong, Wong Jing, and actor Patrick Tse Yin joined the family in the early morning hours. Alex's father, a man who triumphed over many obstacles in his life, now found himself in a position he could not control. Cheung Yan-lung displayed a gesture of hopelessness as his weeping wife choked back tears. The staff was concerned she would not be able to cope with the devastating situation, and the lead physician felt it best if she didn't see her son in his current state. The Cheungs had no choice but to put their fate in the surgeons and pray for a positive outcome.

The hands on the clock in the waiting room crept forward. Each second was an eternity of the deepest lament and hope. His parents' minds raced to remember. A lively boy. A rebellious teen. A successful man. To the world, he was Fu Sheng. Favored son of Chang Cheh. Star of Shaw Brothers Studio. To Angela and Benton, he was their cherished ninth child.

He was their Alex. At 3:43am, the head surgeon came with just a shake of his head. His parents understood. Alexander Cheung Fu-Sheng was dead.

---

[1] Chung's father-in-law was Chu Shu-hwa, a pioneer in Hong Kong's Mandarin-language film industry, who co-founded Great China Film Company, Yung Hwa Motion Picture Industries, and assisted in establishing International Films Distributing Agency which was later restructured as MP&GI. In 1966, he left MP&GI for Shaw Brothers, launching its official magazine "Hong Kong Movie News" as Editor-in-Chief and supervising its actors' training program.
[2] Southern Screen Dec 1982: 20-21.
[3] See Web and More, "Fu Sing & Yan Nei," page 21.
[4] Ibid.
[5] Ibid.
[6] Mei Foo Sun Cheun is a large private housing estate in Lai Chi Kok, Kowloon which was a half hour drive from the couple's home.
[7] Steven Liu was the composer for Heaven and Hell (1980).
[8] See Web and More, "Fu Sing & Yan Nei," page 21.
[9] Ibid., 23.
[10] First runner-up in the 1982 Miss Hong Kong Pageant.
[11] See Web and More, "Fu Sing & Yan Nei," page 23.
[12] Ibid., 21.
[13] Ibid., 23.
[14] Tsuen Wan Bowling Centre was also used during the production of Hong Kong Playboys (1983).
[15] Many reports list the accident occurring on Clearwater Bay Road when in fact it was Tai Au Mun Road. The possible reason for this error is that Tai Au Mun was built in 1982/83 for the opening of Clearwater Bay Club. The road was very new, simply an extension of the Clearwater Bay Road, and some reporters at that time didn't discern them as separate roads.
[16] Seatbelt legislation was announced on July 7, 1982 (one year before Alex's death) but would not go into effect until October 1983.
[17] See Web and More, One Step Beyond (1992)

23

The Funeral of Fu Sheng

Tokyo. Jenny began to receive phone messages in the early dawn hours from family members. She was initially in denial of the accident, until several calls were received, in which the singer and her sister hurriedly packed and rushed to Narita Airport. Their JL001 flight landed at Kai Tak around 9:40pm on Thursday where Run Run Shaw and members of the press greeted them. While reporters crowded the mogul for an update, the diversion allowed Jenny to sneak off through another exit. She was dressed all in white and wore large black sunglasses. One reporter, who caught a glimpse of her before she disappeared into the night, remarked that Jenny looked as if she had died as well. Unknown to her, Alex's body had already been moved to the mortuary and there was confusion as to where his remains were stored. This only exasperated the situation for Jenny.

"I wanted to see Alex but my family didn't allow me. There were many drawers at the mortuary but I didn't know which one Alex was kept in. I was screaming and shouting for him but he wouldn't show himself."[1]

Friday, July 8. Jenny was fully aware of the circumstances of how she and Alex parted company and the difficulties the couple were facing. Now, it seemed so trivial. She affirmed that Alex was still the single most important person in her world and her heart was completely shattered. The widow returned to the mortuary Friday morning after a sleepless night. Rows and rows of entombed bodies lie in the catacomb of drawers as the staff directed her to the location of her beloved Alex. Jenny paused to gather her thoughts.

"He lied there calmly as if he were sleeping. I touched his face and he was cold. Ice cold. I laid on his body, face to face, and asked him why he left without a word. I could feel that he was crying too. His brother said it was just moisture seeping from his eyes. But I didn't want to believe it."[2]

The news of Alex's death spread across the colony like wild fire and sent shockwaves throughout the entertainment industry. Production came to a halt at Movietown as 120 staff members assisted with the funeral proceedings. Lau Kar-fai recalled how he was awakened by a phone call in the middle of the night with the grave news. He stated what many were feeling: Disbelief. Denial. Bargaining. Guilt. Anger. Depression.

"Little Sheng didn't have any untreatable illness or confined to his bed. He used to be healthy and strong. It was just too hard to accept."[3]

Saturday, July 9. Alex's elder brother initially went to United Christian but was later transferred to the ICU at Hong Kong Baptist Hospital in fair condition. Horatio Chun-Sing regained consciousness that Saturday and spoke with Jenny. He recalled leaving the country club but believed the cars weren't racing and traveling less than 25mph. Nothing appeared out of the ordinary until they drew closer to the bus stop. That's where his tale took a turn for the otherworldly.

One sensationalized report at the time alleges that a strong gust kicked up and it felt as if a spirit forced Horatio's right foot down onto the accelerator.[4] He was paralyzed and unable to move his leg. Panicked, he turned to Alex whose gaze was on a group of shadows. Alex turned to his elder brother and stated he was going on a trip with the spirits. Horatio attempted to drag his foot away from the accelerator, losing his leather shoe in the process, and struggled to take control of the vehicle. Moments later, the Porsche careened into the hillside.

While skeptics find this recounting questionable, there were multiple sightings of Alex after that fatal evening. Some residents swore they witnessed a young man, who fit Fu Sheng's description, jogging with his head down at night. When the observers moved towards the jogger, to better identify him, the elusive vision receded into the shadows. An elderly man also said he saw the ghost of Alex three days after the accident. He commented that the film star was driving his white Porsche around the bend and then abruptly vanished without explanation.[5]

Over the weekend, the post mortem exam came into question. It wasn't customary to perform an autopsy in a fatal traffic accident and the Coroner's Court of Hong Kong would decide on a case-by-case basis. When Alex's file reached the assigned coroner's desk, his phone began to ring off the hook. Legislator Maria Tam was among several prominent legal and civic individuals who contacted Ian Polson to dissuade the post mortem. The opposing parties stated the family was hoping to forgo the exam as they had a superstition that the body must be buried intact. Coroner Polson remarked to the author,

"It seemed there could be some civil litigation arising from this death. That being the case, I felt drugs or alcohol may be a factor and an examination should be done to investigate that possibility. I couldn't help suspect someone was trying to cover up or conceal something."[6]

Tuesday, July 12. After some delays, the autopsy was performed on Monday the 11th, and the next day, the post mortem report by Dr. Simon at United Christian was released. The pathologist noted that a road construction team was in the process of erecting a metal gate at the bottom of the hill where Alex's vehicle impacted. Two steel rails had been placed on the side of the curb and the automobile struck the poles at an angle which caused the car to flip. The Porsche slant nose turbo had its battery located under the dashboard of the passenger side which became dislodged during the collision. The report revealed extensive injuries to Alex's upper right torso, including a collapsed lung and a ruptured liver, which caused severe hemorrhaging.

Some sources close to the crash investigation stated the post mortem was inconclusive on establishing the driver and the police were still investigating the matter. Solicitor Fred Lee conveyed that the Cheung family was satisfied with the autopsy findings, and if the coroner decided an inquest was required, they wouldn't oppose it despite their initial objections to the post mortem. Nearly six days since the accident, Horatio's condition upgraded from fair to stable. This was welcoming news to the family as they prepared for Thursday's burial ceremony.

Wednesday, July 13. It is a traditional belief that the soul of a crash victim leaves the body and wanders about the scene of the accident. David Cheung and elder brother Edmund Leung-Sing arrived at the crash site that morning to partake in a Taoist ritual to locate Alex's spirit. David was outfitted by the priest with white mourning clothes and a soul-summoning flag to lead Alex back to the funeral parlor. Abundant sunshine basked the area throughout the morning but all that changed once the ceremony commenced. The sky turned dark as the priest chanted the spells to evoke the spirit of the departed. The rays of sun turned to drops of rain as a chilled wind kicked up. The crowd of onlookers shivered in the downpour as the 15-minute ritual concluded.

Back in Hung Hom, the final touches were set in place for the next day's service. An overabundance of wreaths spilled out of the Universal Funeral Parlor and onto the city pavement. As per tradition, members of the family stayed with Alex to protect his body, and Ti Lung had the bittersweet honor of spending the night to guard the corpse of his best friend. Cheung Yan-lung and wife Angela said their final goodbyes to their beloved son this day, as it was customary for elders to not attend the funeral of the younger generation. It was an emotional evening for all those present as the funeral parlor echoed Angela's repetitive sobs of *"I want my Alex back."*[7]

Thursday, July 14. As early as 6:00am, a few dozen onlookers had already lined the street across from the funeral home. The numbers grew as the morning progressed and authorities estimated upwards of 3000 people descended upon Cheong Hang Road. More than fifty uniformed officers were posted to keep the multitudes behind barricades as hundreds of relatives, friends, and co-workers filtered into the parlor's largest hall. The press would later report that the colony had not seen such a funeral turnout since the equally untimely death of Bruce Lee.

Inside the parlor, rows of mourners sat in remorse, shock, and hopelessness as a steady stream of people filed into the great hall to say their last farewells. Alex's preferred portrait hung at the center of the room while a trio of large banners displayed the words, "Loss of Talent," "A Wise Man Has Passed," and "A Super Star Has Fallen." All of Alex's beloved foods were staged on a banquet table in front of his portrait. Chinese steamed rice noodle rolls, beef mince ball, instant noodles, and even a pack of Marlboro Reds. Chang Cheh was especially heartbroken and composed a poem for his late apprentice. Loosely translated it read, *"Losing a great son of mine made my hair turn white in one day. Like a broken piece of jade or star no longer in the galaxy."*[8]

The funeral service began at 11:00am and brother David was responsible for the Dam Fan Mai Shui.[9] Alex was dressed in a white suit with heavy makeup though a bruise could still be noticed on the right side of his face. When the monk asked Jenny to kowtow three times in front of the coffin, the singer couldn't contain her emotions, so others assisted her as she offered her final respects. Jenny's wailing triggered several onlookers to become caught up in the moment and found themselves grieving with the new widow.

"I don't always like this world. But Alex, he loved his life. He was interested in everything around him. Why—why God is so unfair to take away his life . . . but leave me alive!?"[10]

The service took under an hour and the family departed around noon as the monk performed his final chants and rituals. Alex's coffin was accompanied by his good friends and trusted co-workers. The men who answered the call were Lam Fai-Wong, Wong Jing, Wang Lung-Wei, Nat Chan Pak-Cheung, Lam Kai-tai, Hui Jun-ling, Liu Ho-yi, and Chan Chak-mu. The pallbearers carried the departed outside to the waiting hearse as the ceremony moved to the Cape Collinson Crematorium in Tai Tam.

When all the parties arrived at the crematory, the eight men transported Fu Sheng to the burning pavilion. Alex's relatives burned incense and paper money as the priest rhythmically struck a muyu with a wooden stick. He recanted Buddhist chants that state we are born and die with nothing in our hands, which implies that life is but a process and death is inescapable. The mourners then splashed wine onto coins so the enchanted monies could untie the knots of the soul and drive away evil spirits. When the soul was freed from the netherworld, the ceremony came to an end. David paused, took a heavy breath, and reached out for the furnace button. With a single finger stroke, Alex's remains inched forward into the incinerator.

After the coffin was consumed, the family removed their white ceremonial clothes and tossed them into the fire. Alex had been living in Meifoo just before he died, so they proceeded there to complete the worshipping ritual. Jenny continued to suffer from severe stomach cramps throughout the day, and after the service her relatives took her back to Taipei to recover. It was the end of a grim day of an extremely gloomy week that many preferred not to reflect on. A family member lamented,

"It's such a sad day. If only he had lived. He was always there to *cheer things up when we were down and give us words of comfort."*[11]

Fu Sheng was an auto fanatic as many of his friends confirmed. He drove numerous sports cars and the walls of his Shaw dressing room were adorned with photographs of auto racing vehicles. Alex's passion for the fast lane caught up with him multiple times, with several convictions for speeding, but he continued to drive at excessive speeds. This factor, coupled with the case that his license was suspended just 12 hours before the crash, rose many questions on who was driving the wrecked 911.

On August 21, the coroner upheld the results of the police report and confirmed that Alex was not the driver. His brother instead was charged with careless driving, and on December 9, a magistrate decided his fate. The Honorable Gerard Muttrie concluded there was evidence the 911 was travelling upwards of 50mph but this was not a reckless speed. The magistrate determined Horatio Chun-Sing had been punished enough by the death of his brother and dismissed all charges. This was a great relief to the family who already suffered so much.

Back at Movietown, the passing of one of their most treasured left a demoralizing void across the studio. Fu Sheng's Dressing Room H was converted into a shrine and the management forbade its use unless David Cheung was at the studio for shooting. Run Run Shaw also erected a stone cenotaph at the crash site bearing inscriptions adapted from a Buddhist prayer.[12] According to the mogul, it was to serve as a memorial to the actor and a reminder to motorists to drive safely. The six characters inscribed on the cenotaph are part of a Buddhist chant (Namo Amituofo) for the deceased and a greeting among the monks. Amituofo is the common salutation of the Shaolin Temple disciples and lay practitioners and an important part of their culture. *Wits of the Brats* co-star and close friend Wong Yu reflected on Alex's absence from the studio lot.

"I pretend as if he's emigrated to a country far away. Many people who move overseas never come back. I don't want to believe he is dead."[13]

Fu Sheng's unexpected departure left a handful of projects in limbo, and some had to be terminated. One such film was Wong Jing's tentatively titled *The Tricksters*. The director abandoned the production believing no one could replace little Sheng. Another endeavor canceled was the joint Shaw-Japanese musical comedy in which Alex was to co-star with Hideki

Saijo. There were also two partially finished films that had to be addressed. Wong took over directorial duties on *Wits of the Brats* and shot the remaining sequences while *The 8 Diagram Pole Fighter* went on a lengthy hiatus as Lau Kar-Leung needed time to come to terms with the death of his favored student. His master wept,

"After I heard of the news of little Sheng's death, I was shocked and couldn't believe it was true. How could the life of such a cute, energetic, and strong boy be so fragile?"[14]

The night Lau received news of the accident, he and an unnamed actress immediately went to the hospital in separate vehicles. They proceeded north on Prince Margaret Road when they happened upon an earlier wreck. Lau nor the actress had enough time to brake and both collided at the accident scene, but luckily for them, no one else was injured. Lau inevitably shut down production on *Disciples of the 36th Chamber (1985)* as well and mourned for nearly two months.

Shooting resumed on *The 8 Diagram Pole Fighter* at Studio #10 in the first week of September. The cast and crew gathered outside where they set up an incense table with offerings of roasted pork, chicken, cans of cola, and cigarette packs. They prepared joss papers hoping Fu Sheng's spirit would give blessings to this unfinished work. Lau tried to light the incense sticks but each time his attempt failed. He put on a slight scowl, looked down, and muttered under his breath, *"Be serious. Don't play anymore!"*[15] Though it may seem farfetched, the sticks lit up without a hitch on the next match strike. The director told reporters,

"I hope we can finish the movie as soon as possible. We'll try our best to perfect it, so the audience can see the charisma of little Sheng again. I believe he will be satisfied too."[16]

Leading actor Lau Kar-fai also found it a challenge to get back into routine when the project began anew. Lee Tai-Hang took over aspects of the action, much of the crew had changed, plus there were rumors that the Jinsha Beach scene was cursed. Believers stated it depicted the massacre of the male Yangs which was an actual omen to Alex's untimely death. Lau Kar-fai admitted it was a popular tale at the time as the showbiz community in Hong Kong struggled to accept that their most charmed was no more.

"Everybody loved Fu Sheng. He was a genuine trickster on and off the set and often joked about the supernatural. But nobody really knows if that had anything to do with his death."[17]

Alex's passing brought another major problem for his old master, as for how the movie could complete without the departed star. The original ending was much more light-hearted as Fu Sheng and Lau Kar-fai's characters reunited and defeated the treacherous leader of the Liao Army. But now, Alex's character would vanish mid-film without explanation as the revised finale assigned emphasis on Yang 5th brother and Yang 8th sister; played by Hui Ying-hung.

"The director rewrote all of Fu Sheng's part for me," Hui explained. *"Fu Sheng is the one who worked with me on my first day of work [The Brave Archer] thus he was very significant. My heart ached in every scene where I was playing his part. I was determined to help him finish it."*[18]

Lau Kar-Leung's plot change provided a touch of bitter melancholy, as the emotional strain of their lost team member weighed heavily on the production crew's hearts. The climax challenged the cast's physical limits which made them feel like they had braved weeks of hard-labor. Lau Kar-fai disclosed that in a few of the more emotive scenes *"some of the tears were real"* for his fallen co-star.[19] The project wrapped Halloween 1983, and the following February, *The 8 Diagram Pole Fighter* raked in nearly $3.8 million. Reviewer Keith Allison, who compiled the early internet Shaw Brothers Movie FAQ, summarized the final product as,

"...an explosion of emotion: anger, frustration, disappointment, madness, confusion, and maybe a little hope. The humor Lau often used is non-existent. The compassion is lost in the madness of the situation as the characters are swept up in the uncontrollable firestorm of rage. It is bleak, depressing, and ultimately open-ended."[20]

Wong Jong would finalize *Wits of the Brats* two days before Christmas 1983. The film became the concluding picture featuring the late, Alexander Fu Sheng. With his big brother now gone, co-star David Cheung called it quits soon thereafter. His last movie, *This Man Is Dangerous (1985),* was a modern crime drama by Wang Lung-Wei that released March 16, 1985.

Alas, by this point, Shaw Brothers Studio too was nearing an end.

Asia's largest film production company subsequently restructured its resources into television broadcasting after producing several hundred movies over the previous quarter century. With its favorite son gone and the population's viewing habits changing, Movietown's own coffin also appeared nailed shut.

---

[1] Cinemart 164 Aug 1983: 24-25.
[2] Ibid.
[3] Southern Screen Sept 1983: 55.
[4] Yuk Long TV Weekly 304 Jul 1983: 10-11.
[5] Some locals have coined this part of Tai Au Mun as "Fu Sheng Bend."
[6] "Ian Polson and the post mortem." Personal interview. 6 Jan. 2015.
[7] Yuk Long TV Weekly 304 Jul 1983: 9.
[8] Ibid., 7.
[9] Chinese funeral ritual that a male relative of the departed will carry a flag and help the deceased to enter heaven.
[10] Cinemart 164 Aug 1983: 24-25.
[11] Facebook post.
[12] GPS coordinates: 22°17'12.8"N 114°17'12.4"E.
[13] Southern Screen Sept 1983: 73.
[14] Ibid, 22.
[15] Ibid.
[16] Ibid., 23.
[17] The 8 Diagram Pole Fighter (1984). Dir. Lau Kar-Leung. 2004. DVD (insert), Region 3 IVL.
[18] See Film Reviews and Interviews, "Kara Hui Exclusive Interview - My Young Auntie."
[19] See Film Reviews and Interviews, "Gordon Liu Chia Hui."
[20] See Film Reviews and Interviews, "Movie Reviews Eight Diagram Pole Fighter."

24

Jenny after Alex

The couple's Clear Water Bay home reminded Jenny too much of Alex. That summer, she took up residence near the Governor's house and strived to patch the pieces of her broken heart. She shunned the spotlight for several months but it proved a daunting task. The gossip columnists had a free-for-all dissecting their private lives and the events leading to their separation and impending divorce. The tabloids portrayed Jenny as a domineering wife whom Alex was unable to tame.

The following January, Jenny emerged from her isolation and returned to the stage for a charity concert at New York City's Lincoln Center for the Performing Arts. The Avery Fisher Hall event, hosted by New York journalist Kaity Tong, was a much-needed boost of confidence to help Jenny return to the Hong Kong scene. As part of her comeback, CBS-HK released her latest album to coincide with her Spring '84 concerts. This new album contained the poignant song, "Lonely Again," causing the seasoned singer to well up on stage mid-performance, when the memories of her beloved Alex came crashing in.[1]

The next three years proved to be a blessing for the singer as her career rekindled with multiple hits and sold out shows. However, nothing compared to the news of the small miracle she made public in early 1987. Jenny announced she was pregnant, and on July 7 in the United States, gave birth to a daughter. Despite previous misfortunes, the songstress beamed that baby Melody clung to her, and after the birth, announced that her daughter was a gift from God. Jenny kept the identity of the father a secret, much to the irritation of the paparazzi press, and only revealed that he was a married man.

With Jenny's latest album *Cold Autumn* on top of the Hong Kong pop charts, the new mother had a full slate of promotions, TV appearances, concerts, and recordings. She also continued to invest in various businesses and became manager to singer Linda Wong Hin Ping, daughter of *One-Armed Swordsman* Jimmy Wang Yu. This relationship terminated in 1994 after a bitter lawsuit over mismanagement, and without fail, the tabloids once more meddled into Jenny's private life. This time, with a daughter at home, Jenny decided that enough was enough. The singer packed her bags and took Melody to the U.S. where she maintained a relatively low profile for the remainder of the decade. Jenny commented on her semi-retirement,

"I did the cleaning, washing, scrubbing and cooking at home; the whole nine yards. Since Melody was still young, I wanted to make sure she was brought up in the right manner."[2]

When Melody turned 13, she encouraged her mom to take back the mic. She knew her mother was a natural stage performer and should do what she loves best. Jenny headed back to the colony to perform in the Hui Wong Charity Concerts at the Hong Kong Coliseum, and a few months after, held three sold out concerts that marked her official comeback. As for Melody, who was under the care of her aunts in Taiwan while her mother rekindled her career, the identity of her father remained a mystery. In a 2005 interview, Jenny commented on her miscarriages with Alex and how the final one caused her to be bedridden for five months.

"We went through various checkups so I could conceive. When my husband suddenly passed, I felt like dying. I needed a child and was grateful when I got my wish. It's because of her that I've had the courage to live on for the past 18 years."[3]

Publicly, Jenny remained closed lip as to the father's identify, but it was alleged she confided in a good friend; Taiwanese singer Chen Ying-chieh. Stories would continue to circulate over the next several years, and it wasn't until a 2011 Mingpao interview in which the identity of the mystery man became known. The following year, Jenny appeared as a guest on the Taiwanese talk show, *Mei Wei Sheng Huo*, where she confirmed for the cameras who the father was — none other than her late husband, Fu Sheng.

Skeptics were quick to pick apart her revelation pointing out that Alex died four years before Melody's birth. Jenny defended the inconsistency by clarifying that many martial arts actors were concerned they might be rendered impotent due to perilous work conditions. As a precaution, some had their sperm frozen in the off-chance a tragedy were to occur. Sperm cryopreservation had been around as early as the 1940s, when cattle breeders and veterinarians refined the process of cryopreserving bull semen and artificially inseminating heifers. In the 1950s, the methods for cryopreserving human semen and artificial insemination were improved until scientists produced the first human births.

Despite her explanation, doubters remained unconvinced and believed the truth had yet to be told. Jenny was engaged in 1985-86 and there was the lingering question of whether her ex-fiancé, Yong Bing Leung, could be the father. Others though were elated by the announcement that their beloved star lived on through Melody, who eventually relocated to Manhattan and graduated from Parsons, The New School for Design. While it remains to be seen if irrefutable evidence will ever come to light, dispelling all doubts, the reality of the situation is that Jenny loves her daughter no matter what the public believes.

As for Jenny, her later years were split between her career, enthralling fans with concerts across the globe, and developing an organic farm in Taoyuan, Taiwan. In 2012, she reflected in an interview,

"I made my debut at 17 and it feels just like yesterday that I had to divide my time between studying and recording. As I age, I find that material wealth isn't what matters the most. It's being able to do what you like and being surrounded by friends and family."[4]

Despite her hectic schedule, Jenny and daughter Melody always made time to return to Fanling and visit Alex's burial site at Fung Ying Seen Koon.[5] Though the couple have been apart for over three decades, there is still a precious bond between them that only Jenny and Alex will truly ever understand.

"His death has affected me very deeply because, despite the impending separation, he still has a place in my heart. It does not change anything as long as I live. Yes, I still love him in my own special way."[6]

---

[1] Adapted from Taiwanese songstress Ouyang Fei Fei's "Love is Over."
[2] Ricky Yap. "Welcome back, Jenny!" New Straits Times [Singapore] 22 May 2000: 34.
[3] See Web and More, "Jenny Tseng's Best Friend Blurts Truth about Her Daughter."
[4] Wai Ting Loong. "Trip Down Memory Lane" New Straits Times [Singapore] 15 Dec

2012: np.

[5] Located in Fanling in the N.T., the temple is easily accessible by the East Rail Line of the Hong Kong MTR.

[6] See Web and More, Shaw Brothers Fanzine, Special Edition SB Stars # 01.

25

Fu Sheng's Legacy

Despite Movietown's historic rise and inevitable fall, the martial arts film industry forged ahead. New directors and stars from all corners of the globe vied for a share of the marketplace as the older, Shaw produced films drifted into obscurity. After their theatrical runs in the 1970s & '80s, and television syndication thereafter, Alex's movies stayed afloat thanks to a small but dedicated fan base. Once the 1990s arrived, most of the Shaw's catalog appeared lost, and those that survived were on life-support via bootlegged VHS tapes. Glorious Shawscope imagery was now hacked with slip shoddy edits, laughable Anglicized dubbing, and indistinct subtitles from generation loss. The broadcasted versions of these magnificent films were bludgeoned into a pan and scan format where the widescreen vision of the filmmaker was constricted to an unforgiving, "edited for television" 4:3 format. Times were bleak for fans.

Back in Hong Kong, the Shaw Brothers Studio vaults were closed to the public. Reels of film stock sat in rusting canisters in forgotten storage rooms. The once beloved movies fell into various states of decay as each year of neglect passed, and nothing short of a miracle would salvage these archives. Then the new millennium came and the Pan-Asian company, Celestial Pictures Ltd., made a welcoming revelation. They revealed that 760 Shaw films were to undergo a state-of-the-art digitization process and become available for the first time on DVD and VCD formats. The restoration procedure would take three years and involve a team of three dozen professionals working around-the-clock to restore the visual and sound quality of each frame from the Shaw library. CEO William Pfeiffer proudly announced,

"Celestial Pictures is honored to launch the Shaw Brothers library in the restored digital format. Modern audiences worldwide will now have a unique opportunity to own these masterpieces of Chinese cinema."[1]

Starting in late 2002, film spectators across the planet were set to experience the magic of Shaw Brothers Studio once again. For the first time ever, fans could now own a comprehensive set of Alex's 43 produced films in remastered quality; some which hadn't been seen since their initial release. Despite his untimely death, Movietown hadn't forgotten their beloved son and neither had his fans, friends, or family. A close relative of Alex commented on Facebook,

"Good people tend to die young. I don't think he would enjoy growing old and grey like me. He helped me to see life and death as just the process of life in which none can escape. It's more important to live a life that's full of adventure, than bale out at an old age in a nursing home."[2]

In more recent years, the fate of Shaw Brothers Studio has been up in the air. For more than a decade, Shaw Brothers and the SCMP Group, co-owner of the site, failed to win over Hong Kong's Town Planning Board to develop the property. If they had their way, the Clear Water Bay location would have been converted into a 750-unit low-rise luxury residential project. In May 2014, TVB owner Charles Chan sold Shaw Brothers Studio to Shanghai-based conglomerate Fosun International. The price tag was reported to be $1.5 billion though the exact figure has not been disclosed. That November, real estate developers were given permission to renovate the area for commercial purposes but withdrew their plans the following year, after the Antiquities Advisory Board classified Movietown as a Grade 1 Historical site.

With the deaths of Lau Kar-Leung in 2013, Run Run Shaw the following year, and Mona Fong in 2017, the bright lights of Movietown continue to ebb into the shadows. The studio has long been labeled by its detractors as a film factory that subjected its talent to low wages and lengthy contracts. They asserted that the staff was constrained by the cookie-cutter studio system which stifled their personal and creative freedom. Some talent was so embittered they broke their contracts (Lo Lieh, Jimmy Wang Yu, King Hu), fled to create new companies (Leonard Ho), or just refused to sign because of tight-fistedness (Bruce Lee). However, many Shaw veterans saw it differently.

Ti Lung recalled those early days as a paradise in which the Shaw stables provided him horse-riding lessons in the hills behind the studio.[3]

Chiang Da-Wei agreed and commented that, in exchange for so-called freedom, the actors were provided with a sense of security, while Hui Ying-hung likened herself to a flower in a greenhouse. Once they parted company, they realized Movietown was family and missed the sanctuary it provided. Lau Kar-fai said he saw Run Run Shaw as a father figure while Lily Li admired how the Shaws made their make-believe worlds feel true-to-life. Cheng Pei-Pei verbalized her memories with a metaphor of how a lone, young tree from her early days was now mature when she returned for *Painted Faces (1988)*. She likened it to seeing a child all grown up after many years of absence.

Despite Movietown's recent classification as a protected estate, the future of the cinema graveyard is still uncertain as of this writing. While grading determines the heritage value of historic buildings, the grading system is merely an administrative exercise as opposed to actual law. Even buildings with grade one status, the highest level on the government's heritage grading system, are not safe from demolition by the property's owners. A grim reminder of this came to pass in the summer of 2016 for the studio's most sacred shrine. While Dressing Room H had endured for 33 years, construction workers dismantled the long-standing memorial of Alexander Fu Sheng that June. There was no announcement. Zero fanfare.

Although this may be the end of our commemorated journey of the life and times of Alexander Fu Sheng, and the aftermath of his untimely passing, his spirit will carry on for decades to come through the magic of cinema. Thanks to the preservation efforts by Celestial Pictures Ltd., a new generation of film lovers will discover the thrilling world of Shaw Brothers and Alex's longevity on screen will survive after most of us are long gone.

"The key to immortality is first living a life worth remembering," Bruce Lee once declared.[4]

So long as Alexander remains in the hearts of his family and fans, Cheung Fu-Sheng's legacy will truly live on forever.

---

[1] See Web and More, "Celestial Pictures Presents Shaw Brothers Masterpieces Digitally Restored Starting December 5, 2002."
[2] Facebook post.
[3] See Books, Ng. Oral History Series (7): Ti Lung, page 129.
[4] The Pierre Berton Show, 9 December 1971.

Film Summaries
(in production order)

Terrence J. Brady

TITLE: The 14 Amazons

DIRECTOR: Cheng Kang, Charles Tung Shao-Yung

PRODUCER: Run Run Shaw

ACTION DIRECTOR: Ching Siu-Tung, Leung Siu-Chung

ASS'T DIRECTOR: Stanley Siu Wing

CINEMATOGRAPHER: Charles Tung Shao-Yung + 6 others

EDITOR: Chiang Hsing-Lung, Fan Kung-Ming

SCRIPT: Cheng Kang

CAST:
Lisa Lu Yan . . . . Grand Dame/She Tai Chun
Ivy Ling Po . . . . Mu Kuei Ying
Lily Ho Li-Li . . . . Yang Wen Kuan
Yueh Hua . . . . Lu Chao
Yeung Chi-Hing . . . . Minister Kou Chun
Cheng Miu . . . . Minister Wang Ching
Li Ching . . . . Yang Pa Mei
Fan Mei-Sheng . . . . General Chiao Ting Kuai
Wong Chung-Shun . . . . General Meng Huai Yuan
Lo Lieh . . . . Fifth Prince of West Hsia
Tien Feng . . . . King Wang Wen of West Hsia

RELEASE DATE: July 27, 1972

BOX OFFICE: $2,569,100 (ranked #4 for 1972)

TRIVIA: Fu Sheng appeared in cameo as a Hsia soldier

TRIVIA: Won four Golden Horse Awards in 1973

TRIVIA: 140,000 feet of celluloid was shot for this film

TRIVIA: Ching Siu-Tung's first action-director credit

"Such a cunning bitch! Looks like I've been defeated (hahaha)."

Cheng Kang directs this multi award-winning epic which features many of Hong Kong's finest actresses in Shaw Brothers Studio's most extravagant and costliest production of its time.

Set nearly a millennium ago, Commander Yang Tsung Pao is brutally slain by the Western Xia invaders during the defense of the northern frontier. The Song Emperor is reluctant to send new troops to the border and avenge this disastrous defeat, so the Yang family decides to take matters into their own hands.

Led by the clan's matriarch Grand Madame (Lisa Lu), and the widow Mu Kei Ying (Ivy Ling Po), a sorority of patriots take to arms and launch a sneak attack against Western Xia's base camp. Assisted by a runaway slave (Yueh Hua), and a small band of female warriors, the Yangs endure a series of engagements that test their courage and resolve. The Yang heroines are driven by love of country, and despite several setbacks, reach their destination as both armies engage in a gory free-for-all.

The 14 Amazons is a monumental tale of piety and patriotic sacrifice. The Yangs represent some of China's noblest patriots who believed it was their filial duty to defend the people and the land.

TITLE: The Thunderbolt Fist

DIRECTOR: Chang I-Hu (aka) Jang Il-Ho

PRODUCER: Runme Shaw

ACTION DIRECTOR: Leung Siu-Chung

ASS'T DIRECTOR: Chen Chin-Yu

CINEMATOGRAPHER: Wang Ti, Wang Tien-Yu

EDITOR: Chiang Hsing-Lung

SCRIPT: Li Cho-Chien

CAST:
Shih Szu . . . . Die Er
Chuen Yuen . . . . Fang Tie Wa
James Nam Gung-Fan . . . . . Gu Gang
Wong Gam-Fung . . . . Feng Niou
Tung Lam . . . . Da Xiong
Fang Mian . . . . Master Fang Ping Bai
Chen Feng-Chen . . . . Gu Lan
Gam Kei-Chu . . . . Gin Chi
Wong Ching-Ho . . . . Old Wang
Austin Wai Tin-Chi . . . . Tie Wa (young)
Stephen Tung Wai . . . . Gu Gang (young)

RELEASE DATE: December 30, 1972

BOX OFFICE: $217,969 (ranked #69 for 1972)

TRIVIA: Fu Sheng makes a two second cameo at 00:13:36

TRIVIA: Cameos by Bruce Leung, Tommy Lee, Sammo Hung

TRIVIA: Chiang Hsing-Lung was editor of nearly 600 films

TRIVIA: Red brick building was also used in *Boxer from Shantung*

"Run! The Japanese are coming!"

Prominent Korean director Chang I-Hu helms this 1972 basher, which addresses the Chinese struggle against the hordes of invading Japanese in the early 20th century.

In a small village of Northeast China, a vicious band of Japanese fighters terrorize the local citizens. One of the residents (Fang Mian) is a martial artist who takes up the challenge to pit himself in an open-air tournament against their leader. Master Fang Ping Bai is victorious and kills his opponent only to be murdered by the resentful Japanese.

His young son, entrusted with a secret kung fu manual, escapes to the mountains to join a group of Chinese patriots in hiding. Years pass and Fang Tie Wa (Chuen Yuen) has become a skilled fighter who returns to town to seek his vengeance. The new leader of the Japanese, Gu Gang, is the son of the man Master Fang Ping Bai had defeated years earlier. Gu Gang proves to be even more treacherous, and the finale highlights the next generation in the same arena their fathers had fought to the death.

Similar to the themes found in Jet Li's *Fearless*, Bruce Lee's *Fist of Fury,* and King Hu's *Sons of Good Earth, The Thunderbolt Fist* is a tragic affair steeped in melodrama and innocence lost.

TITLE: Young People

DIRECTOR: Chang Cheh

PRODUCER: Run Run Shaw

ACTION DIRECTOR: Tong Gai, Lau Kar-wing

ASS'T DIRECTOR: Godfrey Ho Chih Chiang, John Woo

CINEMATOGRAPHER: Kung Mu-To

EDITOR: Kwok Ting Hung

SCRIPT: Chang Cheh, Ni Kuang

CAST:
Chiang Da-Wei	Hung Wai
Ti Lung	Lam Tat
Chen Kuan-Tai	Ho Tai
Agnes Chan Mei-Ling	Po-Erh
Irene Chen Yi-Ling	Princess
Wu Ma	Gao
Chin Feng	Hung Wai's brother
Lo Dik	Basketball Couch Wong
Wong Ching	Cheung Wai Shing
Lau Kar-wing	Johnny Lau
Alexander Fu Sheng	Drum player

RELEASE DATE: July 7, 1972

BOX OFFICE: $1,223,950 (ranked #10 for 1972)

TRIVIA: Fu Sheng's first on-screen fight

TRIVIA: Gran Prix was held in Sekkong, NT over three days

TRIVIA: Filmed on location at Chung Chi College

TRIVIA: Agnes Chan Mei-Ling's intro film

"I think Princess will follow everyone . . . except Gao."

Ni Kuang co-scripts this early 1970s melodrama featuring a large cast of popular Shaw Brothers Studio performers. Shot in various locations throughout Hong Kong, Chang Cheh's vision creates a unique time-capsule of collegiate life from this bygone era.

Our tale takes place on the campus of Chung Chi College where three groups of students are divided by their interests. Hung Wai (Chiang Da-Wei) is the leader of a performing arts club that is caught in the middle of a competition between the jocks and the martial artists. Lam Tat (Ti Lung) is the basketball captain and the big-man-on-campus who finds himself at odds with Ho Tai (Chen Kuan-tai). Ho is the leader of the kung fu crew and a man of few words. Despite their differences, the warring factions come to value cooperation over rivalry in which they represent their school in an exhilarating Gran Prix event.

Young People is a docu-drama depiction of '70s college life. Sports, music, and dance are intertwined to create a good time vibe similar to the Frankie and Annette beach party movies. Filled with whimsical fluff and dated styles, the film maintains a level of innocence and charm.

TITLE: Four Riders

DIRECTOR: Chang Cheh

PRODUCER: Runme Shaw

ACTION DIRECTOR: Lau Kar-Leung, Tong Gai

ASS'T DIRECTOR: Godfrey Ho Chih Chiang, John Woo

CINEMATOGRAPHER: Kung Mu-To

EDITOR: Kwok Ting Hung

SCRIPT: Chang Cheh and Ni Kuang

CAST:
Chiang Da-Wei . . . . Jin Yi
Ti Lung. . . . . Feng Xia
Chen Kuan-Tai . . . . Li Wei-Shi
Wong Chung . . . . Gao Yin-Han
Lily Li Li-Li . . . . Wen Si
Ching Li . . . . Song Hua
Kurata Yasuaki . . . . Lei Tai
Tina Chin Fei . . . . Yin Hua
Andre Marquis . . . . Mr. Hawkes
Lo Dik . . . . Korean MP leader
Alexander Fu Sheng . . . . . . Soldier in bar

RELEASE DATE: December 22, 1972

BOX OFFICE: $1,095,137 (ranked #18 for 1972)

TRIVIA: Fu Sheng has cameos in the Hello John Bar

TRIVIA: Premiere was a midnight showing attended by Chang Cheh

TRIVIA: Filmed on location in and around Seoul, Korea

TRIVIA: Flying Tigers merged into FedEx in 1989

"No, that's the money you sold yourself for."

Chang Cheh and team travel to South Korea to shoot this anti-war picture that features hauntingly stunning snow-clad landscapes lensed by cinematographer Kung Mu-To aka Miyaki Yukio.

The time is July 1953. The battle of Korea waged for three years and a ceasefire has finally ended hostilities. With major combat over, a group of UN troops leave the snow trapped north and head south to Seoul in search of relief from the anxieties of war.

Feng Xia (Ti Lung) discovers that even in civilization, crimes against humanity continue. He confronts a gang of men pummeling an American GI who refused to smuggle drugs for their cartel. Though valiant in his efforts, Feng is outnumbered and falls victim to the gang led by enforcer Lei Tai (Yasuaki Kurata). Framed for the soldier's murder, Feng is arrested and it's up to his close friend Jin Yi (Chiang Da-Wei) and war vets Gao Yinhan (Wong Chung) and Li Weishi (Chen Kuan-tai) to free him from his captives and expose the truth about the drug cartel.

An often-overlooked film, Chang's apocalyptic vision was shot in the midst of the Second Indochina War, though relatable for any time period, as his four heroes do their best to rid their world of its evils and the corruption that warfare brings.

TITLE: Man of Iron

DIRECTOR: Chang Cheh, Pao Hsueh-Li

PRODUCER: Run Run Shaw

ACTION DIRECTOR: Lau Kar-Leung, Chan Chuen

ASS'T DIRECTOR: Chung Liang, Cheung Ging-Boh

CINEMATOGRAPHER: Yuen Teng-Bong

EDITOR: Kwok Ting Hung

SCRIPT: Chang Cheh and Ni Kuang

CAST:
Chen Kuan-Tai . . . . Qiu Lian-Huan
Ching Li . . . . Shen Ju-Fang
Wong Chung . . . . Lin Geng-Sheng
Chu Mu . . . . Boss Chang Gen Bao
Tin Ching . . . . Yu Chow-Kai
Bolo Yeung Sze . . . . Jin Xi-Fu
Yeung Chi-Hing . . . . Boss Yu Zhen-Ting
Wang Kuang-Yu . . . . Boss Chang's assistant
Cheung Ging-Boh . . . . Boss Chang's assistant
Tung Choi-Bo . . . . Ah Mo
Alexander Fu Sheng . . . . . . Teenager on bike

RELEASE DATE: October, 14 1972

BOX OFFICE: $1,059,092 (ranked #20 for 1972)

TRIVIA: Fu Sheng's first lines of dialogue

TRIVIA: Follow-up to *Boxer from Shantung* though not a sequel

TRIVIA: Chan Chuen appeared in Bruce Lee's *Fist of Fury*

TRIVIA: Alias is "Warrior of Steel"

"Master Qiu. Many people came to your home but haven't left."

Chang Cheh and Pao Hsueh-Li reunite in capitalizing on their blockbuster, *Boxer from Shantung*, to create an equally intense film about an upstart gangster's rise and fall in early 20th century Shanghai.

In the prior film, Ma Yung Chen (Chen Kuan-tai) took on overpowering numbers in his attempt to rules the streets. His struggle became the stuff of legends in Shanghai, and some twenty years later, boxer Qiu Lian-Huan (also played by CKT), has decided to follow in his predecessor's footsteps.

Qiu Lian-Huan begins by taming the wastrel Yu Chow-Kai (Tin Ching) who is a bit of an embarrassment for his father, crime Boss Yu Zhen-Ting (Yeung Chi-Hing). Boss Yu concedes to the newcomer which allows an opportunity for Boss Yu's lieutenant, Chang Gen Bao (Chu Mu), to gain control of the city's criminal network. Wounded in battle by Boss Chang's thugs, Qiu is nursed back to health by socialite mistress Shen Ju-Fang (Ching Li) which leads to a superhuman battle as one man takes on an army.

The on-screen chemistry between Chen Kuan-tai and Ching Li creates a balanced story which features fisticuffs, knives, buckets of blood, and Chen wielding a 65-pound bike as if it were an aluminum bat. Keep an eye out for Alex's small cameo as he delivers his first ever words of screen dialogue.

TITLE: The Generation Gap

DIRECTOR: Chang Cheh

PRODUCER: Runme Shaw

ACTION DIRECTOR: Lau Kar-Leung, Tong Gai

ASS'T DIRECTOR: Ting Chih-Fang

CINEMATOGRAPHER: Kung Mu-To

EDITOR: Kwok Ting Hung

SCRIPT: Chang Cheh, Ni Kuang

CAST:
Chiang Da-Wei . . . . Ling Xi
Agnes Chan Mei-Ling . . . . . Cindy Xin
Ti Lung . . . . Ling Zhao
Lo Dik . . . . Ling Yuan-Neng
Yeung Chi-Hing . . . . Xin Zhen-Qiang
Kong Ling . . . . Yun-Ling
Chiang Tao . . . . Xiao Zhou
Alexander Fu Sheng . . . . . . Ah Qiang
Dean Shek Tin . . . . Club waiter
Lee Sau-Kei . . . . Police officer
Lin Jing . . . . Cindy's mother

RELEASE DATE: April 20, 1973

BOX OFFICE: $698,165 (ranked #26 for 1973)

TRIVIA: Fu Sheng's last film as a school trainee

TRIVIA: Working title was "The Rebel"

TRIVIA: Ti Lung & Chiang Da-Wei won awards for their roles

TRIVIA: Soundtrack from "Original I (A New Beginning)"

"She's living with a teddy boy."

Chang Cheh continues to explore the youth genre with this contemporary drama that features a rebellious couple who regretfully discover that love does not conquer all.

Ling Xi (Chiang Da-Wei) is a young man with a bright future on his hands. He comes from a good home, has plenty of friends, and a promising future abroad as a college student. Ling though prefers to concentrate on cars, nightclubs, and underaged girlfriend Cindy Xin (Agnes Chan), which sparks an unsavory predicament for both households.

When the adolescent couple decides to move out on their own, their families and society turn against them. Even Ling's older brother, Ling Zhao (Ti Lung), cannot persuade him to understand the irrational path he is taking. When Cindy is finally forced back to her parents' care, Ling begins his dark descent into the underworld. The results put him in a fateful confrontation between the hooligans he has befriended and the Royal Hong Kong Police Force.

Colorful props and sets mixed with early 1970s fashion seem to date this film. However, the message of impetuous youth versus the establishment is still as current as ever. Trainee Fu Sheng receives a lengthy role here and his first on-screen name.

TITLE: Police Force

DIRECTOR: Chang Cheh, Ulysses Au-Yeung Jun

PRODUCER: Runme Shaw

ACTION DIRECTOR: Lau Kar-Leung, Tong Gai

ASS'T DIRECTOR: Godfrey Ho Jeung-Keung

CINEMATOGRAPHER: Kuang Han-Lu, Mai Ho-Hei

EDITOR: Kwok Ting Hung

SCRIPT: Chang Cheh, Ni Kuang

CAST:
Wong Chung . . . . Huang Gao Tung
Lily Li Li-Li . . . . Shen Yan
Alexander Fu Sheng . . . . . . Liang Kuan
Wang Kuang-Yu . . . . Kao Tu
Wong Shu-Tong . . . . Kao Tu's partner
Wang Hsieh . . . . Boss Sun Zuozhong
Tung Lam . . . . Inspector Cheung Sing
Fung Hak-On . . . . Police Officer
Ko Ti-Hua . . . . Su Ling
Fung Ngai . . . . Police Academy Instructor
Chu Gam . . . . Detective

RELEASE DATE: June 16, 1973

BOX OFFICE: $657,076 (ranked #31 for 1972)

TRIVIA: Opening titles "introduced" Alexander Fu Sheng

TRIVIA: Shot with the participation of the Royal HK Police Force

TRIVIA: Ulysses Au-Yeung Jun directed *Prodigal Boxer* in 1972

TRIVIA: Hong Kong Marine Police was established in 1841

"He's the Karate Kid!"

Chang Cheh co-directs this early crime drama, a decade before the genre took Hong Kong screens by storm with such critical hits like Jackie Chan's *Police Story (1985)* and John Woo's *A Better Tomorrow (1986)*.

When karate champ Liang Kuan (Fu Sheng) is murdered in an attempted robbery, his best friend Huang Gao Tung (Wong Chung) elects to seek retribution by joining up with the Royal Hong Kong Police Force. Several years pass as Huang moves up in the ranks to inspector, where he leads a task force investigating a ring of counterfeiters. Huang discovers that a member of this gang, Kao Tu (Wang Kuang-Yu), is the man responsible for his friend's death.

When Huang captures the thug, he struggles between the promise he made to his murdered friend, and his pledge to society as a law enforcer. To the shock of Liang's old girlfriend, Shen Yan (Lily Li), Huang decides not to execute Kao but use him to weed out the head of the counterfeiters. The finale is an all-out epic chase and battle on the high seas.

With its impressive production values for a film of this period, Chang and company have put together a compelling tale of vengeance, gunplay, martial arts, and action.

TITLE: Friends

DIRECTOR: Chang Cheh

PRODUCER: Run Run Shaw

ACTION DIRECTOR: Lau Kar-Leung, Tong Gai

ASS'T DIRECTOR: Godfrey Ho Jeung-Keung, Chang Chien

CINEMATOGRAPHER: Kung Mu-To

EDITOR: Kwok Ting Hung

SCRIPT: Chang Cheh, Ni Kuang

CAST:
Chiang Da-Wei . . . . Hua Heng
Alexander Fu Sheng . . . . . . Du Jia-Ji
Lily Li Li-Li . . . . Gao Xin
Lo Dik . . . . Du Dong-Tai
Wai Wang . . . . Ma Wei-Hong
Matsuoka Minoru . . . . Boss Huang Da-Cheng
Ko Ti-Hua . . . . Mary
Lee Yung-Git . . . . Lin Si-Bao
Danny Chow Yun-Kin . . . . . Meng Gui
Chen Wo-Fu . . . . Jin Bing-Da
Bruce Tong Yim-Chaan . . . . Chen Xing

RELEASE DATE: June 29, 1974

BOX OFFICE: $470,687 (ranked #49 for 1974)

TRIVIA: Lowest box-office gross in Fu Sheng's career

TRIVIA: Chang Cheh composed the music for this film

TRIVIA: Chen Wo-Fu committed suicide at 24

TRIVIA: Fu Sheng won Most Hopeful Young Actor Award

"Young Master please. Those were Mickey Mouse moves."

Director Chang Cheh's final film on the youth genre movement. This lesser known effort co-stars the up-and-coming Alexander Fu Sheng, who received an award for his efforts at the 20th Asian Film Festival.

Hua Heng (Chiang Da-Wei) is a struggling artist and the quasi-leader of a motley band of brothers who toil through their low-paying day jobs while dreaming of better lives. On the opposite end of the spectrum is Du Jia-Ji (Fu Sheng), who is the son of billionaire Dong-Tai (Lo Dik). Du nonetheless is smothered by his social status and restless with teen angst until he finds solace with Hua and his group of acquaintances.

The happy times are short-lived though when Hua's girlfriend (Lily Li) reveals to Du Jia-Ji that she will be sold into prostitution to settle a debt with Boss Huang Da-Cheng. The newcomer suggests a scheme to fake his own kidnapping and extort the money from his wealthy father to pay off the loan. The ploy works until Boss Huang's gang discovers Du's true identity and hatches a plan to make the kidnapping real. Hua and friends are then called into action to take on Boss Huang and his cohorts to rescue their new associate from certain death.

Themes of brotherhood resonate in Chang's larger films, but here too we witness his yanggang philosophy as bonds of friendship are tried and tested. A good dose of martial arts rounds out this sleeper film.

TITLE: Na Cha the Great

DIRECTOR: Chang Cheh

PRODUCER: Lin Hsiang-Fan

ACTION DIRECTOR: Lau Kar-Leung, Tong Gai

ASS'T DIRECTOR: Lee Wing-Cheung, Lam Chin-Wai, Shao Hao

CINEMATOGRAPHER: Kung Mu-To

EDITOR: Kwok Ting Hung

SCRIPT: Chang Cheh, Ni Kuang

CAST:
Alexander Fu Sheng . . . . . . Na Cha
Lo Dik . . . . General Li Chi
Lam Jing . . . . Na Cha's Mother
Chiang Tao . . . . Auguang of the East Sea
Fung Hak-On . . . . Third Prince
Jamie Luk Kim-Ming . . . . . Yecha Li Gen
Li Chen-Piao . . . . Yang Gen
Yuen Man-Tzu . . . . Su Juan
Sze-Ma Wah-Lung . . . . Na Cha's Teacher
Stephan Yip Tin-Hang . . . . Jin Cha
Cheung Yue-Tong . . . . Mu Cha

RELEASE DATE: September 27, 1974

BOX OFFICE: $516,604 (ranked #44 for 1974)

TRIVIA: Loosely based on a 16th century Chinese novel

TRIVIA: 20 months from production start to release date

TRIVIA: Fu Sheng's first (produced) Changgong film

TRIVIA: David Cheung's favorite film of his brother

"I'm smelly so I'm having a bath"

Chang Cheh launches his semi-independent career with this retelling of a centuries old folktale featuring martial arts, fantasy, demons, and inventive special effects for its day.

Fun loving Na Cha (Fu Sheng) is bored with his sheltered home life and obstinate father; General Li Chi (Lo Dik). He sneaks away to experience the real world where he discovers the local villagers are being abused by demons and corrupt officials — which includes his own father.

Na Cha decides to take matters in his own hands when a pair of demons in human guise create difficulties for a young couple. He slays Third Prince (Fung Hak-On) and Yecha Li Gen (Jamie Luk Kim-Ming) in a pair of battles which outrage the King Dragon aka Auguang of the East Sea (Chiang Tao). To save the village and his family from King Dragon's wrath, Na Cha agrees to take his own life in a ritual slaying but is soon after resurrected. Na Cha the deity returns as the community's protector and engages in an epic battle with both the god who demanded his death and his father who would not stand up for him.

Na Cha the Great is a fun, fantasy romp with low-budget pantomime special effects. This was also the first time Fu Sheng plays a film lead.

TITLE: Heroes Two

DIRECTOR: Chang Cheh

PRODUCER: Lin Hsing Fan

ACTION DIRECTOR: Lau Kar-Leung, Tong Gai

ASS'T DIRECTOR: Shao Hao

CINEMATOGRAPHER: Kung Mu-To

EDITOR: Kwok Ting Hung

SCRIPT: Chang Cheh, Ni Kuang

CAST:
Alexander Fu Sheng . . . . . . Fang Shih-yu
Chen Kuan-Tai . . . . Hung Hsi Kuan
Fong Sam . . . . 3rd Sister
Bruce Tong Yim-Chaan . . . Nien Shui Ching
Chu Mu . . . . General Che Kang
Wong Ching . . . . Lord Teh Hsiang
Fung Ngai . . . . Mai Hsin
Fung Hak-On . . . . Hsiang Chao Hui
Chiang Nan . . . . Ho Chu
Wu Chi-Chin . . . . Li Shih Chung
Jamie Luk Kim-Ming . . . . . Ming Patriot

RELEASE DATE: January 19, 1974

BOX OFFICE: $1,363,602 (ranked #12 for 1974)

TRIVIA: Chang Cheh's first (released) Shaolin Cycle film

TRIVIA: Chu Mu was Jackie Chan's first director before Lo Wei

TRIVIA: Earliest record of a Fang Shih-yu film is from 1938

TRIVIA: Kung Mu-To lensed 45 films for Chang Cheh

"I despise guys like you. Go away!"

The trailblazing inaugural film of Chang's Shaolin Cycle in which the "tomato director" explores the courageous tales of the legendary fighters: Fang Shih-yu and Hung Hsi Kuan.

The story opens with the burning of the revered Shaolin Temple. Shaolin patriot Hung Hsi Kuan (Chen Kuan-tai) wages a fierce stand against the marauding Manchus before escaping from the blaze. He disappears into the countryside in hopes of reuniting with some of his Shaolin brothers but the reunion is far from what he had planned.

Fang Shih-yu (Fu Sheng) has never met Hung Hsi Kuan, so he believes the Manchus when they tell him that Hung is a bloodthirsty robber. Fang overcomes Hung Hsi Kuan in battle who is then taken to a Manchu stronghold run by General Che Kang (Chu Mu) where he's imprisoned in their dungeon. Fang later meets up with fellow Shaolin students and boasts of his victory but they inform him of his grave error. With Hung's life on the line, Fang commits himself to a desperate plan to rescue his Shaolin brother.

This film features plenty of authentic martial arts action, courtesy of Tong Gai and Lau Kar-Leung, which bolsters a rousing story of Shaolin warriors seeking retribution for the burning of their temple. Moreover, this is the first of several films in a loosely based series.

TITLE: Men from the Monastery

DIRECTOR: Chang Cheh

PRODUCER: Lin Hsing Fan

ACTION DIRECTOR: Lau Kar-Leung, Tong Gai

ASS'T DIRECTOR: Shao Hao

CINEMATOGRAPHER: Kung Mu-To

EDITOR: Kwok Ting Hung

SCRIPT: Chang Cheh, Ni Kuang

CAST:
Alexander Fu Sheng . . . . . . Fang Shih-yu
Chen Kuan-Tai . . . . Hung Hsi Kuan
Chi Kuan-Chun . . . . Hu Hui-Chien
Chiang Tao. . . . . Gao Jin Zhong
Lo Dik . . . . Feng Dao De
Bruce Tong Yim-Chaan . . . Nian Rui Qing
Wu Hsueh-Yan . . . . Li Cui-Ping
Wong Ching . . . . Lei Da Pang
Wu Chi-Chin . . . . Hu Yiu Ding
Tang Tak-Cheung . . . . He Da Yong
Lam Fai-Wong . . . . Li Er Wan

RELEASE DATE: April 3, 1974

BOX OFFICE: $822,329 (ranked #28 for 1974)

TRIVIA: Filmed consecutively with *Heroes Two*

TRIVIA: Chi Kuan-Chun's film debut

TRIVIA: Chang expanded on this film with *Shaolin Avengers*

TRIVIA: Over 50% of the film's running time is action based

"Even if you're a king, no mercy is shown here."

Chang Cheh's second entry in his Shaolin Cycle consists of four short movies in one. We are introduced to the three main players, in parts 1-3, before the trio join forces for the final act in a life or death clash against the dreaded Manchus.

The first section centers on Fang Shih-yu (Fu Sheng) as a member of the Shaolin Monastery. He is falsely accused of murder and must battle his temple brothers in the Wooden Men Alley to rejoin the outside world.

The action shifts to Hu Huei Chien (Chi Kuan-Chun) for the second act. He's a reckless youngster on a mission to avenge his father's death, but despite his valor is unable to defeat his adversaries. Fang intercedes and directs him to the temple where he can receive proper training for his revenge. We then meet famed patriot Hung Hsi Kuan (Chen Kuan-tai) in the third chapter. In the finale, the Shaolin band of comrades-in-arms come together to engage those forces that seek to destroy them.

With its novel approach to storytelling and clever use of sepia tones and red filters in the climax, *Men from the Monastery* looks at events that caused the rift between the Shaolin and Wudang schools.

TITLE: Shaolin Martial Arts

DIRECTOR: Chang Cheh

PRODUCER: Lin Hsiang Fan

ACTION DIRECTOR: Lau Kar-Leung, Tong Gai

ASS'T DIRECTOR: Lee Wing-Cheung + 3 others

CINEMATOGRAPHER: Kung Mu-To

EDITOR: Kwok Ting Hung

SCRIPT: Chang Cheh, Ni Kuang

CAST:
Alexander Fu Sheng . . . . . . Li Yao
Chi Kuan-Chun . . . . Chen Bao Rong
Irene Chen Yi-Ling . . . . Lin Zhen Ziou
Yuen Man-Tzu . . . . Ah Wai
Lo Dik . . . . Master Lin Zan Tin
Chiang Tao . . . . Master Wu Chung-Ping
Simon Yuen Siu-Tin . . . . . . Master Liang Hong
Fung Hak-On . . . . He Lian
Leung Kar-Yan . . . . Ba Kang
Johnny Wang Lung-Wei . . . Yu Pi
Gordon Lau Kar-fai . . . . . . He Zhen Gang

RELEASE DATE: August 3, 1974

BOX OFFICE: $1,283,178 (ranked #15 for 1974)

TRIVIA: Yuen Hsiao Tien is father of the famed Yuen Clan

TRIVIA: Film introduced several upcoming Shaw stars

TRIVIA: Lo Dik appeared in 13 of Alex's initial films with Chang

TRIVIA: Production started 3 days after *Heroes Two* concluded

"Talking to you is no better than talking to a rock."

Chang Cheh and Lau Kar-Leung raise the bar with this superior production that is jam-packed with genuine kung fu. The powerfully constructed choreography, compelling storyline, and ensemble cast in this third of Chang's Shaolin Cycle is one for the ages.

The days of Fang Shih-yu and Hung Si Kwan are long gone. However, the rivalry between the remnants of Shaolin and the Manchus is still a heated one. When the opposing parties clash at a ceremony, the Manchus enlist two formidable martial artists whose superior kung fu is no match for the anemic members of the once powerful monastery.

The leader of the Shaolin (Lo Dik) dispatches two of his best fighters (Gordon Lau Kar-fai and Bruce Tong) to study under a pair of old masters. Their training though is of no consequence, for when they return, they are easily routed by their Manchu adversaries (played by newcomers Leung Kar-Yan and Wang Lung-Wei). It is then up to Shaolin student Li Yao (Fu Sheng) and Chen Bao Rong (Chi Kuan-Chun) to undergo intensive training of their own to attain retribution for their slain brothers and the reputation of Shaolin.

Shaolin Martial Arts is a compelling tale of loyalty and brotherhood. The production is one of the first films in which the narrative focuses on the martial arts training required to overcome another's martial style.

TITLE: Disciples of Shaolin

DIRECTOR: Chang Cheh

PRODUCER: Chu Gang, Peng Shih-Wei

ACTION DIRECTOR: Lau Kar-Leung

ASS'T DIRECTOR: Fan Sau-Yee, Wu Yueh-Ling, Chou Hsiao-Pei

CINEMATOGRAPHER: Kung Mu-To, Chui Tak-Lei

EDITOR: Kwok Ting Hung

SCRIPT: Chang Cheh, Ni Kuang

CAST:
Alexander Fu Sheng ...... Guan Feng Yi
Chi Kuan-Chun .... Wang Hon
Chen Ming-Li .... Xiao Ying
Wong Ging-Ping .... Chu Hong
Lo Dik .... Boss He
Chiang Tao .... Boss Ha He Bu
Fung Hak-On .... Lun Ying Tu
Han Chiang .... Supervisor Tan Da Bao
Fan Sau-Yee .... Supervisor Chen Zheng
Lam Fai-Wong .... Boss He's door guard
Jamie Luk Kim-Ming ..... Boss He's door guard

RELEASE DATE: June 28, 1975

BOX OFFICE: $1,319,161 (ranked #8 for 1975)

TRIVIA: AD Fan Sau-Yee also played Supervisor Chen Zheng

TRIVIA: Production started in HK but finished in Taiwan

TRIVIA: Theme was revisited in *Chinatown Kid*

TRIVIA: Original working title was "Hung Fist Takes the World"

"Who else wants to borrow the machines?"

Despite the movie's title, this fourth installment of the Shaolin Cycle does not have any affiliation with the legendary temple. Nonetheless, the dynamic pairing of Fu Sheng and Chi Kuan-Chun make this production a fan favorite.

Guan Feng Yi (Fu Sheng) plays a penniless bumpkin who travels to the city in search of his kung fu brother, Wang Hon (Chi Kuan-Chun). Wang gets Guan a job at the textile mill where he works; however, life is not so simple in the big city. An ongoing battle with a competing mill causes Guan to resort to his martial arts skills when trouble breaks out.

Despite Wang's pleas not to become involved, Guan battles and soundly defeats the two bosses of the competing mill (Chiang Tao and Fung Hak-On). Guan's fighting abilities put him in good with the big boss (Lo Dik) who provides him the lifestyle he's only dreamt of, but his newfound position and wealth creates friction with Wang Hon. When the defeated mill bosses exact revenge on Guan for embarrassing them, a whirlwind battle ensues in which Guan pays a heavy toll.

The rise and fall of a rags-to-riches type creates a gripping tale laced with first-rate action, entertaining comedy, and a good dose of drama.

TITLE: Five Shaolin Masters

DIRECTOR: Chang Cheh

PRODUCER: Peng Shih-Wei, Chu Gang

ACTION DIRECTOR: Lau Kar-Leung, Lau Kar-wing

ASS'T DIRECTOR: Wu Yueh Ling

CINEMATOGRAPHER: Kung Mu-To, Hsu Te Li

EDITOR: Kwok Ting Hung

SCRIPT: Ni Kuang

CAST:
Chiang Da-Wei . . . . Hu Te-Ti
Ti Lung . . . . Tsai Te-Chung
Alexander Fu Sheng . . . . . . Ma Chao-Hsing
Chi Kuan-Chun . . . . Li Shih-Kai
Meng Fei. . . . . Fang Ta-Hung
Leung Kar-Yan . . . . Chien San
Fung Hak-On . . . . Chang Chin-Chiu
Tsai Hung . . . . Pao Yu-Lung
Johnny Wang Lung-Wei . . . Ma Fu-Yi
Chiang Tao . . . . General Chen Wen-Yao
Lo Dik . . . . Ma Chin-Yung

RELEASE DATE: December 25, 1974

BOX OFFICE: $1,693,684 (ranked #5 for 1974)

TRIVIA: Chang's first film shot in Taiwan

TRIVIA: Tentative title was "5 Exponents of Shaolin Boxing"

TRIVIA: Budget was $2,000,000

TRIVIA: There are no actresses in this film

"I especially came up with this . . . for you sons of bitches."

The first film of Changgong to be shot in Taiwan, *Five Shaolin Masters* includes an all-star cast, as a group of five refugees from the razed Shaolin Temple are pitted against a superior force of Manchus.

After the Qing army destroys their beloved temple, surviving members of Shaolin are scattered across the countryside and hunted by the opposition. Five heroes led by Hu Te-Ti (Chiang Da-Wei) recognize they aren't a match for the group of overwhelming Manchus that includes the Shaolin traitor, Ma Fu-Yi (played by Wang Lung-Wei).

The five patriots return to their charred temple and each perfect a skill which can be used to counter their opponents' style. With time running out, and the Manchu warriors seeking their whereabouts, the monks come out of hiding to faceoff with their arch-enemies in five separate, one-on-one battles. While some of the Shaolin fighters succeed, others pay the ultimate price.

Five Shaolin Masters is part of a quasi-trilogy with the earlier *Shaolin Martial Arts* and later *Shaolin Temple*. Chang Cheh's story of survival is deftly peppered with intricate and vibrant choreography by the Lau brothers, and the film's lengthy set of training sequences are just some of the highlights.

TITLE: Boxer Rebellion

DIRECTOR: Chang Cheh

PRODUCER: Peng Shih-Wei, Chu Gang, Tsu Kang

ACTION DIRECTOR: Lau Kar-Leung

ASST DIR: Wu Yueh-Ling, Fan Sau-Yee, Liu Wei-Kang

CINEMATOGRAPHER: Kung Mu-To, Hsu Te Li

EDITOR: Kwok Ting Hung

SCRIPT: Chang Cheh, Ni Kuang

CAST:
Alexander Fu Sheng . . . . . . Tsang Hin Hon
Chi Kuan-Chun . . . . Shuai Fang Yun
Leung Kar-Yan . . . . Chen Chang
Jenny Tseng . . . . Xiao Jiu
Hu Chin . . . . Master Cai
Johnny Wang Lung-Wei . . . Li Jung Ching
Bruce Tong Yim-Chaan . . . Chang Chun Jiang
Li Li-Hua . . . . Empress Dowager
Suen Yuet . . . . Xiao Li
Chui Fook-Sang . . . . Lord Kong Ngai
Richard Harrison . . . . General Waldersee

RELEASE DATE: January 29, 1976

BOX OFFICE: $1,172,519 (ranked #17 for 1976)

TRIVIA: Initially banned in Hong Kong

TRIVIA: Liu Wei-Bin co-directed *The Naval Commandos*

TRIVIA: Waldersee was actually 68-years-old in 1900

TRIVIA: "Bloody Avengers" is the alternate title in the West

"If she's Master Cai, then we're all women."

Based on historical events, Chang Cheh oversees his most lavish and expansive film which centers on several fighters caught up in the Boxer Rebellion of 1899-1901. A sizeable cast and high production values help create this larger-than-life production.

Three martial artists (Fu Sheng, Chi Kuan-Chun, Leung Kar-Yan) decide to join up with other fellow patriots after a wave of foreigners infiltrate their beloved China. They team up with a sect of Boxers led by Li Jung Ching (Wang Lung-Wei) who deceives his followers into thinking magical spirits will make them impervious to the foreigner's gunfire. Ching even misleads the Empress Dowager (Li Li-Hua) into believing that his Boxers are invulnerable and can turn the tide against the invaders. Despite their best efforts, Beijing is overrun by the non-nationals who begin to pillage the capital city.

Master Cai (Hu Chin) strikes up a dialogue with the leader of the invaders, General Waldersee (Richard Harrison), in hopes of halting these atrocities. Though Cai succeeds, Waldersee turns his sights toward two staunch Chinese patriots (Fu Sheng, Chi Kuan-Chun). Escape from the city is their only option even though an army awaits them.

TITLE: Marco Polo

DIRECTOR: Chang Cheh

PRODUCER: Peng Shih-Wei, Chu Gang, Tsu Kang

ACTION DIRECTOR: Hsieh Hsing, Chan San-Yat

ASST DIR: Wu Yueh-Ling, Chou Hsiao-Pei, John Woo

CINEMATOGRAPHER: Kung Mu-To

EDITOR: Kwok Ting Hung

SCRIPT: Chang Cheh, Ni Kuang

CAST:
Alexander Fu Sheng . . . . . . Li Xiongfeng
Chi Kuan-Chun . . . . Zhou Xingzheng
Bruce Tong Yim-Chaan . . . Huang Zonghan
Kwok Chun-Fung . . . . Chen Jie
Richard Harrison . . . . Marco Polo
Shih Szu . . . . Mrs Zu
Gordon Lau Kar-fai . . . . . . Abulahua
Leung Kar-Yan . . . . Caldalu
Johnny Wang Lung-Wei . . . Dulldan
Li Tong-Chun . . . . Kublai Khan
Carter Wong Ka-Tat . . . . . . Zu Jianmin

RELEASE DATE: December 25, 1975

BOX OFFICE: $1,198,860 (ranked #11 for 1975)

TRIVIA: Kwok Chun-Fung's "introduction" credit

TRIVIA: Li Tong-Chun was the father of Li Yi-Min

TRIVIA: Carter Wong's only appearance in a Shaw film

TRIVIA: Fu Sheng's second film to open Christmas Day

"These beans make me itch."

This is another historical based film that presents the Venetian traveler Marco Polo and his relationship with Kublai Khan, grandson of Genghis Khan, who established the Yuan Dynasty.

After three years of exploring the Chinese countryside and reporting his findings to Mongolian Emperor Khan (Li Tong-Chun), Marco Polo (Richard Harrison) is appointed governor of Yangzhou. When two Han warriors attempt to assassinate the Khan, Marco and his men track down and capture the wife (Shih Szu) of one of the would-be assassins. While being escorted back to Yangzhou, she is rescued by the four sworn brothers of her deceased husband who swear to payback the Mongols.

They escape to the Tien Tao Mansion where they undergo grueling, unorthodox martial arts training. Marco is somewhat skeptical of the mansion's leader Chief Wang (Lo Dik) and suspects he may be hiding the four rebels and the fugitive woman. Several months pass as Marco plans his attack on the mansion, but not before he first sneaks inside the compound where he is witness to several events that sway his allegiance from the Khan.

While his book, *The Travels of Marco Polo*, has been criticized by some as fictional, Chang Cheh and company depict this ancient traveler as a man of righteousness and compassion.

TITLE: Heaven and Hell

DIRECTOR: Chang Cheh

PRODUCER: Run Run Shaw

ACTION DIRECTOR: Lu Feng, Robert Tai Chi-Hsien, Leung Ting

ASS'T DIRECTOR: Chiang Sheng, Chan Yau-Man

CINEMATOGRAPHER: Kung Mu-To

EDITOR: Chiang Hsing-Lung

SCRIPT: Chang Cheh, Ni Kuang, Chou Lang

CAST:
Li Yi-Min .... Xin Ling
Lin Chen-Chi .... Red Dress
Alexander Fu Sheng ..... Chen Ding
Jenny Tseng .... Shi Qi
Lo Mang .... Wei Han Ting
Bruce Tong Yim-Chaan ... Yan Tinzan
Sun Chien .... Lin Wei Gang
Kwok Chun-Fung .... Cheng Tien Yang
Chiang Sheng .... Na Cha
Lu Feng .... Chang Jiaxiang
Chiang Da-Wei .... Zhou Bao

RELEASE DATE: January 19, 1980

BOX OFFICE: $556,912 (ranked #104 for 1980)

TRIVIA: Fu Sheng's only film not in the Top 100 box office

TRIVIA: Started in 1975 and completed in 1977

TRIVIA: Shih Szu was originally cast as Red Dress

TRIVIA: Alias title is "Shaolin Hell Gate"

"There's no justice on Earth. And no justice in Hell."

Chang Cheh embarks on perhaps his greatest oddity in 1975 in which his cast and crew travel through the realms of Heaven, Earth, and Hades in this multi-genre feast for the eyes.

Xin Ling (Li Yi-Min) is a heavenly guard who allows a pair of angelic lovers to escape from Paradise against the wishes of his superiors. For his insubordination, he is banished to Earth and encounters another couple (Fu Sheng and Jenny Tseng) in need. Despite his good intentions, Xin Ling's mortal body dies in a gun battle and his spirit is sent further down the line to Hell where he meets Red Dress (Lin Chen-Chi).

The couple journey through the netherworld, witnessing numerous sinners undergo their eternal penance, until the Buddha of Mercy makes his annual appearance. The deity instructs the twosome to recruit several warriors, all wrongly cast to Hell, and together they might be able to escape this monstrous nightmare. Before undergoing their crusade against the netherworld, each recants a tale of how they arrived in the abyss and those who have wronged them in their prior lives.

A psychedelic concoction of genres, *Heaven and Hell* contains a nightmarish mix of martial arts, musicals, and fantasy. Complimented with colorful art direction, this disjointed film is probably the most misunderstood entry in Chang's repertoire

TITLE: Seven Man Army

DIRECTOR: Chang Cheh, Wu Ma, Hung Ting-Miu

PRODUCER: Peng Shih-Wei, Chu Gang, Tsu Kang

ACTION DIRECTOR: Chan San Yat, Hsieh Hsing

ASS'T DIRECTOR: Wu Yueh-Ling, Hsiao-Pei, Yeh Te-Sheng

CINEMATOGRAPHER: Kung Mu-To

EDITOR: Kwok Ting Hung

SCRIPT: Chang Cheh, Ni Kuang

CAST:
Ti Lung . . . . Commander Wu Chan Zheng
Chiang Da-Wei . . . . PFC Bai Zhang Xing
Alexander Fu Sheng . . . . . . Pvt. He Hong Fa
Chen Kuan-Tai . . . . Pvt. Jiang Ming Kun
Li Yi-Min . . . . Pvt. Pan Bing Lin
Chi Kuan-Chun . . . . Pvt. Chu Tiancheng
Pai Ying . . . . Pvt. Jia Fu Sheng
Ting Wa-Chung . . . . Xiao Shun Zi
Leung Kar-Yan . . . . Mongolian Colonel Hu Qi
Johnny Wang Lung-Wei . . . Mongolian mercenary
Gordon Lau Kar-fai . . . . . . Mongolian mercenary

RELEASE DATE: April 16, 1976

BOX OFFICE: $789,574 (ranked #37 for 1976)

TRIVIA: Outstanding Feature at the 13th Golden Horse Awards

TRIVIA: Based on factual events of 1933

TRIVIA: Filmed on location at Chenggong Ling in Taiwan

TRIVIA: *Chinatown Kid* went into pre-planning during this shoot

"The captured nation is a soldier's disgrace."

Based on the real-life events of April 1933, this Sino-Japanese mêlée showcases a cast of thousands supported by the Taiwanese military who provided troops, aircraft, and artillery.

After conquering China's Northeast provinces and creating the puppet state of Manchukuo, Japanese troops are massed to begin a full-scale invasion into the heart of China. On New Year's Day, the invaders mobilize and attack the strategic passes along the Great Wall before they set their eyes on the capital of Beijing. That spring, a group of seven Chinese soldiers are the last remaining members of the decimated Chinese army to guard the corridor known as Pa Tou Lou Tzu.

Led by Battalion Commander Wu Chan Zheng (Ti Lung), they continue to fight and repel several waves of invaders despite being overwhelmed by sheer numbers and firepower. With mini flashbacks providing background details on how each soldier joined the army, the seven combatants, aided by an orphan child, develop a strong bond as they fight for their nation and for each other.

Chang Cheh pulls out all the stops in the monumental production featuring explosive war games and heroic bloodshed.

TITLE: New Shaolin Boxer

DIRECTOR: Chang Cheh, Wu Ma

PRODUCER: Peng Shih-Wei, Tsu Kang

ACTION DIRECTOR: Hsieh Hsing, Chan San-Yat, Chen Jih-Liang

ASS'T DIR: Hsiao-Pei, Yeh Te-Sheng, Yue-Leung, Wu Yueh-Ling

CINEMATOGRAPHER: Kung Mu-To

EDITOR: Chiang Hsing-Lung

SCRIPT: Chang Cheh, Ni Kuang

CAST:
Alexander Fu Sheng . . . . . . Zhong Jian
Jenny Tseng . . . . Ms. Huang
Johnny Wang Lung-Wei . . . Feng Tian-Shan
Lo Dik . . . . Zhong Zhi-Mun
Leung Kar-Yan . . . . Feng's associate
Jamie Luk Kim-Ming . . . . . Feng's associate
Chan Wai-Lau . . . . Master Zhu
Shan Mao . . . . Master Zhou
Ng Siu-Wai . . . . Xiao Li
Stephan Yip Tin-Hang . . . . . Li Ting
Wong Cheong-Chi . . . . Zhong Jian's boss

RELEASE DATE: September 3, 1976

BOX OFFICE: $909,240 (ranked #28 for 1976)

TRIVIA: Chen Jih-Liang is Jenny Tseng's uncle

TRIVIA: Has at least seven alternate titles

TRIVIA: Leung Kar Yan is credited as "boxer instructor"

TRIVIA: Alex and Jenny appeared in 5 films together

"Even if I die, I'll repay you."

Alexander Fu Sheng took on a solo vehicle displaying a different style of kung fu, Choy Li Fut, in this second film (of an unofficial trilogy) of a man dedicated to championing the cause of the underdog regardless of the consequences.

Zhong Jian (Fu Sheng) is a reckless young carriage driver who cannot tolerate miscreants yet his continued street fights create problems for his family, neighbors, and even his kung fu school. When Zhong clashes with a gang of local knife fighters, the people's champion realizes his skills are no match for their leader, Feng Tian-Shan (Wang Lung-Wei).

Zhong's teacher intervenes and sends the young boxer away from the village to study under a hermit master named Zhu (Chan Wai-Lau) whose specialty is Choy Li Fut. After his training is complete, Zhong returns to his village only to learn that a female friend has been abused and his beloved teacher slain. This sets off the emotionally charged Zhong to rid the town of these hoodlums in which he must face off against leader Feng who's weapon of choice is a lethal hand claw.

Despite the title, *New Shaolin Boxers* has truly nothing to do with the Shaolin Monastery in itself. Nevertheless, the underlying theme of good versus evil is just as pertinent.

TITLE: Shaolin Avengers

DIRECTOR: Chang Cheh, Wu Ma

PRODUCER: Peng Shih-Wei, Chu Gang

ACTION DIRECTOR: Hsieh Hsing, Chan San-Yat

ASS'T DIR: Hsiao-Pei, Yeh Te-Sheng, Yue-Leung, Wu Yueh-Ling

CINEMATOGRAPHER: Kung Mu-To, Hsu Te Li

EDITOR: Kwok Ting Hung

SCRIPT: Chang Cheh, Ni Kuang

CAST:
Alexander Fu Sheng . . . . . . Fang Shih-yu
Chi Kuan-Chun . . . . Hu Hui-Chien
Bruce Tong Yim-Chaan . . . . Fang Xiaoyu
Lung Fei . . . . Lei Laohu
Johnny Wang Lung-Wei . . . Lu Yinbu
Shan Mao . . . . Niu Huajiao
Leung Kar-Yan . . . . Peng Buyun
Jamie Luk Kim-Ming . . . . . Yuan Nan
Chan Wai-Lau . . . . Bak Mei
Tsai Hung . . . . Feng Daode
Ma Chi-Chun . . . . Miao Cuihua

RELEASE DATE: June 18, 1976

BOX OFFICE: $857,983 (ranked #32 for 1976)

TRIVIA: Third film Alex was cast as Fang Shih-yu

TRIVIA: Quasi-remake of the earlier *Men from the Monastery*

TRIVIA: Alex's quickest film. Shot in under 40 days.

TRIVIA: Filmed concurrently with *Magnificent Wanderers*

"Brat Fang Shih-yu. Meet me for a duel on the poles."

Alexander Fu Sheng and Chi Kuan-Chun reprise their roles of Shaolin heroes, Fang Shih-yu and Hu Hui-Chien, in this detailed remake of Chang's earlier film, *Men from the Monastery*.

The film opens with Fang Shih-yu, his brother Fang Xiao-yu (played by Bruce Tong), and Hu Hui-Chien pitted against a liege of Wudang fighters led by the enigmatic Bak Mei (Chan Wai-Lau). Through the use of flashbacks, we learn of the heroes back stories and the course of events that have led them to this field of battle, which include confrontations with Johnny Wang Lung-Wei, Leung Kar-Yan, and Tsai Hung.

Shaolin Avengers delves deeper into the Fang Shih-yu legend encompassing the death of his father, his mother's training and body conditioning, and his deadly match with Tiger Lei (Lung Fei) atop the Plum Lotus piles. Though the story has been told prior, this new rendering provides much more characterization, detailed training, and highlights how Fu Sheng's martial arts skills and Chi Kuan Chun's cinematic faculties have improved since the previously mentioned film.

TITLE: Magnificent Wanderers

DIRECTOR: Chang Cheh, Wu Ma

PRODUCER: Peng Shih-Wei, Chu Gang

ACTION DIRECTOR: Hsieh Hsing, Chan San-Yat

ASS'T DIR: Wu Yueh-Ling, Hsiao-Pei, Yue-Leung, Yeh Te-Sheng

CINEMATOGRAPHER: Kung Mu-To, Hsu Te Li

EDITOR: Kwok Ting Hung, Hsu Te-Li

SCRIPT: Chang Cheh, Ni Kuang

CAST:
Chiang Da-Wei . . . . Chu Tie Xia
Alexander Fu Sheng . . . . . . Lin Shao You
Chi Kuan-Chun . . . . Shi Da Yong
Li Yi-Min . . . . Guan Fei
Shan Mao . . . . Mongol General Lu Bo Hua
Yeung Chung-Man . . . . Mongol General Zhu Da Cheng
Lee Ying . . . . Mongol leader
Lam Fai-Wong . . . . Fried fritter seller
Kwok Chun-Fung . . . . Mongol fighter
Lu Feng . . . . Mongol fighter
Wang Li . . . . Mongol fighter

RELEASE DATE: May 27, 1977

BOX OFFICE: $813,186 (ranked #40 for 1977)

TRIVIA: Wu Ma worked as a co-director on 14 Chang Cheh films

TRIVIA: Not released for nearly 15 months after its completion

TRIVIA: Ranked by many as a weaker effort of Chang's

TRIVIA: Fu Sheng's sixth film (most in one year) to start in 1975

"I'll personally chop off your heads."

Chang Cheh and team take on the Mongol Emperor and his army in this pseudo-comedy shot in Taiwan.

Chu Tie Xia (Chiang Da-Wei) is a wealthy fighter and Ming patriot who allocates his personal fortune to his associates for safe keeping. Unfortunately for Chu, his acquaintances are faithful only to their own greed, and to the Mongol Emperor (Lee Ying), who covets Chu's fortune for himself. True loyalty comes to Chu when he befriends three pauper con artists (Fu Sheng, Chi Kuan-Chun, and Li Yi-Min) who's proficiency in martial arts is equal to his own. Thanks to his new allies, Chu Tie Xia retrieves his assets to the embarrassment of the Emperor's two entrusted generals (Shan Mao and Yeung Chung-Man). Fearful the Emperor will punish them for their failure, they devise a plot to apprehend Chu and recover the misappropriated fortune. Chu manages to avoid capture only to wind up at the stronghold of a Mongol camp where he and his three "magnificent wanderers" are forced to engage with some of the Mongol's greatest warriors.

Widely panned as one of Chang's lowest outputs, the film demonstrates praiseworthy martial arts and provides Fu Sheng an opportunity to display his comedic talents.

TITLE: Shaolin Temple

DIRECTOR: Chang Cheh, Wu Ma

PRODUCER: Runme Shaw, Chen Lieh

ACTION DIRECTOR: Hsieh Hsing, Chen Jih-Liang, Chan San-Yat

ASS'T DIR: Yeh Te-Sheng, Li Baak-Ling

CINEMATOGRAPHER: Kung Mu-To

EDITOR: Chiang Hsing-Lung

SCRIPT: Chang Cheh, Ni Kuang

CAST:
Alexander Fu Sheng . . . . . . Fang Shih-yu
Chi Kuan-Chun . . . . Hu Hui-Chien
Chiang Da-Wei . . . . Hu De Di
Ti Lung . . . . Cai De Zhong
Johnny Wang Lung-Wei . . . Ma Fu Yi
Frankie Wei Hung . . . . Hong Xi Guan
Yueh Hua . . . . Li Se Kai
Wong Chung . . . . Fang Da Hong
Li Yi-Min . . . . Huang Song Han
Bruce Tong Yim-Chaan . . . Zhu Dao
Kwok Chun-Fung . . . . Lin Guang Yao

RELEASE DATE: December 22, 1976

BOX OFFICE: $1,220,594 (ranked #15 for 1976)

TRIVIA: Chang's first film upon his return to HK from Taiwan

TRIVIA: Fu Sheng's fourth and final app as Fang Shih-yu

TRIVIA: Master Chiu Wai was the masked monk who trains FSY

TRIVIA: Receipts weakened due to Hui's *The Private Eyes* (#1 film)

"Shaolin is finished. Surrender or die."

The traitor Ma Fu Yi (Wang Lung-Wei) sums up the plot with his quote above. Simply, this film is a Chang Cheh blockbuster that exhibits an impressive lineup of Shaw talent at the summit of the kung fu genre.

Three dedicated fighters (Fu Sheng, Chi Kuan-Chun, and Wei Hung) wait outside the Shaolin Temple in its final days. The monks inside realize that, for the Shaolin tradition to continue, they must recruit new members. Eventually, the trio passes the initial test and can enter the monastery. Once inside, they embark on the arduous task of learning the arts.

As word spreads that Shaolin is instructing outsiders, the ruling Qing government is concerned the temple may become too powerful and resolves that it must be abolished. With the assistance of Shaolin Master Hui Xian (Shan Mao) and turncoat Ma Fu Yi, the Manchu scheme to poison the monks and then attack the temple. Two of its latest recruits, Fang Shih-yu and Hu Hui-Chien, learn of the destructive plot and race back to Shaolin to help save their martial brothers.

This film is one of Chang Cheh's last hurrahs. It combines powerful choreography, a stellar cast, and a gripping tale of the legendary temple.

TITLE: The Naval Commandos

DIRECTOR: Chang Cheh, Wu Ma, Pao Hsueh-Li, Lau Wai Ban

PRODUCER: Run Run Shaw, Chen Lieh, Chow Cheong-Wa

ACTION DIRECTOR: Hsieh Hsing, Lee Ka-Ting, Robert Tai

ASS'T DIR: Yang Tzu-Chi, Yeh Te-Sheng, Wang Jing

CINEMATOGRAPHER: Kung Mu-To

EDITOR: Chiang Hsing-Lung

SCRIPT: Cheung Wing-Cheung

CAST:
Lau Wing . . . . Vice Admiral An Qi Bang
Chi Kuan-Chun . . . . Capt. Hu Jing Duan
Chiang Da-Wei . . . . Song San
Alexander Fu Sheng . . . . . . Xiao Liu
Shih Szu . . . . Cui Hsia
Ti Lung . . . . Captain Liang Guan Qin
Bruce Tong Yim-Chaan . . . . Sgt. Shao Kang Fa
Chiang Sheng . . . . Sgt. Jiang Ping Guang
Kwok Chun-Fung . . . . Sgt. She Gan
Lu Feng . . . . Sgt. Xu Xiang Lin
Shan Mao . . . . Japanese Naval Officer Hiroda

RELEASE DATE: April 7, 1977

BOX OFFICE: $694,326 (ranked #46 for 1977)

TRIVIA: Alex and Jenny wed while in production

TRIVIA: The Izuma was sunk on July 28, 1945

TRIVIA: Taiwan provided naval support ships and aircraft

TRIVIA: Co-produced with Taiwan's China Film Studio

"We came to Shanghai for a big fish."

Chang Cheh, in his last big budget production, demonstrates the military might of the Taiwanese Navy and an arsenal of Shaw regulars in this historical epic based on real-life events.

Set at the onset of the Second Sino-Japanese War, Chinese Naval Captain Hu Jing Duan (Chi Kuan-Chun) and four brave sailors (Bruce Tong, Chiang Sheng, Kwok Chun-Fung, Lu Feng) take on a suicide mission by entering Japanese controlled Shanghai. When their torpedo boat is destroyed, they must revise their stratagem and seek out the assistance of Song San (Chiang Da-Wei), a local Chinese Triad who has won the trust of the Japanese oppressors.

Along with Song San's aide (Fu Sheng), the sailors hatch a scheme to destroy the Japanese flagship Izuma moored in the harbor. Once aboard, the Chinese seamen face overpowering odds and Izuma's best military fighter, karate champion and Japanese Naval Officer Hiroda (Shan Mao).

Loaded with patriotic fervor, *The Naval Commandos* is another example of Chang's message of brotherhood and staunch masculinity (yanggang) in which his stars face a life and death struggle.

TITLE: Chinatown Kid

DIRECTOR: Chang Cheh

PRODUCER: Run Run Shaw, Chen Lieh, Mona Fong Yat-Wa

ACTION DIRECTOR: Lee Ka-Ting, Robert Tai Chi-Hsien

ASS'T DIR: Yeung Chi-Gat, Yeh Te-Sheng

CINEMATOGRAPHER: Kung Mu-To, Cho Wai-Kei

EDITOR: Chiang Hsing-Lung

SCRIPT: Chang Cheh, Ni Kuang, James Wong Jim

CAST:
Alexander Fu Sheng . . . . Tang Dong
Sun Chien . . . . Yang Jian Wen
Kwok Chun-Fung . . . . White Dragon
Lo Mang . . . . Green Dragon
Jenny Tseng . . . . Yvonne / Li Hua Feng
Shirley Yu Sha-Li . . . . Lana Chen
Johnny Wang Lung-Wei . . . Xu Hao
Yeung Chi-Hing . . . . Restaurant owner Chen
Wong Ching-Ho . . . . Uncle Tang
Siu Yam-Yam . . . . Sylvia
Wang Han-Chen . . . . Chef Ye

RELEASE DATE: December 2, 1977

BOX OFFICE: $1,537,867 (ranked #21 for 1977)

TRIVIA: Production began in Taiwan in 1975 but halted

TRIVIA: B-roll footage shot in San Francisco

TRIVIA: Script was rewritten to include Golden Dragon Massacre

TRIVIA: The international release was 118 minutes

"When you are poor, you must struggle."

A fan favorite in the West, Chang Cheh and Fu Sheng tackle the ever-growing struggles in the real-life Chinatowns throughout America.

Tang Dong (Fu Sheng) is a newly arrived immigrant to Hong Kong who can't find work due to his illegal status. Despite his grandfather's benevolence, Tang gets himself into trouble with a local crime boss, Xu Hao (Wang Lung-Wei). The elder Tang (Wong Ching-Ho) decides that the best way to save his grandson is by putting him on a merchant marine vessel and escape to the United States.

In San Francisco's Chinatown, Tang Dong lands a job at a restaurant where he meets another new arrival, Yang Jian Wen (Sun Chien), who is also adapting to his host country. Despite his best intentions, Tang gets mixed up with the local Green Dragon gang headed by Lo Mang. After he defeats his new adversaries, the rival White Dragon gang (led by Kwok Chun-Fung) recruits him as their main enforcer. Tang soon becomes infamous in Chinatown, enjoying his new luxuriant lifestyle, but then discoveries that the White Dragon's drugs are harming Yang Jian Wen, so he opts to initiate his own war.

This modern-day tale depicts the brutality of Chinatown and the ever-growing drug trafficking problems many there endure.

TITLE: The Brave Archer

DIRECTOR: Chang Cheh

PRODUCER: Runme Shaw, Chen Lieh, Mona Fong Yat-Wa

ACTION DIRECTOR: Lee Ka-Ting, Robert Tai Chi-Hsien

ASS'T DIR: Yeh Te-Sheng, Yang Tzu-Chi

CINEMATOGRAPHER: Kung Mu-To

EDITOR: Chiang Hsing-Lung

SCRIPT: Ni Kuang, Louis Cha (original story)

CAST:
Alexander Fu Sheng . . . . . . Guo Jing
Tien Niu . . . . Huang Rong
Kwok Chun-Fung . . . . Chao Pai-Tun
Ku Feng . . . . Northern Beggar Hung Chi-Kung
Goo Goon-Chung . . . . Eastern Devil Wong Lung-Su
Johnny Wang Lung-Wei . . . Western Poison Ouyang Fung
Danny Lee Sau-Yin . . . . Ouyang Ke
Li Yi-Min . . . . Yang Kang
Dick Wei . . . . Yang Tieh-Sin
Lau Wai-Ling . . . . Bau Shi-Ruo
Tsai Hung . . . . Flying Bat

RELEASE DATE: July 30, 1977

BOX OFFICE: $1,540,867 (ranked #20 for 1977)

TRIVIA: Chapters 1-18 of *Legend of Condor Heroes* (1957)

TRIVIA: Chang Cheh shot over 18,000 feet of film

TRIVIA: Edged out *Chinatown Kid* by only $3000 at the box office

TRIVIA: Hui Ying-hung was only 16 when production began

"You drank my snake's blood. Now I'll drink yours!"

This is the first film in a three-part series adaptation of Louis Cha's 1957 wuxia novel, *The Legend of the Condor Heroes*.

Guo Jing (Fu Sheng) and Yang Kang (Li Yi-Min) are two infant boys reared by separate masters. Guo Jing receives tutelage under the Seven Freaks (led by Choi Hung), while Yang Kang is trained by the Jin's 6th prince (Yue Wing). It is agreed that when the boys reach adulthood, they'll meet and do battle to determine which teacher has the superior kung fu.

As the years pass, Guo's martial capabilities are mediocre at best until he befriends a street beggar named Huang Rong (Tien Niu). The pauper turns out to be the daughter of Eastern Devil Wong Lung-Su, a villain who rules Peach Blossom Island. The pair travel to the island, and along the way cross paths with different masters who help Guo become a more capable martial artist. When they arrive at Peach Island, Guo must put his skills to the test when he faces off against Ouyang Ke (Danny Lee), who has been promised Huang's hand in marriage.

A sprawling costume drama hampered with a huge cast, *The Brave Archer* features a complicated plot which may need multiple viewings to digest all that unfolds on the screen.

TITLE: Life Gamble

DIRECTOR: Chang Cheh

PRODUCER: Runme Shaw, Chen Lieh, Mona Fong Yat-Wa

ACTION DIRECTOR: Leung Ting, Lu Feng

ASS'T DIR: Chiang Sheng

CINEMATOGRAPHER: Kung Mu-To

EDITOR: Chiang Hsing-Lung

SCRIPT: Chang Cheh, Ni Kuang

CAST:
Alexander Fu Sheng . . . . . . Yun Xiang
Lo Mang . . . . Mo Jun-Feng
Kwok Chun-Fung . . . . Qiu Zi-Yu
Johnny Wang Lung-Wei . . . Mao Kai-Yuan
Hui Ying-hung . . . . Xiao Hong
Li Yi-Min . . . . Master Nan
Lin Chen-Chi . . . . Xiao Qiang
Shirley Yu Sha-Li . . . . Peng Shuang-Shuang
Ku Feng . . . . Chief Constable Xiao
Suen Shu-Pau . . . . Cheng Zhang-Po
Dick Wei . . . . Jin Ba

RELEASE DATE: February 22, 1979

BOX OFFICE: $1,228,770 (ranked #39 for 1979)

TRIVIA: Chang's 1990 film *Hidden Hero* is a remake of this film

TRIVIA: Robert Tai worked as action director but not credited

TRIVIA: AD Chiang Sheng is credited as Chao Kang-Sheng

TRIVIA: Released in Taiwan on 4/26/78 as "Poison for Poison"

"Why this impetuous use of weapons as soon as we meet?"

A tale of shifting alliances with ill-gotten fortune that involves an ensemble cast of Shaw talent including all members of the Venoms team; minus Sun Chien.

When four notorious outlaws acquire a precious jade heirloom, they resolve not to split their bounty into four equal parts. Instead, they enter a winner-takes-all game of chance at the house of a famous gambler, Golden Lion Mao (Wang Lung-Wei). The gem catches the eye of many who covet the treasure, including the local Chief Constable (Ku Feng) who places his daughter, Xiao Hong (Hui Ying-Hung), inside the gambling den as a hired hand. It is there that she befriends Mao's in-house assassin, Yun Xiang (Fu Sheng), a master of the throwing knives.

Once the game of luck begins, each of the outlaws is promptly killed off as more players enter this risky venture. The den owner's greed even gets the best of him and Yun Xiang must take on another famous knife-thrower, Mo Jun-Feng (Lo Mang), in a classic Wild West shootout of blades.

Life Gamble is a convoluted yarn of ulterior motives, assassins, and swirling alliances. The film contains a wide array of unique martial arts weapons: whips, deadly hairpins, even a prosthetic hand that fires darts.

TITLE: The Brave Archer Part II

DIRECTOR: Chang Cheh

PRODUCER: Runme Shaw, Chen Lieh, Mona Fong Yat-Wa

ACTION DIRECTOR: Lu Feng, Robert Tai Chi-Hsien, Leung Ting

ASS'T DIR: Chiang Sheng, Chan Yau-Man

CINEMATOGRAPHER: Kung Mu-To

EDITOR: Chiang Hsing-Lung

SCRIPT: Ni Kuang, Louis Cha (original story)

CAST:
Alexander Fu Sheng . . . . . . Guo Jing
Esther Niu Niu . . . . Huang Rong
Ku Feng . . . . Hung Chi Kung
Kwok Chun-Fung . . . . Chao Pai Tun
Johnny Wang Lung-Wei . . . Ouyang Fung
Danny Lee Sau-Yin . . . . Ouyang Ke
Li Yi-Min . . . . Yang Kang
Shirley Yu Sha-Li . . . . Kuk's daughter
Goo Goon-Chung . . . . Huang Lung Su
Lo Mang . . . . Iron Palm Master Kau
Lu Feng . . . . Beggar Clan elder

RELEASE DATE: May 13, 1978

BOX OFFICE: $1,491,458 (ranked #19 for 1978)

TRIVIA: Production was complete in 12 weeks

TRIVIA: Niu Niu replaced Tien Niu as the lead actress

TRIVIA: Shirley Yu totaled her car driving to the set

TRIVIA: Alex's 25th consecutive film with Chang Cheh

"My kung fu has been crippled."

This film is the second installment of Louis Cha's wuxia novel, *The Legend of the Condor Heroes*, which depicts the continued adventures of Guo Jing and Huang Rong.

The sequel opens with a brisk recap. The various parties leave Peach Island but are caught in a storm at sea. Huang Rong (Esther Niu) is captured by Western Poison (Wang Lung-Wei), who demands that Guo Jing (Fu Sheng) write out the details of the Jiao Jin manual. Guo complies but provides him with a false rendering, and in the aftermath, Western Poison severely wounds Guo's teacher with his Toad Fist. "Nine Finger Beggar" Hung Chi Kung (Ku Feng) then passes the leadership, his dog beating stick, of the Beggar Clan to Huang.

Quite the opportunist, Yang Kang (Li Yi-Min) maliciously wounds Guo Jing and later obtains the coveted beggar chief's stick with plans to take over the Beggar Clan. Yang tells the clan that Huang Rong's father was responsible for the death of Nine Finger Beggar. The captured Huang and Guo Jing are to be executed but its temporarily stalled when the Iron Palm sect, led by Master Kau (Lo Mang), arrive at the clan's gathering.

Featuring an elaborate storyline like its predecessor, *The Brave Archer Part II* introduces many sub-plots, and a grand line up of characters who enter in and out the film as if it were a stage play.

TITLE: The Avenging Eagle

DIRECTOR: Sun Chung

PRODUCER: Runme Shaw, Mona Fong Yat-Wa, Chan Yim-Kuen

ACTION DIRECTOR: Tong Gai, Wong Pau-Gei

ASS'T DIR: Min Min

CINEMATOGRAPHER: Lam Nai-Choi

EDITOR: Chiang Hsing-Lung, Yu Siu-Fung

SCRIPT: Ni Kuang, Louis Cha (story)

CAST:
Ti Lung . . . . Black Eagle Chik Ming Sing
Alexander Fu Sheng . . . . . . Double Sword Sleeve Cheuk Yi Fan
Ku Feng . . . . Yoh Xi Hung
Johnny Wang Lung-Wei . . . Vulture Eagle Yien Lin
Eddy Ko Hung . . . . Blue Eagle Wan Da
Austin Wai Tin-Chi . . . . Owl Eagle Cao Gao Shing
Shih Szu . . . . Siu Fung
Yue Wing . . . . Devil's Plight Wang An
Yeung Chi-Hing . . . . Se Ma Sun
Jenny Tseng . . . . Se Ma Yu Chin
Tong Gai . . . . Golden Spear Tao De Biu

RELEASE DATE: September 13, 1978

BOX OFFICE: $2,028,488 (ranked #13 for 1978)

TRIVIA: Fu Sheng's first film to break $2M at box office

TRIVIA: Remade as *The 13 Cold-Blooded Eagles (1993)*

TRIVIA: Wong Pau-Gei is the brother of Tong Gai

TRIVIA: The AD was also an extra with Alex in *Man of Iron*

"You better save your strength . . . to report in hell."

In this international fan favorite, Sun Chung pairs two of Shaw Brothers Studio's biggest stars, Ti Lung and Alexander Fu Sheng.

Two martial artists form an unlikely partnership after one discovers the other on the verge of death in the desert. Black Eagle (Ti Lung) is a notorious outlaw from the Iron Boat Gang who is fleeing from their company. The other is the mysterious Cheuk Yi Fan (Fu Sheng), who befriends the man on the run; however, the lone warrior appears to have an agenda of his own.

Black Eagle divulges his tale to his new companion of the nefarious Yoh Xi Hung (Ku Feng), who taught him and his fellow disciples to create misery in their quest for secular gains. After Black Eagle is injured during a heist, he is nursed back to health by a household whose eldest daughter (Shih Szu) becomes smitten with him. When the gang plots to assassinate the family that saved him, Black Eagle must oppose his crew and take the battle to them, which leads to a climactic clash with Yoh Xi Hung.

Sun Chung creates an atmospheric thriller with lush sets, vibrant costumes, and outlandish weaponry in this film that went on to become a box office success. Notably, this is Fu Sheng's first film with a new director after a 25-film stint with Chang Cheh.

TITLE: Ten Tigers of Kwantung

DIRECTOR: Chang Cheh

PRODUCER: Run Run Shaw, Mona Fong Yat-Wa, Chen Lieh

ACTION DIRECTOR: Leung Ting, Chiang Sheng, Lu Feng

ASS'T DIR: Chiang Sheng, Chan Yau-Man

CINEMATOGRAPHER: Cho Wai-Kei

EDITOR: Chiang Hsing-Lung, Lee Yim-Hoi

SCRIPT: Chang Cheh, Ni Kuang

CAST:
Ti Lung . . . . Li Chen Chow
Alexander Fu Sheng . . . . . . Tam Min
Sun Chien . . . . Wang Yin Lin
Lu Feng . . . . Su Hei Hu
Kwok Chun-Fung . . . . Beggar So Chen
Lo Mang . . . . Iron Fingers Chen Tie Fou
Yeung Hung . . . . Tieh Chow San
Ku Feng . . . . Chai Min Yi
Johnny Wang Lung-Wei . . . General Liang Sz Guei
Wong Lik . . . . Tung Chi
Chin Siu-Ho . . . . Lin Fu Shing

RELEASE DATE: Released in 1980

BOX OFFICE: *unknown*

TRIVIA: Final production ended on Leap Day 1980

TRIVIA: The real "10" never appeared at the same time as a group

TRIVIA: Cho Wai-Kei was cinematographer on 19 Venom films

TRIVIA: The real "10" were Shaolin lay disciples

"I want to see how good your Wudang swordsmanship is."

Chang Cheh brings together an imposing ensemble cast of Shaw Brothers Studio martial artists in this account of the legendary fighters from Canton who lived during the late Qing Dynasty.

Chai Min Yi (Ku Feng) is a revolutionary on the run who takes refuge with fellow patriot and kung fu expert Li Chen Chow (Ti Lung). In order for Chai to continue his struggles against the Qing, Li must gather additional loyalists (Ten Tigers) to help Chai escape from the city and make his way out of the country. Overseeing the hunt for the rebel is General Liang Sz Guei (Wang Lung-Wei), who aligns himself with a local merchant to divide the heroes and weed out Chai. When the Tigers become aware of the subversion, they unite and a bloody showdown ensues between the treacherous Qing and the revered group of martial heroes.

Flash forward to the future. A Qing official named Tung Chi (Wong Lik) and the son of the now deceased General Liang Sz Guei plot revenge on the Tigers' descendants. They systematically assassinate their adversaries until two of the original Tigers return to take on their old foes.

Told through several flash-backs, the multi-generational tale is one of the last times we see so many Shaw stars on the same stage.

TITLE: The Deadly Breaking Sword

DIRECTOR: Sun Chung

PRODUCER: Run Run Shaw, Mona Fong Yat-Wa, Chan Yim-Kuen

ACTION DIRECTOR: Tong Gai, Wong Pau-Gei

ASS'T DIR: Min Min

CINEMATOGRAPHER: Cho On-Sun, Lam Nai-Choi

EDITOR: Chiang Hsing-Lung, Yu Siu-Fung

SCRIPT: Ni Kuang

CAST:
Ti Lung . . . . Tuan Changqing
Alexander Fu Sheng . . . . . . Xiao Dao
Shih Szu . . . . Liu Yinxu
Ku Feng . . . . Killer Doctor Guo Tiansheng
Michael Chan Wai-Man . . . Lian San
Lily Li Li-Li . . . . Luo Jinhua
Shum Lo . . . . Boss Luo
Chan Shen . . . . Officer Fan Fei
Ngaai Fei . . . . Chen Yinggang
Teresa Ha Ping . . . . Madam Li Xing
Hui Ying-hung . . . . Xiaoqin

RELEASE DATE: April 12, 1979

BOX OFFICE: $2,716,494 (ranked #12 for 1979)

TRIVIA: Fu Sheng suffered a head concussion during production

TRIVIA: Jenny Tseng was the singer of the film's title track

TRIVIA: Working title was Romantic Dagger and Little Dagger

TRIVIA: Brothers Tong and Wong co-choreographed 34 films

"Compared to Ms. Liu's bed, yours doesn't look so comfy."

    Sun Chung reunites his two stars (Ti Lung and Fu Sheng) from the highly successful *The Avenging Eagle* in this lavish costume drama that highlights a merger of weapons, boxing, and comedy.

    Ti Lung plays Tuan Changqing, who is known as "The Deadly Breaking Swordsman." He is a cocksure martial arts expert who greets his opponents with a trio of gifts: a lavish set of new clothes, a promise, and a coffin for their body. At the other end of the spectrum is the unsophisticated fighter Xiao Dao (Fu Sheng) who has a passion for gambling but unfortunately also a knack for losing.

    Tuan Changqing and Xiao Dao cross paths when a regal prostitute Liu Yinxu (Shih Szu) sets up shop in the local brothel. She conspires to exploit the fighters and bring an evil doctor, Guo Tiansheng (Ku Feng), to justice for imprisoning her brother years earlier. Dr. Guo though is far from vulnerable as his ally is the hell-bent Lian San (Michael Chan Wai-Man) who has his own score to settle with Tuan Changqing.

    Sun Chung makes a valiant attempt here with *The Deadly Breaking Sword* to create a bridge of wuxia pian with the up-and-coming chuckle-fu genre that dominated the HK film industry for the late 1970s & '80s.

TITLE: The Proud Twins

DIRECTOR: Chor Yuen

PRODUCER: Run Run Shaw, Mona Fong Yat-Wa, Chen Lieh

ACTION DIRECTOR: Tong Gai, Wong Pau-Gei

ASS'T DIR: Chang Chuan-Tsan, Fang Tze-Ch

CINEMATOGRAPHER: Hung Chieh

EDITOR: Chiang Hsing-Lung, Yu Siu-Fung

SCRIPT: Chor Yuen, Gu Long (original story)

CAST:
Alexander Fu Sheng . . . . . . Jiang Xiao Yu
Wu Wei-Kuo . . . . Hua Mu Juet
Wong Yung . . . . Yin Nan Tien
Candy Wen Xue-Er . . . . Tieh Sin Nan
Au-Yeung Pui-San . . . . Green Fairy
Kitty Meng Chui . . . . Princess of Yi Hua Palace
Tang Ching . . . . Jiang Chin
Goo Goon-Chung . . . . Jiang Yu Long
Cheng Miu . . . . Dr. Wan Chuen Liu
Chan Shen . . . . Chief of 10 Villains
Lau Wai-Ling . . . . Siao Mi Mi

RELEASE DATE: July 19, 1979

BOX OFFICE: $4,009,486 (ranked #4 for 1979)

TRIVIA: Wong Chit lensed nearly 1/3 of Chor Yuen's 124 films

TRIVIA: Fu Sheng's highest-ranking film in any given year

TRIVIA: A remake of *The Jade Faced Assassin (1971)*

TRIVIA: *Legendary Siblings* was 127 chapters

"Either take us to look for the treasure or I'll let Li eat you."

Chor Yuen adapted the wuxia classic for the silver screen featuring his unique vision and heralding the triumphant return of Alexander Fu Sheng after his crushing neck injury a few months prior.

Jiang Xiao Yu (Fu Sheng) and Hua Mu Juet (Wu Wei-Kuo) are twin boys separated after their parents are slain by the Princess of Yi Hua Palace (Kitty Meng Chui). To seal her revenge, she raises one child as her own while sending off the other to be brought up by a band of evil men. When the siblings reach a certain age, it's the princess' intention to have the twins destroy one another.

While the malcontent raise baby Jiang, he grows up having a kind and unselfish disposition with a good understanding between the moral and the malevolent. After he tricks and overcomes his evil uncles, Jiang sets out into the world where he encounters Tieh Sin Nan (Candy Wen Xue-Er). She leads him on a treasure hunt where they encounter a variety of individuals including Jiang's now grown twin. The duo become fast friends, unaware of each other's identity until all is revealed, which leads to a rousing confrontation between the scheming parties.

Fu Sheng excelled in this comeback film with witty wordplay and comedic rhythm. His contributions uplift the fantasy laden drama and deliver a charming and stirring adventure.

TITLE: My Rebellious Son

DIRECTOR: Sun Chung

PRODUCER: Mona Fong Yat-Wa, Wong Ka-Hee, Chan Yim-Kuen

ACTION DIRECTOR: Tong Gai, Wong Pau-Gei

ASS'T DIR: Hoh Kei-Shing

CINEMATOGRAPHER: Lam Nai-Choi, Cho On-Sun

EDITOR: Siu Fung, Chiu Cheuk-Man, Ma Chung-Yiu

SCRIPT: Sun Chung, Ni Kuang

CAST:
Alexander Fu Sheng ...... Chang Siu Tai
Ku Feng .... Chang Tak Tai
Tang Ching .... Chairman Tang
Johnny Wang Lung-Wei ... Robert Tang
Cecilia Wong Hang-Sau ... Judy Shum Shao Ling
Ngaai Fei .... Sam Shum
Michael Chan Wai-Man .... Yamaguchi
Tin Ching .... Mr. Chun
Walter Tso Tat-Wah ...... Master Jiang
Yuen Wah .... Matsuzaka
Ng Hong-Sang .... Tomoasa

RELEASE DATE: November 26, 1982

BOX OFFICE: $2,884,408 (ranked #52 for 1982)

TRIVIA: 1 of 5 productions put on hold due to Alex's leg injury

TRIVIA: Sun Chung opened a Chinese restaurant in Chicago in 1990

TRIVIA: Yuen Wah was Bruce Lee's stunt double

TRIVIA: Jenny Tseng was originally cast but later cut

"Who cares if they're foreigners or Japanese, we'll use kung fu."

Sun Chung's third and final outing with Alexander Fu Sheng is a production that was prolonged nearly four years due to the actor's second Black September injury.

Chang Siu Tai (Fu Sheng) struggles to be the filial son of Chang Tak Tai (Ku Feng), a man who operates a well-known health clinic during a time when China is experiencing an influx of foreigners. Siu Tai is restless with his day-to-day responsibilities and finds himself at odds with both the outsiders and the local turncoats who've adopted their Western ways.

Siu Tai catches the eye of Judy Shum (Cecilia Wong), the girlfriend of Robert Tang (Wang Lung-Wei), who is the leader of a pro-foreigner alliance. When the village temple's idol is desired by one of the self-indulgent non-nationals, Siu Tai and friends take it upon themselves to hide their sacred statue. The gesture is short-lived, and the icon is recovered by Tang and his Westernized group of locals. This forces the two crews into a confrontation that includes a pair of Japanese Kendo experts who are keen on dismembering Siu Tai.

With a mixture of kung fu comedy and martial arts action, this production showcased the brilliant pairing of Shaw Brothers Studio megastars Fu Sheng and Ku Feng in their final (released) film together.

TITLE: The Brave Archer Part III (1981)

DIRECTOR: Chang Cheh

PRODUCER: Mona Fong Yat-Wa, Chen Lieh

ACTION DIRECTOR: Kwok Chun-Fung, Chiang Sheng, Lu Feng

ASS'T DIR: Chiang Sheng, Lo Yuen-Ming

CINEMATOGRAPHER: Cho Wai-Kei

EDITOR: Chiang Hsing-Lung, Lee Yim-Hoi

SCRIPT: Chang Cheh, Ni Kuang

CAST:
Alexander Fu Sheng . . . . . . Guo Jing
Esther Niu Niu. . . . . Huang Rong
Ti Lung . . . . Emperor Duan
Ching Li . . . . Auntie Ying/Lady Liu
Kwok Chun-Fung . . . . Chao Pai Tung
Lu Feng . . . . The Woodcutter
Sun Chien . . . . .The Scholar
Wong Lik . . . . The Tiller
Chiang Sheng . . . . The Fisherman
Lo Mang . . . . .Qiu Qian-ren
Chu Ko . . . . .Qiu Li

RELEASE DATE: November 12, 1981

BOX OFFICE: $1,889,396 (ranked #47 for 1981)

TRIVIA: 1 of 5 productions stalled due to Alex's leg injury

TRIVIA: Final installment of *The Legend of the Condor Heroes*

TRIVIA: The highest grossing of the four *Brave Archer* films

TRIVIA: Blast of the Iron Palm was the popular title in the West

"Old Naughty has a Little Naughty."

The Brave Archer Part III is the final installment of Louis Cha's *The Legend of the Condor Heroes* wuxia novel which resumes the further escapades of Guo Jing and Huang Rong.

Guo Jing (Fu Sheng) and Huang Rong (Niu Niu) discover the location to a secret manual deep inside the Iron Palm Clan territory. When Huang is mortally wounded by Iron Palm Chief Qiu Qian-ren (Lo Mang), she and Guo take refuge in the home of hermit Auntie Ying (Ching Li). The recluse reveals that the only person who can save her is Emperor Duan (Ti Lung) who resides on a fortified mountain. The duo set off for the mount unaware that Ying plans to use them for her own sordid plot of revenge.

After a serious of challenges along the way, Guo Jing and Huang Rong reach Duan's palace where the Emperor agrees to administer his life-saving healing process. This act though makes Duan defenseless and a hapless target for Auntie Ying who has also traveled to the mountain. Ying must now decide if she should slay Duan, who allowed her child to die years prior, or the man who actually killed her baby, Chief Qiu Qian-ren.

While many of the characters are gone from the original film, this third chapter of *The Brave Archer* holds up on its own and includes a grand finale featuring all five main Venom actors.

TITLE: Return of the Sentimental Swordsman (1981)

DIRECTOR: Chor Yuen

PRODUCER: Run Run Shaw, Mona Fong Yat-Wa, Chen Lieh

ACTION DIRECTOR: Tong Gai

ASS'T DIR: Chang Chuan-Tsan, Fang Tze-Chi

CINEMATOGRAPHER: Hung Chieh

EDITOR: Yu Siu-Fung, Chiang Hsing-Lung

SCRIPT: Chor Yuen, Gu Long (original story)

CAST:
Ti Lung . . . . Li Xunhuan
Alexander Fu Sheng . . . . . . Jing Wuming
Derek Yee Tung-Sing . . . . . A' Fei
Ching Li . . . . Lin Shiyin
Lo Lieh . . . . Hu Bugui
Ku Feng . . . . Shangguan Jinhong
Choh Seung-Wan . . . . Lin Xianer
Goo Goon-Chung . . . . Shangguan Fei
Hui Ying-hung . . . . Sun Xiaohong
Lau Wing . . . . Lu Fengxian
Cheng Miu . . . . Bai Xiao Sheng

RELEASE DATE: January 31, 1981

BOX OFFICE: $4,302,930 (ranked #15 for 1981)

TRIVIA: Sequel to *The Sentimental Swordsman*

TRIVIA: Based on Gu Long's *Xiaoli Feidao* series of novels

TRIVIA: Filmed concurrently with *Mark of the Eagle*

TRIVIA: Only time Fu Sheng shares the screen with Lo Lieh

"Mine is a knife that shears off all emotion."

This is director Chor Yuen's adaptation of the Gu Long novel that inspired his highly successful *The Sentimental Swordsman,* a film that brought in over $1.6 million at the local box office in October 1977.

The renowned swordsman, Li Xunhuan (Ti Lung), has withdrawn from the martial arts world and his lover, Lin Shiyin (Ching Li), after the final contest with Plum Blossom. Unfortunately, his legendary flying daggers still rate third in the imperial examination which makes the martial expert's retirement not as permanent as he had hoped.

Enter the chief of the powerful Money Clan, Shangguan Jinhong (Ku Feng), who aspires to rule the martial arts world. His lethal dragon-phoenix rings rate second, and at his side is the eccentric left-handed warrior, Jing Wuming (Fu Sheng). To stop the Money Clan in their quest, Li Xunhuan is forced out of retirement to find his long-lost ally Ah Fei (Derek Yee). Nevertheless, another person of interest has different plans for Ah Fei who wields powers of persuasion to satisfy her own agenda.

Multiple duels and scandalous affairs pit the greatest warriors in the martial arts world and rewrite history anew. An exceptional cast, fluctuating alliances, and decorative sets fashion this impressive sequel.

TITLE: Heroes Shed No Tears (1980)

DIRECTOR: Chor Yuen

PRODUCER: Run Run Shaw, Mona Fong Yat-Wa, Chen Lieh

ACTION DIRECTOR: Tong Gai, Wong Pau-Gei

ASS'T DIR: Chang Chuan-Tsan, Fang Tze-Chi

CINEMATOGRAPHER: Hung Chieh

EDITOR: Yu Siu-Fung, Chiang Hsing-Lung

SCRIPT: Chor Yuen, Gu Long (original story)

CAST:
Alexander Fu Sheng . . . . . . Kao Chien Fei
Jason Pai Piao . . . . Sze Ma Chao Chun
Derek Yee Tung-Sing . . . . . Zhou Tung Lai
Ku Feng . . . . Chu Meng
Yueh Hua . . . . Hsiao Lei Hsueh
Angie Chiu Nga-Chi . . . . . . Graceful
Lau Wai-Ling . . . . Sze Ma Chao Chun's wife
Wang Sha . . . . Hsiao Kong Tsi
Cheng Miu . . . . Kao Chien Fei's Master
Goo Goon-Chung . . . . Tsai Chung
Keung Hon . . . . Yang Chian

RELEASE DATE: July 24, 1980

BOX OFFICE: $2,077,577 (ranked #24 for 1980)

TRIVIA: Fu Sheng broke his right leg during filming

TRIVIA: Based on Gu Long's novel *A Hero Without Tears*

TRIVIA: Jenny Tseng sang for Angie Chiu's dance scene

TRIVIA: Jason Pai Piao's only film with Fu Sheng

"This is the leg that you liked. I'm giving it to you."

Chor Yeun's reworking of another classic Gu Long novel, *Ying Xiong Wu Lei*, unveils a complex, soap opera-like narrative.

Kao Chien Fei (Fu Sheng) is an expert swordsman entrusted with a peculiar mission by his elderly master (Cheng Miu). He is given the fabled Teardrop Sword which Kao must bring to the martial world in order to decide the fate of this presumably cursed weapon.

Kao descends from his mountain retreat to stumble into a massive dispute between clans and their fabled chiefs. The charismatic Zhuo Donglai (Derek Yee), with his condescending monologues, is the unscrupulous and cunning chess master. Zhuo desires to become master of the martial arts world and launches a scheme to pit the various heroes against one another. Kao becomes a player in this game of deceit which includes Sima Chaoqun (Jason Pai Piao), Zhumeng (Ku Feng), and Xiao Leixue (Yueh Hua) aka the man with the wooden box. Xiao Leixue's celebrity derives from the small crate of 37 special weapons he carries, which makes him a dependable ally or treacherous adversary.

Heroes Shed No Tears features an exemplary troupe of actors who engage in a dramatic yarn which encompasses mystery, love lost, and characters whose motives change in the blink of an eye.

TITLE: Treasure Hunters (1981)

DIRECTOR: Lau Kar-wing

PRODUCER: Mona Fong, Lawrence Wong, Chan Lee-Wah

ACTION DIRECTOR: Lau Kar-wing, Li King-Chu

ASS'T DIR:

CINEMATOGRAPHER: Au Gaam-Hung

EDITOR: Chiang Hsing-Lung, Lee Yim-Hoi

SCRIPT: Wong Jing

CAST:
Alexander Fu Sheng ...... Chi Ta Po
David Cheung Chin-Pang .. Chow Su Chi
Johnny Wang Lung-Wei ... Lord Mo Cong
Lau Kar-wing .... Lu
To Siu-Ming .... Chief Zhu San
Gordon Lau Kar-fai ...... Monk Wu Sun
Yeung Jing-Jing .... Lord Mo's assistant
Wilson Tong Wai-Shing ... Chief Chao Hung
Lam Wai .... Librarian
Li King-Chu .... Chief Xu
Lam Fai-Wong .... Phantom

RELEASE DATE: July 9, 1981

BOX OFFICE: $1,396,271 (ranked #60 for 1981)

TRIVIA: Fu Sheng's first film after breaking his leg

TRIVIA: Fu Sheng is only 14 months older than his co-star sibling

TRIVIA: David Cheung studied under director Lau Kar-wing

TRIVIA: "Master of Disaster" is alternate title

"Didn't you know 11 out of 10 old men got to pee at midnight?"

Alexander Fu Sheng teams up with director Lau Kar-wing, famed brother of Lau Kar-Leung, for the first of three films which also introduces newcomer and Alex's real-life sibling, David Cheung Chin-Pang.

Chi Tao Pao (Fu Sheng) is a cunning kung fu conman and low-level thief who befriends the affluent but spoiled socialite, Chao Chu Chi (David Cheung). The pair form a close bond through tomfoolery and attempt to seize some letters from an antique merchant, in the belief these dispatches will lead to an undisclosed treasure. However, they aren't the only ones.

The ruthless Lord Mo (Wang Lung-Wei) and his henchwoman assistant (Yeung Jing-Jing) also seek this fortune. They kill off everyone in their quest and make it appear that the head priest of the Fahua Temple (Gordon Lau Kar-fai) is the culprit. When Lord Mo's scheme becomes clear to both the priest and the two bumbling thieves, they combine forces against Lord Mo and his female cohort in a deadly encounter.

Based on Louis Cha's script, *Treasure Hunters* is an agreeable blend of serious, hard kung fu with comedic antics that many films of the time had adopted. Though this is David Cheung's introduction film, he held his own in both physical flair and slapstick comedy.

TITLE: Legendary Weapons of China (1982)

DIRECTOR: Lau Kar-Leung

PRODUCER: Mona Fong Yat-Wa, Chan Lee-Wah

ACTION DIRECTOR: Lau Kar-Leung, Hsiao Ho, Li King-Chu

ASS'T DIR: Lee Tai-Hang

CINEMATOGRAPHER: Peter Ngor Chi-Kwan

EDITOR: Chiang Hsing-Lung, Lee Yim-Hoi

SCRIPT: Lau Kar-Leung, Lee Tai-Hang

CAST:
Lau Kar-Leung . . . . Lui Gung
Hsiao Ho . . . . Tien Hao
Hui Ying-hung . . . . Fang Shau-Ching
Lau Kar-wing . . . . Lui Yung
Alexander Fu Sheng . . . . . . Mo
Gordon Lau Kar-fai . . . . . . Ti Tan
Jue Tit-Woh . . . . Tieh Tien
Wong Ching-Ho . . . . Chief Eunuch Li Lien Ying
Li King-Chu . . . . Leader of Earth Clan
Cheung Chok-Chow . . . . . . Boss of Fu An Inn
Wang Han-Chen . . . . Boss of eatery

RELEASE DATE: January 21, 1982

BOX OFFICE: $9,913,242 (ranked #9 for 1982)

TRIVIA: Fu Sheng's biggest box office gross

TRIVIA: Fu Sheng's first film under director Lau Kar-Leung

TRIVIA: Faced stiff competition in theaters as it was released the same week as *Aces Go Places* (#1), Jackie Chan's *Dragon Lord* (#2), and Jet Li's *Shaolin Temple* (#4).

"You're in shit and not worthy to fight me."

Fu Sheng's first of three productions with his real-life master, Lau Kar-Leung, validates his comedic talents in a supporting role.

With the country overrun by foreigners, the Empress Dowager demands that the Yi Ho Boxer Society make their fighters invulnerable to gunfire. While these Boxers become invincible to many weapons, they're simply no match for the invader's superior firearms. Lui Gung (Lau Kar-Leung) has foreseen this so he disbands his own army of Boxers to save them and goes into reclusion as a simple woodcutter.

The unctuous Chief Eunuch Li Lien Ying declares Lui Gung's abandonment an act of treason and sends a select group of fighters to assassinate him. Tien Hao (Hsiao Ho) is the first hitman who falls ill after a feces-strewn battle with a charlatan Boxer (Fu Sheng), and is nursed back to health by Lui. The next assassin, Heaven Clan's Ti Tan (Gordon Lau Kar-Fai), is soundly defeated by Liu but his life is spared. Tien Hao sees the error of his ways, and along with spiritual Boxer Fang Shau-Ching (Hui Ying-hung), assists the retired spirit warrior in preparation for a final duel against a yet to be seen assassin.

Legendary Weapons of China's title denotes the 18 traditional weapons of wushu which is represented throughout the movie. In making this film, director Lau Kar-Leung creates a historical record that's both visually exhilarating and informative.

TITLE: The Brave Archer and his Mate (1982)

DIRECTOR: Chang Cheh

PRODUCER: Mona Fong Yat-Wa, Chen Lieh

ACTION DIRECTOR: Kwok Chun-Fung, Lu Feng, Chiang Sheng,

ASS'T DIR: Chiang Sheng, Lo Yuen-Ming

CINEMATOGRAPHER: Cho Wai-Kei

EDITOR: Chiang Hsing-Lung, Lee Yim-Hoi

SCRIPT: Chang Cheh, Ni Kuang, Louis Cha (original story)

CAST:
Kwok Chun-Fung . . . . Guo Jing
Gigi Wong Suk-Yee . . . . . . Huang Rong
Alexander Fu Sheng . . . . . . Yang Guo
Chin Siu-Ho . . . . Wu Sau Man
Lung Tien-Hsiang . . . . Yang Kang
Wong Lik . . . . Western Poison Ouyang Fung
Chan Shen . . . . Senior Teacher Or
Chiang Sheng . . . . Prince of Fu To
Chu Ko . . . . Da Er Ba
Lu Feng . . . . Priest Chi King
Danny Lee Sau-Yin . . . . Ouyang Ke

RELEASE DATE: February 25, 1982

BOX OFFICE: $1,627,031 (ranked #76 for 1982)

TRIVIA: Based on Louis Cha's *The Return of the Condor Heroes*

TRIVIA: TVB produced a 50-episode series from the same book

TRIVIA: "Mysterious Island" is an alternate title

TRIVIA: *Little Dragon Maiden* is a retelling of this story

"All gone."

Those are Alexander Fu Sheng's last words as the final Chang Cheh/ Louis Cha adaptation came to a screeching halt — freeze frame and all.

Following in the footsteps of the first three films, this production continues the saga of hero Guo Jing (Kwok Chun-Fung) and his wife Huang Rong (Gigi Wong). The couple are now guardians to an orphaned child, Yang Guo, after a deadly encounter with the nefarious Ouyang Fung (Wong Lik) in Iron Spear Temple.

Years later, Yang Guo (Fu Sheng) is a playful loafer residing on Peach Island. Guo Jing and Huang Rong have refrained from teaching martial arts to Yang concerned that he may follow in his real father's footsteps. This doesn't dissuade Yang from finding someone who will teach him kung fu, and sneaks off to Iron Spear Temple where he encounters Ouyang Fung, whose mind is impaired from studying the Jin Jan manual in error. Ouyang instructs Yang Guo in the powerful frog style and then convinces him that his actual father was a hero murdered by the couple who raised him.

Despite the title, this final *Brave Archer* film by Chang is less about the adventures of Guo Jing and Huang Rong and more about Yang Guo and his coming of age. The film features superb fights by three of the remaining Venoms.

TITLE: The 8 Diagram Pole Fighter (1984)

DIRECTOR: Lau Kar-Leung

PRODUCER: Mona Fong Yat-Wa, Wong Ka-Hay, Chan Lee-Wah

ACTION DIRECTOR: Lau Kar-Leung, Hsiao Ho, Li King-Chu

ASS'T DIR: Chan Yau-Man, Wong Bat-Ging, Wong Kwok-Wai

CINEMATOGRAPHER: Cho On-Sun

EDITOR: Chiang Hsing-Lung, Lee Yim-Hoi

SCRIPT: Ni Kuang, Lau Kar-Leung

CAST:
Gordon Lau Kar-fai . . . . . . Yang 5th brother
Alexander Fu Sheng . . . . . . Yang 6th brother
Hui Ying-hung . . . . Yang 8th sister
Lily Li Li-Li . . . . Mother Yang
Yeung Jing-Jing . . . . Yang 9th sister
Phillip Ko Fei . . . . Temple Abbot
Li King-Chu . . . . Temple Abbot Zhihong
Lam Hak-Ming . . . . General Pan Mei
Johnny Wang Lung-Wei . . . Prince Yeh Li Lin
Lau Kar-Leung . . . . Hunter
Wong Ching-Ho . . . . Innkeeper

RELEASE DATE: February 17, 1984

BOX OFFICE: $3,792,852 (ranked #47 for 1984)

TRIVIA: Began production in early 1981

TRIVIA: LKL was director/choreographer/actor/writer

TRIVIA: Original ending was for Lau Kar-fai to save Fu Sheng

TRIVIA: Received a nomination for Best Action Choreography at the 4th HKFA but lost to Jackie Chan's *Project A (1983)*

"*Seven gone, Six returned.*"

This is Lau Kar-Leung's gripping drama of the Yang Clan and the cataclysmic betrayal that ripped apart their family.

The Yangs are stalwart supporters of the reigning Song Dynasty. Their lives unravel after falling into a trap set by the traitorous general Pan Mei. The turncoat has sided with the barbarous Tartars to overthrow the Emperor, and a one-sided battle leaves only two of the Yang patriots to escape the carnage.

The first survivor is Yang 6th brother (Fu Sheng), who returns home driven by an uncontrollable rage and bloodlust. Unknown to him or the others, Yang 5th brother (Lau Kar-fai) also survives and attempts to take refuge in a Buddhist temple where he begs entry as a monk.

Yang 5th brother is equally traumatized by the battle and the Abbott determines his ferocity clashes with the pacific nature of the monk lifestyle. The Abbott informs the Yang family and Yang 8th sister (Hui Ying-hung) is sent off to retrieve her brother, but falls into the hands of Pan Mei and his Tartar allies. Yang 5th brother has no choice but to come out of hiding to rescue his sister and exact revenge.

A raw and powerful film, there is no doubt Fu Sheng's real-life death helped fuel Lau Kar-Leung's finest yet darkest cinematic accomplishment.

TITLE: Fake Ghost Catchers (1982)

DIRECTOR: Lau Kar-wing

PRODUCER: Mona Fong Yat-Wa, Chan Lee-Wah

ACTION DIRECTOR: Lau Kar-wing, Li King-Chu

ASS'T DIR: Chang Kwok-Tse, Wong Ying-Git

CINEMATOGRAPHER: Wong Wing-Lung

EDITOR: Chiang Hsing-Lung, Lee Yim-Hoi

SCRIPT: Wong Jing

CAST:
David Cheung Chin-Pang . . Zhou Peng
Hsiao Ho . . . . Bao Tuo
Alexander Fu Sheng . . . . . . Wu Shunchao
Johnny Wang Lung-Wei . . . Zhuge Sen
Lily Li Li-Li . . . . Mrs. Lin Huanzhu
To Siu-Ming . . . . Luo Wuhai
Lam Fai-Wong . . . . Master Zhang
Yeung Chi-Hing . . . . Official Gongsun
Wong Ching-Ho . . . . Old Master Lin
Shum Lo . . . . Magistrate
Lung Tien-Hsiang . . . . Du Luo

RELEASE DATE: July 30, 1982

BOX OFFICE: $3,622,7423 (ranked #40 for 1982)

TRIVIA: David Cheung's second lead role

TRIVIA: Fu Sheng nearly quit the studio during production

TRIVIA: Lily Li's seventh and last film with Fu Sheng

TRIVIA: DP Wong's first credit was *Temple of the Red Lotus*

"I found your husband hence the emergency landing."

Alexander Fu Sheng teams up with his real-life brother in this tale of ghouls, gags, and giggles penned by one of Hong Kong's most diligent and controversial filmmakers.

Bao Tuo (Hsiao Ho) is a pupil of Master Zhang (Lam Fai-Wong), a local conman who claims connections to the afterlife. When Zhang leaves town for a few days, Bao and his cousin Zhou Peng (David Cheung) endeavor to make some easy money by staging a faux exorcism. Unknown to them, Mrs. Lin (Lily Li Li-Li) is truly possessed by her scorned lover, Du Luo (Lung Tien-Hsiang), and the con duo soon find themselves in way over their heads. Bao and Zhou must flee for their lives after the demon kills its host and a group of monks who attempt to expel the evil spirit.

Their freedom is short lived when the ghost of Mrs. Lin tracks the pair down and demands to be taken to Lin's twin sister's home. They reluctantly agree with Du Luo's ghost and enlist cursed opera star Wu Chuntao (Fu Sheng) to assist them. What complicates matters further for Bao Tuo and Zhou Peng is a corrupt government official (Wang Lung-Wei) and his posse who are hot on their trail.

Fake Ghost Catchers is an entertaining mix of supernatural fantasy and kung fu choreography which is further enhanced with some rather creative special effects.

TITLE: Cat vs Rat (1982)

DIRECTOR: Lau Kar-Leung

PRODUCER: Mona Fong Yat-Wa, Chan Lee-Wah, Wong Ka-Hay

ACTION DIRECTOR: Lau Kar-Leung, Li King-Chu, Hsiao Ho

ASS'T DIR: Lee Tai-Hang, Wong Bat-Ging

CINEMATOGRAPHER: Cho On-Sun, Cho Wai-Kei

EDITOR: Lee Yim-Hoi, Chiang Hsing-Lung

SCRIPT: Ni Kuang

CAST:
Adam Cheng Siu-Chow . . . Jien Chiu
Alexander Fu Sheng . . . . . . Bai Yu Tong
Hsiao Ho . . . . Cheung Ping
Hui Ying-hung . . . . Jien Yu Lan
Lau Kar-wing . . . . Master Si Da Fu
Gordon Lau Kar-fai . . . . . . Emperor Yang Xi
Wong Ching-Ho . . . . Minister Huang
Lydia Shum Tin-Ha . . . . Bai's mother
Johnny Wang Lung-Wei . . . Pierce Mountain Rat
Li King-Chu . . . . Ground Rat
David Cheung Chin-Pang . . Sky Rat

RELEASE DATE: September 30, 1982

BOX OFFICE: $4,472,000 (ranked #27 for 1982)

TRIVIA: Plot based on the novel *Seven Heroes and Five Gallants*

TRIVIA: Fu Sheng's final collaboration with the Lau brothers

TRIVIA: Alex and Adam's competition extended beyond the set

TRIVIA: Only 24 days from end of production to theatrical release

"A cat ultimately thwarts a rat's treachery."

Alexander Fu Sheng and Adam Cheng pair up for their only on-screen performance in a maniac comedy featuring superb choreography that only the Lau brothers could concoct.

Jien Chiu aka The Cat (Adam Cheng) and Bai Yu Tong aka The Rat (Fu Sheng) are from competing households despite having the same teacher; Master Si Da Fu (Lau Kar-wing). Although their master declares they are equally matched, Jien and Bai continue to engage one another in a series of challenges.

When Emperor Yang Xi (Lau Kar-fai) arrives in the area, he's ambushed by bandits but saved by Jien Chiu. Emperor Yang praises his savior and bestows him with the honor of a royal guard. This infuriates Bai Yu Tong who hatches an elaborate scheme to not only steal the emperor's jade seal but place the blame on his kung fu brother. The plan backfires when his rat gang (Wang Lung-Wei, Li King-Chu, and David Cheung) leave Bai behind in the act. Caught red-handed by the Emperor, Jien and Bai set aside their personal grievances to find the real thieves and retrieve the jade seal.

Lau Kar-Leung served up a dizzying combination of cartoonish comedy and silly slapstick with some superb weapons fighting in his final film with Alex.

TITLE: Hong Kong Playboys (1983)

DIRECTOR: Wong Jing

PRODUCER: Mona Fong Yat-Wa, Tse Ga-Wai, Wong Ka-Hay

ACTION DIRECTOR: Yuen Bun

ASS'T DIR: Leung Sing-Kuen, Mau Kin-Tak

CINEMATOGRAPHER: Lee San-Yip

EDITOR: Lau Shiu-Gwong, Chiang Hsing-Lung

SCRIPT: Wong Jing

CAST:
Alexander Fu Sheng . . . . . . Yan Quan Sheng
Patrick Tse Yin . . . . Valentine
Nat Chan Pak-Cheung . . . . . Lolanto
Cherie Chung Cho-Hung . . . Ah Mei
Leanne Lau Suet-Wah . . . . . Rachel Yu
Lee Heung-Kam . . . . Sheng's Mother
Winnie Chin Wai-Yee . . . . . Mao Ying Ying
Sek Kin . . . . Mao Ying Ying's Father
Lam Fai-Wong . . . . Lolanto's assistant
Margaret Lee Din-Long . . . . Aunt Mao
Chiang Kam . . . . Fatty

RELEASE DATE: June 18, 1983

BOX OFFICE: $7,373,743 (ranked #13 for 1983)

TRIVIA: Fu Sheng's second highest grossing film

TRIVIA: Film's last day in theaters was July 6, 1983

TRIVIA: In production for over 14 months

TRIVIA: Fu Sheng's actual Porsche was used for the film

"There's four steps in dating a girl: Watch. Chase. Date. Dump."

Alexander Fu Sheng stars in this comedic look at the trials and tribulations of bachelor life, written and directed by Wong Jing, in one of Wong's earlier efforts behind the camera.

Yan Quan Sheng (Fu Sheng) is a well-to-do playboy who leads a carefree existence in which his home, cars, and lifestyle cater to his primary necessity; female companionship. When his socialite mother returns from overseas, his routine is miserably turned upside down. What makes matters worse is his mother's private nurse, Ah Mei (Cherie Chung Cho-Hung), who quickly finds herself at odds with Yan's womanizing ways.

Instead of perusing a meaningful relationship with the straitlaced Ah Mei, Yan is caught up in a skirt-chasing competition with the debonair Valentine (Patrick Tse) and likable loser Lolanto (Nat Chan Bak-Cheung). The object of their rivalry is the lovely Mao Ying Ying (Winnie Chin Wai-Yee), who has a spinster guardian (Li Tien-lang), and a Triad for a dad (Shih Kien). Amidst all the scheming, Yan realizes his heart doesn't lie with any woman except one, Ah Mei, who he may have lost for good due to his player ways.

Charming and witty, this rom-com featured some early '80s hi-tech gadgetry plus lots of now dated fashion statements.

TITLE: Wits of the Brats (1984)

DIRECTOR: Lau Kar-wing, Fu Sheng, Wong Jing

PRODUCER: Mona Fong Yat-Wa, Tse Ga-Wai, Wong Ka-Hay

ACTION DIRECTOR: Lau Kar-wing, Yeung Sai-Gwan

ASS'T DIR: Leung Sing-Kuen, Yung Leng-Wai

CINEMATOGRAPHER: Lee San-Yip

EDITOR: Lau Shiu-Gwong, Cheung Siu-Hei, Chan Gan-Shing

SCRIPT: Wong Jing

CAST:
David Cheung Chin-Pang . . Tou Kuan
Lam Fai-Wong . . . . Mai Song
Johnny Wang Lung-Wei . . . Three Eyes
Alexander Fu Sheng . . . . . . Che Zai
Wong Yu . . . . Three Hands
Chan Shen . . . . Shih Chun
Wong Jing . . . . Mr. Blinker
Li King-Chu . . . . Master Lai
To Siu-Ming . . . . Rendao Tajirou
Nat Chan Pak-Cheung . . . . . Ren Zhen-Hao
Lee Hoi-Sang . . . . Four Eyes

RELEASE DATE: May 24, 1984

BOX OFFICE: $2,195,764 (ranked #66 for 1984)

TRIVIA: 1 of 3 films uncompleted at the time of Fu Sheng's death

TRIVIA: Last "released film" in Fu Sheng's filmography

TRIVIA: Fu Sheng's only (released) directorial effort

TRIVIA: Lam Fai-Wong appeared in 26 films with Fu Sheng

"What? Both of them can't handle her?"

Alexander Fu Sheng and David Cheung star in their final on-screen collaboration. Alex also shares directing duties with the ever-versatile Lau Kar-wing and sometimes vulgar Wong Jing.

Tou Kuan (David Cheung) is the spoiled brat of a wealthy Guangdong family who cannot find any fighters in Southern China that match his skills. Tou's mother decides she has tolerated his immature behavior for long enough and packs him off to Beijing to find a new bride. Nonetheless, Tou's only ambition is to challenge masters from the north to test his martial arts expertise.

The obnoxious young scholar's first encounter is with a shrewd charlatan, Che Zai (Fu Sheng), who shows Tou that he is no match for his wits and lands the Guangdong native in hot water. Tou soon after meets his next rival, dubbed Terrific (Nat Chan Pak-Cheung), in wooing a Russian Ambassador's daughter, and later is pitted against master thief Three Hands (Wong Yu). While all these competitions are harmless, Tou is unaware that a formidable assassin named Three Eyes (Wang Lung-Wei) has been hired by his scheming uncle, so Tou will need his new allies to battle this dangerous adversary.

Kung fu and "Mo-lei-tau" brand of comedy combines in this energetic tale, which due to Fu Sheng's untimely death, was finished post-mortem by filmmakers Lau Kar-wing and Wong Jing.

BIBLIOGRAPHY

BOOKS

Akers-Jones, David. Feeling the Stones: Reminiscences. Hong Kong: Hong Kong UP, 2004.

Baker, Hugh D. R. A Chinese Lineage Village: Sheung Shui. Stanford, CA: Stanford UP, 1968.

Bettinson, Gary. Directory of World Cinema. China 2. Bristol, UK: Intellect, 2015.

Block, Alex Ben. The Legend of Bruce Lee. St. Albans, Herts.: Mayflower, 1974. 56-68.

Blyth, Sally, and Ian Wotherspoon. "Cheung Yan Lung: Rural Politics." Hong Kong Remembers. New York: Oxford UP, 1996. 36.

Booth, Martin. The Dragon Syndicates: The Global Phenomenon of the Triads. New York: Carroll & Graf, 2001.

Bordwell, David. Planet Hong Kong: Popular Cinema and the Art of Entertainment. Cambridge, MA: Harvard UP, 2003.

Bray, Denis. Hong Kong Metamorphosis. Hong Kong: Hong Kong University Press, 2001.

Canzonieri, Salvatore. "Shaolin's Fighting Monks - The Buddhist/Taoist Legacy of Shaolin's Fighting Monks." Kung Fu Qigong Magazine Apr-May 1996.

Charles, John. The Hong Kong Filmography, 1977-1997: A Complete Reference to 1,100 Films Produced by British Hong Kong Studios. Jefferson, NC: McFarland, 2000.

Cheuk-to, Li, ed. A Tribute to Action Choreographers. N.p.: Hong Kong International Film Festival Society, 2006.

Cohen, Paul A. History in Three Keys: The Boxers as Events, Experience, and Myth. New York, NY: Columbia UP, 1997.

Cheung, Chi-sing, Po Fung, and May Ng. Oral History Series (7): Hong Kong Cinema of the 1970s. Hong Kong: Hong Kong Film Archive, 2018.

Chu, Yuan, Jingning Guo, and Grace Ng. Oral History Series (3): Director Chor Yuen. Hong Kong: Hong Kong Film Archive, 2006.

Editors of Kung-Fu Monthly. Who Killed Bruce Lee? N.p.: Castle, 1978.

Esherick, Joseph W. The Origins of the Boxer Uprising. Berkeley, Calif.: U of Calif. Pr., 1987.

Fu, Poshek. China Forever: The Shaw Brothers and Diasporic Cinema. Urbana: U of Illinois, 2008.

Fu, Poshek, and David Desser. The Cinema of Hong Kong: History, Arts, Identity. Cambridge, U.K.: Cambridge UP, 2000. 99.

Glaessner, Verina. Kung Fu: Cinema of Vengeance. New York: Bounty, 1974.

Hall, Kenneth E. John Woo: The Films. Jefferson, NC: McFarland & Co., 2012.

Hase, Patrick H. The Six-Day War of 1899: Hong Kong in the Age of Imperialism. Hong Kong: Hong Kong University Press, 2008.

Hayes, James. The Great Difference: Hong Kong's New Territories and Its People, 1898-2004. Hong Kong: Hong Kong University Press, 2012.

Hunt, Leon. Kung Fu Cult Masters. London: Wallflower, 2003. 57.

Lent, John A. The Asian Film Industry. Austin: U. of Texas P., 1990.

Leung, Donald. The Making of Martial Arts Films: As Told by Filmmakers and Stars. Hong Kong: Hong Kong Film Archive, 1999.

Lewis, Meredith. Ask for the Moon: Innovations at Shaw Brothers Studio. Morrisville, NC: Lulu Press, Inc., 2018

Li, Daw-ming. Historical Dictionary of Taiwan Cinema. Lanham, MD: Scarecrow P., 2013.

Logan, Bey. Hong Kong Action Cinema. Woodstock, NY: Overlook, 1996.

Long, Gu. Yingxiong Wu Lei Aka A Hero without Tears. Hongkong: Hua Xin Tushu Chubanshe, 1978. Trans. deathblade. (2014): Rpt. in http://www.spcnet.tv/forums/showthread.php/38185-Heroes-Shed-No-Tears-Gu-Long.

Morris, Jan. Hong Kong. New York: Random House, 1988.

Mullen, Kevin J. Chinatown Squad: Policing the Dragon: From the Gold Rush to the 21st Century. Novato, CA: Noir Publications, 2008.

O'Connor, Richard. The Spirit Soldiers. New York, NY: G.P Putnam Sons, 1973.

Preston, Diana. The Boxer Rebellion: The Dramatic Story of China's War on Foreigners That Shook the World in the Summer of 1900. New York: Berkley, 2001.

Reid, Craig. The Ultimate Guide to Martial Arts Movies of the 1970s: 500 Films Loaded with Action, Weapons and Warriors. Santa Clarita, CA: Black Belt, 2010.

Shahar, Meir. The Shaolin Monastery: History, Religion, and the Chinese Martial Arts. Honolulu: U of Hawai'i, 2011.

Stokes, Lisa Odham. Historical Dictionary of Hong Kong Cinema. Lanham: Scarecrow, 2007.

Teo, Stephen. Hong Kong Cinema: The Extra Dimensions. London: British Film Institute, 2007.

Wong, Ain-Ling, and Sam Ho. The Cathay Story. Sai Wan Ho, Hong Kong: Hong Kong Film Archive, 2002.

Wong, Ain-ling, ed. The Shaw Screen: A Preliminary Study. Hong Kong: Hong Kong Film Archive, 2003.

Wu, Dingbo, and Patrick D. Murphy. Handbook of Chinese Popular Culture. Westport, CT: Greenwood, 1994.

Wu, Hao, ed. Nan Er Ben Se = The Heroes. Hong Kong: Joint Publishing, 2005.

Wu, Hao, ed. Wu Xia, Gong Fu Pian = Wu Xia, Kung Fu Films. Hong Kong: Joint Publishing, 2004.

Yang, Jeff, and Art Black. Once upon a Time in China: A Guide to Hong Kong, Taiwanese, and Mainland Chinese Cinema. New York: Atria, 2003.

Youngs, Tim. Rose Nere E Guerrieri Sentimentali: Il Cinema Di Chor Yuen. Udine: Centro Espressioni Cinematografiche, 2004.

Zhang, Che, Ailing Huang, Jingning Guo, May Ng, and Agnes Lam. Chang Cheh: A Memoir. Hong Kong: Hong Kong Film Archive, 2004.

FILM REVIEWS AND INTERVIEWS

Allison, Keith. "Movie Reviews Eight Diagram Pole Fighter." Teleport City. N.p., 2002. Web.

Assayas, Olivier, and Charles Tesson. "Interview with Lau Kar Leung: The Last Shaolin." Trans. Cai Kejian and Yves Gendron. Cahiers Du Cinema (1984): 26-30. Print.

Bettinson, Gary. "Act of Vengeance: an interview with David Chiang." Post Script, Vol. 31, No. 1, 2011. Web.

Bona, Jeffrey. "Five Shaolin Masters aka 5 Masters of Death (1974) Review." Review. City on Fire, 2 Sept. 2011. Web.

Brady, Terrence. "Richard Harrison: Shaw Bros to B-Movie Ninja Films." Jade Screen Mar. 2010: 36-38. Print.

Chang, Tan Han, Lee Dao Ming, and Tse Ching Kwun. "Chang Cheh Talking about Chang Cheh." Trans. Michael Wong. Influence Magazine Apr. 1976: 6-16. Rpt. in http://changcheh.0catch.com N.p.: n.p., 2003. Print.

Davis, Brendan. "Brave Archer 3: The Epic Conclusion (of sorts) of a Wuxia Classic." ShawBrothersUniverse. N.p., 10 Oct. 2016. Web.

"Interview with Chi Kuan-Chun." Taipei Times 1986: N.p. Southern Screen Revisited - The Shaw Brothers Fanzine, Special Edition SB Stars # 01. 2007. Web.

"Kara Hui Exclusive Interview - My Young Auntie." YouTube. Celestial Pictures, 07 Feb. 2017. Web.

Kouf, Will. "Police Force (1973)." Silver Emulsion Film Reviews. N.p., 06 Mar. 2016. Web.

Kouf, Will. "The Boxer from Shantung (1972). "Silver Emulsion Film Reviews. N.p., 30 Aug. 2013. Web.

Lam, Andre. "An Interview with Liu Chia Liang." Real Kung Fu Apr. 1976: 70-77. Print.

Marsh, James. "Paris Cinema IFF Interview: Kara Wai Ying Hung on Kung-Fu and Comebacks." ScreenAnarchy. N.p., 28 June 2012. Web.

"Meeting a Shaw Brothers Legend." Ti Lung at the 2004 Amiens Film Festival. Interview. 11 Nov. 2004: n. page. Hong Kong Cnemagic. Web.

Pollard, Mark. "Heaven and Hell (1980)." Rev. of VHS. Kung Fu Cinema. 2004. Web.

Pollard, Mark. "Men from the Monastery (1974)." Rev. of DVD. Kung Fu Cinema. 2005. Web.

Pollard, Mark. "Na Cha the Great (1974)." Rev. of DVD. Kung Fu Cinema. 2005. Web.

Pollard, Mark. "The Deadly Breaking Sword (1979)." Rev. of VHS. Kung Fu Cinema. 2004. Web.

Reid, Craig. "Chen Kuan-Tai - The Real Iron Monkey." Kung Fu Tai Chi Aug. 2007: 48-52. Print.

Reid, Craig. "Gordon Liu Chia Hui." kungfumagazine.com. N.p., Apr. 2004. Web.

Russell, Toby. "Kuo Chui Interview." Eastern Heroes Special Edition #5. 1985: 28-32. Print.

"Seventy Years of the Shrunken King: Chiang Da-Wai." mtime.com. N.p., 28 Jan. 2012. Web.

Shum, Lydia, host. "Suen Zhong and Kam Fei; Episode 9." Where Are They Now? TVB. Hong Kong, 2006. Television.

Talk Asia. "Interview with Gordon Liu." CNN. Cable News Network, 25 Oct. 2007. Web.

"Thunderbolt Fist, The (1972)." Hong Kong Movie Database. N.p., 9 Aug. 2006. Web.

White, Luke. "Kung Fu with Braudel." Four Riders – Chang Cheh's Apocalyptic Vision. Blogspot.com, 19 Nov. 2011. Web.

Wong, Yan. "Chang Cheh's Directorial Journey." Trans. Min-chi Wong. Influence Magazine Apr. 1976: 17-20. Web.

Yu, Mo-wan. 'Swords, Chivalry and Palm Power: A Brief Survey of the Cantonese Martial at Cinema 1938-1970', in Lau Shing-hon (ed.), A Study of the Hong Kong Swordplay Film (1945-1980), pp. 99-106.

MISCELLANEOUS

Celestial Pictures
Facebook
Hong Kong Cinemagic
Hong Kong Film Archive
Hong Kong Land Registry
Hong Kong Leisure and Cultural Services Dept.
Hong Kong Movie Database
Hong Kong Public Library
Judiciary of the Hong Kong Special Administrative Region
Kung Fu Fandom
Middle Georgia Regional Library System
National Archives of Singapore
New York Public Library
Shaw Organization
Television Broadcasts Limited (TVB)
University of Oxford School of Anthropology and Museum Ethnography
Wuxiasociety

NEWSPAPERS AND PERIODICALS

Chinese University of Hong Kong
Cinemart Magazine
Coast Artillery Journal
Hong Kong Business Daily
Hong Kong Commercial Daily
Hong Kong International Film Festival
Hong Kong Movie News
Lodi News-Sentinel
Los Angeles Times
Milky Way Pictorial
Ming Pao Weekly
NATV Limited

Nanyang Commercial Press
New York Post
Newsweek
Ocala Star-Banner
San Francisco Chronicle
Shaw Brothers Fanzine
Singapore Monitor
South China Morning Post
Southern Screen
The Kung Sheung Evening News
The Straits Times / New Straits Times
Time Magazine
Vancouver Sun
Variety
Yuk Long TV Weekly

WEB AND MORE

"1925: The Start of a Legendary Studio." The Chinese Mirror: A Journal of Chinese History. Chinesemirror.com, n.d. Web.
"A Letter Written by Alex." Silver World 1975: N.p., Rpt. in Cinemart. 164th ed. N.p., 1983. 31. Print.
"About Shaw." Shaw Online. Shaw Organization, 10 Aug. 2001. Web.
Brady, Terrence. "Chinatown Lost: Celestial Pictures vs. Southgate Entertainment." THIRD MILLENNIUM Entertainment. N.p., 14 Mar. 2004. Web.
"Celestial Pictures Presents Shaw Brothers Masterpieces Digitally Restored Starting December 5, 2002." Celestial Pictures. Press Release, Oct. 2002. Web.
Chung, Po-Ying. "Moguls of the Chinese Cinema: The Story of the Shaw Brothers in Shanghai, Hong Kong and Singapore, 1924–2002." Modern Asian Studies Vol. 41, No. 4: 665-682, July 2007. Print.
Dannen, Fredric. "Partners in Crime." New Republic. N.p., 14 June 1997. Web.

Fonoroff, Paul. "A Brief History of Hong Kong Cinema." Renditions 1988: 293-308. Chinese University of Hong Kong. Web.

"From Dancer to Best Actress." Apple Daily. N.p., 18 Jul. 2018. Web.

"Fu Sing & Yan Nei." Hong Kong: NATV Limited. Ng Hing Kee Book & Newspaper Agency, 1983. Print.

Green, Tom. "The Rise and Fall of the House of Shaw." Hong Kong Cinema - View from the Brooklyn Bridge. N.p., 2005. Web.

Hanson, Chris "The Mongol Siege of Xiangyang and Fan-ch'eng and the Song military." De Re Militari. Society for Medieval Military History. N.p., 11 May 2014. Web.

Haven, Cynthia. "Pop Star with a PhD." Stanford Magazine. Stanford Alumni Association, July-Aug. 1999. Web.

"Haywood Cheung Loves Adventure and is Not Afraid of Failure." Takungpao.com. N.p., 27 May 2015. Web.

"Hung Gar History." TCMAInstitute, 3 Sept. 2017, www.chhcanada.com/ history_hung_gar/?lang=en. N.p., Web.

"Jenny Tseng's Best Friend Blurts Truth about Her Daughter." Asian Entertainment News 2011 (Archive). AFspot Forum. 12 May 2011. Web.

Jin, Yong. She Diao Ying Xiong Zhuan. Hong Kong: Hong Kong Commercial Daily, 1957. Trans. Various. (2005): Rpt. in http://www.spcnet.tv/forums/showthread.php/20809-Eagle-Shooting-Hero-Book-4.

Jing, Zheng. "Decline of Cheung Yan-lung and the Heungs." Pixnet. N.p., 8 Aug. 2013. Web.

Kwok, Kam-chu. "Planning for Village Development in the New Territories." Thesis. University of Hong Kong, 1987. N.p., n.d. Web.

Lo, Sonny Shiu-Hing. "The Politics of Cross-border Crime in Greater China Case Studies of Mainland China, Hong Kong, and Macao." Armonk, N.Y: M.E. Sharpe, 2009. Print.

Page, Tony. "The Men Who Make Celluloid Dreams." www.zambagrafix.com/pf_films.htm N.p., 10 Jul 2002. Web.

Palmer, Michael, "Lineage and Urban Development in a New Territories Market Town," in Hugh Baker and Stephen Feuchtwang (eds.), An old state in new settings: studies in the social anthropology of China in memory of Maurice Freedman (Oxford: JASO, 1991), 70-106. Print.

Pang Yi, Norris. South China Morning Post [Hong Kong] Nov. 1976: N.p., Rpt. in Southern Screen Revisited - The Shaw Brothers Fanzine, Special Edition SB Stars # 01. Trans. Marion Mixdorff. 2007. Web.

"Police Officer's Father: Drunk Driver Should Be Sentenced to Prison." Apple Daily. N.p., 18 Mar. 2004. Web.

Renée, V. "A Complete History of CinemaScope with Film Historian David Bordwell." No Film School. N.p., 28 Oct. 2014. Web.

"Resistance Wars." Polticial, Social, Cultural, Historical Analysis of China. Republicanchina.org. N.p., n.d. Web.

"Shandong Ma Yongzhen (1927)." The Chinese Mirror: A Journal of Chinese History. Chinesemirror.com, n.d. Web.

Tsui, Clarence. "Take Two." South China Morning Post. N.p., 05 Apr. 2008. Web.

Unknown [Taiwan] Aug. 1973: N.p., www.chinakongfu.org. 2008. Web.

Wong, Kiew Kit. "Answers to Readers' Questions and Answers - November 1999 Part 1." Shaolin Wahnam Institute. Nov. 1999. Web.

INDEX

14 Amazons, 29-30, 186, 223-224
16th Asian Film Festival, 43
19th Asian Film Festival, 29, 41
20th Asian Film Festival, 47, 238
21st Asian Film Festival, 86
25th Asian Film Festival, 146
28 Reasons, The 199-200
36th Chamber of Shaolin, 78
5 Masters of Death (See Five Shaolin Masters)
8 Diagram Pole Fighter, 5, 186, 188, 195, 211-212, 299-300
A Better Tomorrow, 39, 236
A Brave Girl-Boxer in Shanghai, 41
A Mellow Spring, 42
Adam Cheng, 98, 193, 303-304
Admiral Tsou Chien, 120
Adventures of Fang Shih-yu, 61
Agnes Chan, 36, 41, 227-228, 233-234
Akira Kurosawa, 182
Alain Delon, 38
Alfred von Waldersee, 88
Amy Tao Man-Ming, 77, 98, 125
Andy Lau, 91, 197
Angela Liu, 7-8, 11, 16-17, 124, 178, 181, 203, 208
Anonymous Heroes, 31
Asia-Pacific Film Festival, 39
Assassin, The, 33
Avenger, The, 41
Avenging Eagle, The, 5, 144, 146, 148, 160, 277-278, 282

Bak Mei, 61, 64, 79, 81, 261-262
basher, 39-40, 68, 79, 226
Beggar So, 150, 179, 195-196, 279
Best Young Newcomer Award, 47
Betty Loh Ti, 26
Big Boss, The, 48, 65
Big Sword Society, 89
Black Belt Theater, 130
Black September, 149, 174, 181, 286
Blast of the Iron Palm (See Brave Archer Part III)
Blood Brothers, The, 35, 39, 51
Boxer from Shantung, 39-41, 44, 62-63, 226, 232
Boxer Rebellion, 3, 86-88, 91, 93, 128, 251-252
Brave Archer and His Mate, The, 182, 184-186, 297-298
Brave Archer Part II, The, 139-141, 161, 185, 275, 276
Brave Archer Part III, The, 134, 161-162, 168, 287-288
Brave Archer, The, 5, 47, 132-134, 136, 139-140, 184-185, 212, 271-272
Bruce Lee, 4-5, 23, 30, 38, 43, 57, 68, 72, 74, 88, 130-131, 208, 219-220, 226
Buddhabhadra, 70
Cally Kwong, 200
Carter Wong, 93, 253-254
Cat vs Rat, 5, 193-194, 303-304
Cathay, 65, 158, 167

Celestial Pictures, 30, 131, 136, 141, 218, 220
Chan Ho, 75
Chan Sau Chung, 62
Chan Yat-sen, 20
Chan Yip-Shing, 184-185
Chang Cheh, 3-5, 29, 31-37, 39-41, 43-51, 58-60, 63, 65-66, 68-69, 73-75, 78-79, 81-82, 85-88, 90- 91, 93-94, 97-100, 103, 106-110, 117-122, 125-129, 131-133, 136-141, 143-144, 146, 149, 151-152, 157, 162, 182-185, 190, 192-193, 196, 203, 208, 227-280, 287-288, 297-298
Chang Ho, 185
Changgong, 3, 51, 57, 59-60, 68, 73, 78-79, 85, 91, 93, 103, 109-110, 117, 137, 240, 250
Charles Heung, 18
Chen Jih-Liang, 107, 111, 259-260, 265
Chen Kuan-tai, 4, 34-35, 40, 48, 60, 62-64, 66-68, 82, 98, 104, 106-107, 110-111, 155, 185, 227-232, 241-244, 257
Chen Wo-Fu, 48-49, 237-238
Cheng Gang, 29
Cheng Pei-Pei, 43, 220
Chenggong Ling, 103, 105, 107, 258
Cherie Chung, 197, 200, 307-308
Cheung Chi-hang, 8- 9
Cheung Yan-lung, 8-20, 22, 31, 35, 43, 101, 108, 125, 130, 203, 208
Chi Kuan Chun, 59, 64-67, 72, 87, 93, 104, 109, 121, 243-254, 261-268
Chiang Ching-kuo, 33
Chiang Da-Wei, 4, 27, 31, 34-35, 38-39, 41-43, 47-48, 57, 74-75, 78-79, 91, 98, 100, 104, 109-110, 120-122, 125, 143, 195, 220, 227-230, 233-234, 237-238, 249-250, 255-258, 263-268
Chiang Kai-shek, 33, 62, 90, 125
Chiang Sheng, 78, 109-110, 128, 150, 155, 255-256, 267-268, 273-276, 279-280, 287-288, 297-298
Chiang Tao, 49-50, 233, 239, 245-250
China National Film Studio, 73-74
China United Film, 32
Chinatown Kid, 5, 107, 126-128, 130-132, 136-137
Chinese Boxer, The, 57, 62
Chiu Wai, 65, 68, 149, 266
Chor Yuen, 5, 98, 157-159, 161-162, 164-167, 193, 283-284, 289-292
Choy Lay Fat Kid (See New Shaolin Boxers)
Choy Li Fut, 64, 107-108
Chu Ko, 155, 184, 287-288, 297-298
Chuen Yuen, 31, 225-226
Chung Chi College, 36, 228
Chung-ying Wong, 46
Clans of Intrigue, 165
Condemned,The, 91
Convict Killer, The, 163-164
Crippled Avengers, 63
Danny Lee, 27, 41, 48, 98, 271-

272, 275-276, 297-298
Dato Loke Wan Tho, 65
David Cheung, 17, 108, 159, 177-178, 180-181, 188, 192, 195, 198, 201-202, 207-210, 212, 240, 293-294, 301-306
Dead End, 39, 43
Deadly Breaking Sword, The, 5, 146, 148, 155, 281-282
Deadly Knives, The, 30
Deep Thrust, 57
Delinquent, The, 46, 51
Derek Yee Tung-Sing, 42, 165, 174, 289-292
Devil Bride, 30
Devil's Mirror, The, 144
Dick Wei, 150, 271-274
Disciples of Shaolin, 73-74, 86-87, 91, 107, 247-248
Disciples of the 36th Chamber, 211
Disco Bumpkins, 179
Double Ten Day, 10
Duel between Fang Shih-yu and Hung Hsi, 63
Duel of the Iron Fist, 57
Duel, The, 62
Eastern Han Dynasty, 70, 83
Eastern Zhou Dynasty, 104
Eight-Nation Alliance, 1, 90, 92
Empress Dowager, 1, 89-90, 251-252, 296
Enigmatic Case, The, 197
Executioners from Shaolin, 64
Fake Ghost Catchers, The, 5, 188, 301-302
Fang Da-Hong, 79
Fang De, 60-61
Fang Shih-yu and Misao Cuihua, 61

Fang Shih-yu, 60-64, 66, 72, 82, 109, 241-244, 246, 261-262, 265-266
Fang Yongchun, 64
Fantastic Magic Baby, The, 91, 100, 128
Fearless Fighters, 57
Feng Fei Fei, 77
Fist of Fury, 30, 57, 68, 130, 226, 232
Five Ancestors, The, 79, 81
Five Elders, The, 61, 79-81, 149
Five Fingers of Death (See King Boxer)
Five Great Clans, 7
Five Shaolin Masters, 68, 79-82, 86-87, 91, 249-250
Five Venoms, The, 131, 138, 162
Flying Dagger Series, 165
Four Assassins, The (See Marco Polo)
Four Horsemen of the Apocalypse, 34
Four Riders, 31, 34-35, 140, 229-230
Frankie Chan, 82, 87
Friends, 4, 47-50, 237-238
From the Highway, 65
funeral, 101, 165, 190, 205-209, 213
Fung Dou Dak, 79, 81
Fung Hak-On, 78, 235, 239-241, 245, 247-249
Fung Ying Seen Koon, 216
Gangland Odyssey, 47
Generals of the Yang Family, 29, 30, 186
Generation Gap, The, 41, 43, 47, 51, 233-234

George Lam Chi-Cheung, 197
Gigi Wong Suk-Yee, 184, 297
Globe Films, 130
Golden Bell Awards, 190
Golden Demon, 46
Golden Dragon Restaurant, 127-128, 270
Golden Harvest, 48, 59, 68, 185
Golden Horse Awards, 29, 39, 47, 107, 146, 148, 224, 258
Golden Swallow, 33, 43
Gracy Tong Ka-Lai, 27
Grand Motion Pictures, 73
Great Star Theater, 67
Green Jade Statuette, 82
Griffin Yueh Feng, 158
Gu Long, 158, 164-167, 283, 289-292
Gubeikou, 104-106
Guo Jing, 133-135, 139, 183-185, 271-272, 275-276, 287-288, 297-298
Hakka, 7, 137
Hammer of God, The, 57
Han Ying-Chieh, 65
Hang Lok Theatre, 15
Happenings in Alishan, 32, 69, 79
Have Sword, Will Travel, 46
Heaven and Hell, 91, 99-100 103, 194, 204, 255-256
Helen Li Mei, 33
Hell, The (See Heaven and Hell)
Hellfighters of the East (See Four Riders)
Heroes Shed No Tears, 5, 66, 166, 168, 174, 291-292
Heroes Two, 59-60, 62-63, 67, 241-242, 244, 246
Heroic Ones, The, 31

Heung Chin, 10, 16
Heung Wah-yim, 16-18
Heung Yee Kuk, 12, 20
Hideki Saijo, 210
Hollywood, 25, 42, 65, 74, 137, 198
Hong Kong Baptist, 174, 206
Hong Kong Housing Authority, 15
Hong Kong Jockey Club, 15
Hong Kong Playboys, 5, 197-198, 200, 204, 305-306
Hong Xiguan's Big Brawl at Liu Village, 63
House of 72 Tenants, The, 158
Hsiao Ho, 182, 194, 295-296, 299, 301-303
Hsu Tseng-Hung, 97
Hu Chin, 88, 251-252
Hu De Di, 79, 265
Hu Hui-Chien, 64, 66, 109, 243, 261-262, 265-266
Huang Chieh, 105
Huang Rong, 132, 135, 139, 183-184, 271-272, 275-276, 287-288, 297-298
Hui Ying-hung, 132-133, 180, 182-184, 186, 195, 212, 220, 272-274, 281, 289, 295-296, 299-300, 303
Hung Chung-ho, 61
Hung Gar Kuen, 5, 63-64, 86, 95, 107, 149, 178
Hung Hsi Kuan, 60, 63-64, 66, 72, 151, 241-244
Hung Wei, 42
Invincible Kung Fu Trio, 82
Irene Chen Yi-Ling, 36, 227, 245
Iron Man, The, 30

Iron Monkey, 63, 68
Iron Triangle, The, 121-122
Ivy Ling Po, 26, 29, 98, 223-224
Izumo, 120-122
Jackie Chan, 4, 6, 73, 87-88, 91, 130, 153, 179, 182, 197, 236, 242, 296, 300
Jade Bow, The, 97
James Wong Jim, 126, 269
Jamie Luk, 78, 123, 239-241, 247, 259, 261
Jang Il-Ho, 30-31, 225
Japan(ese), 2, 10-11, 24-25, 30, 32, 36, 71, 92, 95, 99, 103-106, 120-122, 128, 164, 198, 201, 210, 226, 286
Jason Pai Piao, 66, 69, 291-292
Jean Paul Delisle, 19
JenFu Records, 5
Jenny Tseng, 5, 76-77, 84, 87-88, 91-92, 97-101, 103, 107-109, 111, 118-119, 122-126, 130, 138, 145-148, 152, 154, 159, 161, 174-177, 185, 190, 194, 196-197, 199-201, 205-206, 209, 214-216, 251, 255-256, 259-260, 268-269, 277, 282, 286, 292
Ji Sin Sim Si, 64, 79- 81
Jigoku, 99
Jimmy Wang Yu, 4, 26, 30, 38-39, 43, 215, 219
Jin Yong (See Louis Cha)
Jiu Wan, 38
Joe Boys, 127-128
John Woo, 4, 39, 95, 227, 229, 236, 253
Kai Tak, 78, 146, 205
Khitan Empire (See Liao Dynasty)

King Boxer, 30, 57
King Hu, 148, 219, 226
Kingdom and the Beauty, The, 42
Ko Chung-ki, 124
Kong Nee, 157-158
Korea(n), 30-34, 66, 71, 226, 230
Kowloon, 7, 9, 15, 18, 20, 23, 42, 59, 78, 83, 108, 123, 130, 132, 153, 184, 202, 204
Ku Feng, 5, 30, 40, 98, 145-146, 153, 160-161, 165, 179, 271, 273-282, 285-286, 289- 292
Kublai Khan, 94, 253-254
Kuen-wa Chu, 137
Kung Fu Mama, 41
Kung Fu Warlords (See Brave Archer)
Kung Fu, the Invincible Fist, 57
Kuomintang, 9-10, 16, 20, 32, 96
Kwok Chun-Fung, 78, 110, 128, 136, 138, 150, 184, 253-255, 263, 267-271, 273, 275, 279, 287, 297-298
Lam Sai Wing, 96
Lau Jaam, 78, 95-96, 177
Lau Kar-fai, 72, 78, 85, 102, 178, 180, 186, 188, 196, 206, 211-212, 220, 245-246, 253, 257, 293-296, 299-300, 303-304
Lau Kar-Leung, 4-5, 17, 31, 45, 62, 64, 68, 74, 78, 83, 86, 93-97, 102, 122, 125, 128, 160, 174, 177-178, 182-183, 185-188, 192-194, 211-212, 219, 229-251, 294-296, 299-300, 303-304

Lau Kar-wing, 5, 44-45, 177, 179, 181, 188, 191-192, 194, 198, 227, 249, 293-295, 301, 303-306
Lau Soe, 137
Lee Tai-Hang, 182, 211, 295, 303
Legend of the Bat, 165
Legend of the Condor Heroes, The, 134-135, 140, 162, 183, 272, 276, 288
Legendary Weapons of China, 5, 182-183, 193, 295-296
Lei Laohou, 61
Leonard Ho, 25, 59, 219
Leslie Cheung, 185, 197
Leung Kar-Yan, 72, 245-246, 249, 251-253, 257, 259-262
Li Chen-Chow, 150, 279-280
Li Ching, 26, 29, 98, 132, 139, 223
Li Hsing, 144
Li Lihua, 90
Li Shi-Kai, 79, 249
Li Yi-Min, 78, 100, 104, 110, 135, 138, 254-255, 257, 263-265, 271-273, 275-276
Liang Yusheng, 164-165
Liao Dynasty, 186
Liberace, 176
Life Gamble, 136, 273-274
Lily Ho, 29-30, 223
Lily Li, 30, 47, 98, 186, 220, 229, 235-238, 281, 299, 301-302
Linda Lin Dai, 26
Linda Wong Hin Ping, 215
Linn Haynes, 59, 162, 167
Little Dragon Maiden, 185, 298
Liu Chung-kit, 8

Liu Jia Chang, 77
Liu Man Shek Tong, 8
Liu Yuzhang, 105
Lo Lieh, 4, 26, 29-30, 57, 219, 223, 289-290
Lo Mang, 136-138, 150-151, 255, 269-270, 273-276, 279, 287-288
Loews State Theater, 57
Louis Cha, 32, 59, 131-135, 139-140, 162, 164-165, 271-272, 275-277, 288, 294, 297-298
Lu Feng, 78, 109-110, 136, 149-153, 155, 255, 263, 267-268, 273, 275, 279, 287, 297
Lu Kwan Peking Opera School, 128, 152
Lung Tien-Hsiang, 135, 297, 301-302
Ma Chao-Hsing, 79, 82, 249
Ma Yongzhen, 40, 48, 62
Macau, 17, 76
Mad Boy (See New Shaolin Boxers)
Maggie Li Lin-Lin, 74-75, 98, 100
Magnificent Trio, 97
Magnificent Wanderers, 110, 262-264
Man of Iron, 40-41, 231-232, 278
Manchu, 61, 63-64, 71, 80-83, 105, 242, 244, 246, 250, 258, 266 (also see Qing Dynasty)
Marco Polo, 93-95, 98, 128, 253-254
Mark of the Eagle, 163-164, 166, 168, 193, 290
Mel Maron, 130

Melody, 214-216
Member of the Order of the British Empire, 14
Men from the Monastery, 64-67, 72, 109, 243-244, 262
Meng Fei, 82, 249
Ming Dynasty, 23, 49, 63-64, 71, 81, 83, 104
Ming Pao, 134, 140, 183
Ming Patriots, The, 47
Miu Hin, 60-61, 79
Miu Tsui Fa, 61
Mona Fong, 68, 97, 100, 103, 139, 191, 203, 219, 269-307
Monte Carlo, 176
Movietown, 25, 27-28, 30-31, 39, 48, 59, 63, 69, 95, 117, 119, 138-139, 143, 150, 158, 161, 175, 178, 181, 188, 206, 210, 213, 218-220 (also see Shaw Brothers Studio)
MP&GI, 33, 65, 204
My Rebellious Son, 5, 160-161, 168, 194-195, 285-286
Na Cha the Great, 49-50, 100, 107, 239-240
Na Cha versus Red Boy, 192, 195
Nanguo Acting Training Class, 38
Nanyang Productions, 24
Nat Chan Pak-Cheung, 195, 209, 305-308
Naval Commandos, The, 120-122, 252, 267-268
New One-Armed Swordsman, The, 43
New Shaolin Boxers, 107-108, 259-260
New Territories, 4, 7, 11-12, 15, 20, 34, 36, 123, 125, 137-138, 176, 202
Ng Mui, 61, 79
Ni Kuang, 126, 133, 153, 155, 227-265, 269-281, 285, 287, 297, 299, 303
Ning Hai, 121
Niu Niu, 136, 139, 275-276, 287-288
No. 19, 97
Northern & Southern Dynasties, 70
Northern Song, 186
Northern Wei, 70
Northern Zhou, 80
One-Armed Swordsman, 31, 36, 58, 215
Order of St. John, 15
Pa Tou Lou Tzu, 104-106, 258
Pai Ching-jui, 144
Pai Ying, 104, 257
Painted Faces, 220
Palace Theater, 40
Pao Hsueh-Li, 40, 48, 98, 231-232, 267
Patrick Tse Yin, 98, 203, 307-308
Patrick Wayne, 176
Perils of the Sentimental Swordsman, 165
Phillip Ko Fei, 186, 299
Police Force, 4, 45-47, 51, 235-236
Postman Strikes Back, 197
Prodigal Boxer, 46, 85, 236
Proud Twins, The, 5, 157-158, 163, 180, 283-284
Punti, 7
Qin Dynasty, 104
Qing Dynasty, 61, 63, 71, 80-

81, 149, 182, 280 (also see Manchu)
Queen Boxer, The, 41
Queen of Fist, 41
Radio Television Hong Kong, 36, 58
Raymond Chow, 25, 59, 65
Republic Era, 163
Return of the Condors, The, 183, 185, 298
Return of the One-Armed Swordsman, 31, 39, 146
Return of the Sentimental Swordsman, 5, 164, 166, 168, 289-290
Return to the 36th Chamber, 178
Richard Harrison, 88, 93-94, 251-254
Ricky Chan Ga-Suen, 179
Robert Mak, 178
Robert Tai, 31, 78, 100, 137, 139, 149, 155, 255, 267, 269, 271, 274-275
Run Run Shaw, 24-33, 36, 41, 43, 48, 57, 59, 65, 68, 73, 90, 93, 97-98, 100, 103, 105, 110, 117, 124-125, 131, 143, 148, 177-179, 185, 192-193, 205, 210, 219-220, 223, 227, 231, 237, 255, 267, 269, 279, 281, 283, 289, 291
Runde Shaw, 24-25
Runje Shaw, 24, 157
Runme Shaw, 24-25, 59, 225, 229, 233, 235, 265, 271, 273, 275, 277
Sai Jinhua, 88
Sally Yeh, 200
Sammo Hung, 61, 197, 226

San Po Kong, 124, 138, 201
Sand Pebbles, The, 42, 97
Secret of the Shaolin Poles, The, 47
Sek Kei, 4, 33, 140
Sek Yin-Tsi, 61
Sentimental Swordsman, The, 165
Seven Heroes and Five Gallants, The, 193, 304
Seven Man Army, 103-107, 126, 257-258
Seven Shaolin Heroes' Five Ventures into Mount Emei, 63
Seventh Seal, The, 34
Shadow Boxer, The, 48
Shang Dynasty, 49
Shanghai Killers, 57
Shaolin Avengers, The, 67, 109-110, 244, 261-262
Shaolin Cycle, 59, 67, 72, 81, 107, 117, 242, 244, 246, 248
Shaolin Mantis, 195
Shaolin Martial Arts, 72-73, 245-246, 250
Shaolin Prince, 191
Shaolin Temple (film), 80, 117-118, 120-121, 138, 265-266
Shaolin Temple (place), 5, 50, 64, 70-71, 79-81, 117, 210
shapes, 68, 79
Shaw & Sons, Ltd, 24-25
Shaw Brothers Studio, 3-5, 17, 25-27, 29, 33, 36, 39, 45, 47-48, 58-59, 68, 86, 97-98, 117, 120, 132, 143, 148, 152, 160, 178, 195, 203, 212, 218-219, 224, 228, 278, 280, 286 (also see Movietown)
Shaw HK TVB Training Centre,

26, 28, 43, 143
Shawscope, 26, 218
Shek Wu Hui, 9-14, 17, 20
Shenzhen, 8-9, 82
Sheung Shui, 7-11, 13-15, 18-20, 125
Shih Szu, 31, 100, 153, 225, 253-254, 256, 267, 277-278, 281-282
Showdown at the Cotton Mill, 67, 69
Sign of the Eagle (See Mark of the Eagle)
Silly Kid (See New Shaolin Boxers)
Simon Yuen, 73, 160, 167, 179, 245
Simsen International, 15, 19
Singapore, 24-25, 29, 41, 62, 65, 68, 131, 146
Sino-Japanese War, 32, 91, 103, 105, 121, 133, 151, 160, 258, 268
Siu Tai Choi, 9
Smugglers, 66
Snake in the Eagle's Shadow, 73, 179
Song Dynasty, 29, 71, 134, 186, 300
Sons of Good Earth, 226
South Dragon, North Phoenix, 97
Southeast Asian Chinese Martial Arts Tournament, 62
Southern Drama Group, 26
Spirit Boxers, 89
Spiritual Fists (See Boxer Rebellion)
Star Wars, 50, 193
Stephan Yip, 123, 239, 259

Stephen Chow, 91
Stone Lake, 9, 11, 20
Street Gangs of Hong Kong, (See The Delinquent)
Su Hei Hu, 150, 279
Suen Ga-Man, 66, 69
suicide, 48, 51, 238
Summit Film Productions, 144
Sun Chien, 129-131, 150, 255, 269-270, 274, 279, 287
Sun Chung, 5, 143-146, 148, 153, 157, 159-160, 194, 277-278, 281-282, 285-286
Sun Yat-sen University, 10, 157
Sun Yee On, 10, 16-17, 19, 84
Superman, 23, 174
Swordswoman Li Feifei, 24
Tai Au Mun, 202, 204, 213
Taichung, 90, 103
Taipei, 76, 78, 92, 120, 125, 128, 145, 154-155, 209
Taiwan(ese), 5, 16, 29, 31-33, 42, 46, 59, 62, 68, 73-79, 82, 84, 86, 90-91, 99, 101, 103, 108-110, 117-121, 125-126, 128-129, 134, 138, 143, 145, 155, 164, 167, 191, 215-216, 248, 250, 258, 264, 266, 268, 270, 274
Tam Chai-Kwan, 151
Tam Min, 150-151, 279
Tang Dynasty, 80, 125
Temple of the Red Lotus, 97, 302
Ten Tigers of Kwantung, 146, 149-152, 279-280
Teresa Teng, 77
This Man Is Dangerous, 212
Thit Kew Sam, 150
Three Ways of the Hung Fist, 67

Thunderbolt Fist, The, 30-31, 225-226
Thundering Sword, The, 97
Ti Lung, 4-5, 34-36, 38-39, 42-43, 57, 75, 78-80, 98, 104, 106, 109, 111, 118, 121-123, 143-146, 148, 150, 153, 160-161, 163-166, 208, 219-220, 227-230, 233-234, 249, 257-258, 265, 267, 277-282, 287-290
Tianyi Film Co, 24
Tien Niu, 47, 135-136, 139, 271-272, 276
Tit Chee Chan, 150
Tong Gai, 31, 43, 62, 64, 68, 74, 95, 97, 144, 146, 148, 160, 167, 227-229, 233-245, 277-278, 281-291
Tony Wong Yuen-San, 27, 41
Tops in Every Trade, 144, 148
Treasure Hunters, 5, 179, 181-182, 293-294
Triad, 16, 83-84, 129, 268, 308
Tricksters, The, 210
Tsai De-Zhong, 79-80
Tung Ming Shan, 144
TVB, 26-28, 37, 43, 68, 108-109, 124, 143, 185, 194, 196, 219, 298
Twinkle Twinkle Little Star, 197
Tzou Tai, 150
Ulysses Au-Yeung Jun, 46-47, 235-236
Union Film, 42
Unique Film, 24
Unique Lama, The, 82
Vaughan Savidge, 58
Vengeance!, 33, 43, 62
Venoms, 109, 128-129, 138, 162, 185, 274, 280, 288, 298
Wa Daat, 59, 73
Wah Ching, 127-128
Wai Pak, 150
Wang Lung-Wei, 72, 82, 108, 135, 195-196, 209, 212, 245-246, 249-253, 257, 259-262, 265-266, 269-280, 285-286, 293-294, 299-306
Wang Yung-Hau, 82
Water Margin, The, 46, 89
Way of the Dragon, 69
wedding, 75, 98, 108, 123-126, 145, 198
Wei Pin-Ao, 66
White Gold Dragon, 24
White Lotus, 83-84
Wild Fire, 33
Wild Girl, 144, 148
William Pfeiffer, 218
Wing Chun, 38, 61, 149
Winners and Sinners, 197
Winnie Chin Wai-Yee, 200, 307-308
Wits of the Brats, 5, 197, 210-212, 307-308
Wong Ching, 46, 98, 227, 241, 243
Wong Chung, 34, 46, 98, 123, 229-231, 235-236, 265
Wong Fei-hung, 63, 68, 96, 133, 150, 166, 177
Wong Jing, 5, 177, 195, 197-198, 203, 209-210, 293, 301, 305-308
Wong Kei-Ying, 150
Wong Kiew Kit, 80
Wong Yin Lin, 150
Wong Yu, 95, 98, 178, 195, 201-203, 210, 305-306

World Northal Corporation, 130
Wu Chao Zheng, 106
Wu Ma, 4, 69, 95, 98, 132, 141, 227, 257, 259, 261, 263-265, 267
Wudang, 61, 67, 244, 262, 280
xiaozi, 50, 87, 195
Xinhui Clan, 95
Yang Yanzhao, 30
Yang Ye, 30, 186-187, 189
Yanggang, 33, 37, 268
Yeung Hung, 150
Yim Fa, 42-43
Yip Man, 38

Yongzheng Emperor, 80
Young People, 35-36, 47, 140, 227-228
Young Vagabond, The, 195
Yu Tai-Ping, 78, 135
Yuan Dynasty, 8, 110, 254
Yuanshan Hotel, 125
Yueh Hua, 29, 98, 223-224, 265, 291-292
Yuen Woo-ping, 179, 182
Zhang Huichong, 40
Zhen Shushi (See Jenny Tseng)
Zhou Dynasty, 83, 104
Zhu Yu, 136, 163

Terrence J. Brady

ABOUT THE AUTHOR

...In the '60s, I wrote with crayons.
...In the '70s, I wrote on the NYC subway trains.
...In the '80s, I wrote term papers.
...In the '90s, I wrote spec screenplays.
...In the '00s, I wrote all over the net.
...In the '10s, I wrote about Cheung Fu-Sheng.

Terrence Brady a/k/a Teako was born and raised in [the] Bronx, NY, studied film production at Loyola University Chicago, and has been a fan of the martial arts film genre since the late '70s. He's an old-school Irishman who enjoys Steelers football, St. Pauli Girl lager, Silver Age Marvel comics, Hitchcock movies, and a good Chicken Parmigiana.

Teako lives by the seaside with his wife, two daughters, and over 2000 DVDs. He's currently pondering on what to write next, so in the meantime, you'll find him kicking back with some Pink Floyd or on the couch with a few Shaw Brothers discs. Visit him on-line @ www.fushengbio.com

Printed in Dunstable, United Kingdom